Karl Barth's Theology of Relations

Gary W. Deddo

Karl Barth's Theology of Relations

Trinitarian, Christological, and Human:
Towards an
Ethic of the Family

WIPF & STOCK · Eugene, Oregon

Wipf and Stock Publishers
199 W 8th Ave, Suite 3
Eugene, OR 97401

Karl Barth's Theology of Relations, Volume 1
Trinitarian, Christological, and Human: Towards an Ethic of Family
By Deddo, Gary
Copyright©1999 by Deddo, Gary
ISBN 13: 978-1-4982-2878-7
Publication date 5/15/2015
Previously published by Peter Lang, 1999

A note to the reader: This work, originally published as one volume in the Peter Lang series, Issues in Systematic Theology, is now available from Wipf and Stock Publishers in two volumes. Volume one includes the Preface and Introduction for the complete work, along with Chapters One through Five. Volume Two contains Chapters Six through Eleven. Both volumes contain the complete Table of Contents, Bibliography, and Index as it was published in the original single volume work.

Contents

Table of Charts	xi
Acknowledgments	xii
Preface	xiii
Introduction	1

Part One: Barth's Theological Grounding of Anthropology and Ethics — 9

1. The Christological Starting Point for a Theology of Relations — 10
   - The Theological Task: Faith Seeking Understanding of the Word of God — 10
   - The Theological Source: The Word Revealing the Knowledge of God and the Knowledge of Humanity — 10
   - The Shape of our Relations: The *Analogia Relationis* — 15

2. The Trinitarian Relations: Son, Father and Holy Spirit — 18
   - The Shape of Relation in God's Self-Revelation — 19
   - The Christological Knowledge of God in Himself — 22
   - The Shape of Relations in God's Triunity — 22
   - Three Modes (Ways) of God's Being God: The Personal and Relational Nature of God — 23
   - Triunity: Perichoretic Fellowship — 25
   - Ambiguity in *CD* I/1? — 26
   - Christological (Human) Knowing of Father, Son and Spirit *ad extra* as a Relational Reality of Unity and Distinction — 27
   - The Content of Relation is God's Loving Freedom — 27
   - The Triune God: Being-in-Becoming and Creating Loving Fellowship — 28
   - The Triune God: Personifying Person — 30
   - The Triune God: Lovingly Free — 31
   - The Triune God: Freely Loving in all His Ways — 32
   - Summary — 33
   - The "Theo-logic" of Barth's Trinitarian Grammar — 33

3. The Christological Relation: Humankind as Being-Covenant-Partner with God — 36
   - The Relationship of Christology and Anthropology: Barth's General Orientation in *Church Dogmatics* I/1 through III/1 — 36
   - Christology and Anthropology in *Church Dogmatics* III/2 — 38

The Trinitarian Grounding of Anthropology	39
The Obstacles to non-Christological Approaches to Anthropology and the Adequacy of the Revelation in Jesus Christ	40
The Seven Spheres of Relation	41
Jesus Christ: The Revelation and Determination of Humankind as Being-in-Relation with God	42
Barth's Foundational Christology	45
Six Characteristics of the Particular Humanity of Jesus Christ: Being-With-God	51
Christological and Trinitarian Being-in-Relationship	53
Implications for Barth's Doctrine of the Trinity	54
Humankind as Being-in-Relation With God: Six Criteria	56
Being-with-God: Humanity's Relational Form	59
Humanity: Essentially Being *With* and *For* God	62
Being *With* and *For* God through Election	63
Humankind: Elected for Covenant Relation by the Initiative of God	67
Covenant Relationship as a History	71
The Trinitarian Grounding of Humankind in Covenantal Relationship	72
Being-For-God: Covenant Relationship as Being-in-Gratitude	75
Being-For-God: Covenant Relationship as Being-in-Responsibility and Freedom	76
Summary: The Grammar of Karl Barth's Theological Anthropology	81
The Relations of Relations are also Analogous	84

Part Two: Humanity as Co-Humanity: Being in Covenantal Relations One With Another — 87

4. The Christological Determination of Our Co-Humanity	88
Jesus Christ: the "Man for Others"	88
Sin Obscures but Cannot Obliterate God's Purposes	89
The Mystery of Jesus Christ: "Man For God" and so Uniquely "Man For Humanity"	89
Six Implications of the Humanity of Jesus Christ	91
Barth's Grammar of the Triune Relations: *ad intra* and *ad extra*	93
The Correspondence of Relations: The *Analogia Relationis*	94

Imago Dei: Original, First and Second	96
Dissimilarity of the God-Man and Person-Person Relationships	97
Intra-Trinitarian Relations and Our Humanity: Two Dissimilarities	97
The Similarity of Relations: A Co-Humanity	99
Humanity: a Being-With-Others as an Image of Jesus Christ	99
I and Thou: the Form of Humanity	100
The Original Trinitarian Relations and Humanity	103
The Four Elements of Humanity as Being-in-Encounter—Its Content/Action	104
Summary: The Correlation of Relations	105
5. Humanity as Being-in-Communion with Others: the Six-fold Grammar of Relations	**108**
I. Being-in-Communion	108
The Shape of Our Essential Relational Reality	108
Fellowship (yet Differentiation): Humankind as Male and Female	111
The Theological Grounding of Fellowship (yet Distinction)	115
II. Being-in-Relation in a Differentiated Order	119
The Shape of our Differentiated Relations	119
Summary	126
Ordered Communion Grounded in the Humiliation and Exaltation of Jesus Christ	128
Grounded in Christ's Relationship with Israel and the Church	128
Originally Grounded in the Triune Life of God	129
The Ordered Community of Believers	129
III. Being-in-Relationship: Image, Analogy, Correspondence and Witness	130
Barth's Theological Interpretation of *Analogia*	131
Human Relationships as Image and Witness	140
Theological Ethics as Image and Witness	146
Summary: Theological and Anthropological Ethics	151
IV. Personal-Being-in-Covenant-Love	153
Covenant-Love: Reciprocal Life-Giving Exchange	154

Personal and Personifying Covenant Love	159
Personal Being as a Being-in-Loving	166
Covenant Love, Power and Authority	167
Covenant Love: An Unconditional Communion	169
Summary	170
V. Being-in-Becoming	170
Creaturely Being-in-Becoming	170
The Becoming of the Triune God	174
VI. Being-in-Extension-for-Inclusion of the Other	178
The Extension-for-Inclusion of the Triune God	179
Humanity: Extension and Inclusion of the Other in Fellowship	182

Part Three: The Ethics of Parents and Children — 187

6. The Child to Parent Relationship	188
Introduction	188
The Command of God and the Child-to-Parent Aspect	190
The *Analogia Relationis* in the Child-Parent Relationship	200
The Forms of Honoring Parents	209
The Failure of Parents and Temptations to Children: Our Need for Grace	212
The Mediation of Jesus Christ	215
7. Responsible Procreation	221
Involuntary Childlessness	221
1. The Transformation of the OT Command into a Freedom for Procreation	221
2. The Freedom of Childlessness	225
Voluntary Childlessness	229
1. The Question of "Birth Control"	229
2. Voluntary Childlessness: A Threat to Marital Fellowship	230
3. Responsible Discernment and Action	232
4. Grounds for Voluntary Childlessness	236
5. Methods of Contraception and the Basis for Decision Making	237
8. The Parent to Child Relationship	238
The Honor and Duty of Being Parents	238

1. A Special Case and Need for Honoring and Calling to Duty	238
2. Fathering and Mothering	240
Regarding Children as the Children of God	241
1. Parents as the Representatives of God by the Gift of Grace	241
2. Parents as Children of God and so as Elder Brothers and Sisters to their Children	242
3. "Living For Our Children"	244
4. "Exercising Authority over Children"	246
5. "Bringing Up Children"	247
6. The Disciplining of Children	249
7. Using Limited Opportunities	255
8. The Limitations of Parenting	256
9. Readiness for Disruption by Jesus Christ	258
Conclusion	259

Part Four: Implications for Approaches to the Family   261

9. The Fruitfulness of Barth's Theology of Relations for Evaluating Theological and Non-Theological Approaches to the Family	262
Introduction	262
The Criteria of Fruitfulness and Relevance	264
I. A Variety of Contemporary Theological Approaches	266
A Theological Motif Approach: Ross Bender	267
A Theological Inversion Approach: The Family as Hermeneutical Key to the Knowledge of the Triune God: F. D. Maurice and his Interpreters	276
A Theological/Incarnational Approach: Ray S. Anderson and Dennis Guernsey	281
A Pragmatic/Moralist Approach: James Dobson	288
II. Non-Theological Approaches	301
A Sociological Approach: Salvador Minuchin	302
Evaluation	303
A Democratic Approach: Rudolph Dreikhurs and Vicki Soltz	307
Critique	309
Summary	318
Conclusion	318

10. Issues Facing the Contemporary American Family: Nine Explorations	320
Introduction	320
1. The Purpose, Goals and Problems of the Parent-Child Relationship	321
2. New Models of the Family?	338
3. A Theological Interpretation of Procreation	343
4. A Theological Perspective on Adoption	358
5. The Coherence and Unity of the Family and the Place of the Individual	366
6. Child Rearing: Authority, Freedom and the Nature of Discipline	372
7. The Significance of Gender	383
8. Failure and Restoration	391
9. The Place of the Family and the Child in the Church	396
Summary	404
Conclusion	405
11. Conclusion	407
Theological Foundations	407
A Personal and Actional Grammar of Being-in-Relationship	407
Freedom and Fellowship in the Family	408
The Faith-Obedience Connection	408
Barth and His Critics	409
The Question of Legitimate Limits	410
Relevance and Fruitfulness	411
Remaining Questions	412
Summary	419
Selected Bibliography	421
Indexes	434
Names	434
Subjects	436

Table of Charts

Our Personal-Covenantal Being-in-Relation	17
Barth's "Grammar" of the Intra-trinitarian Personal Relations	34
The Seven Spheres of Being-in-Relation	41
The Correspondence of the Trinitarian and Christological Relations	55
Humanity as Determined by Gracious Election	66
The Six Determinations of Humankind as Being-in-Relationship with God	82
The Humanity of Jesus Christ	91
The Intra-triune Relations	93
Marriage as an Image and Witness	141
I and Thou: Being-in-Relationship	155
The Four Elements of Being-in-Encounter	155
The Personal God	164
The Parent-Child Relation	190
The Family and the Six-fold Grammar of Relations	405

Acknowledgments

The basis of this study is the research I completed for doctoral work submitted to King's College, the University of Aberdeen, Scotland. Since that time I undertook additional research, reorganized and rewrote portions of the original thesis.

Considering together both phases of the life of this book, there are so many to whom I am indebted. I could not have begun, much less completed, this endeavor alone. I would like, first of all, to express my gratitude to my wife, Cathy. Her initial enthusiasm for us to take a sabbatical in Scotland and her continuing love and support made the completion of this book possible. I am also grateful for the love and patience shown me by my children, Linda, Gregory, and Krista.

To my mother whose encouragement I have appreciated all along, I want to express my deepest gratitude. This book is dedicated to the memory of my father, Frank Deddo.

Mention must also be made of the many friends we made in Banchory and colleagues found in Aberdeen, Scotland. They enriched our lives while we were there and continue to be a channel of God's blessings to us.

A word of appreciation must said for all our friends here in Princeton, New Jersey. A special note of thanks is due to Lenore Pfutzner for her all her assistance in proof reading the manuscript.

I wish to thank a long-time mentor, Dr. Ray S. Anderson of Fuller Theological Seminary, Pasadena and Dr. George Hunsinger of the Center for Karl Barth Studies, Princeton Theological Seminary for their invaluable comments and suggestions along the way.

However, it is due to the inspiration, both intellectual and spiritual, of the Rev. Prof. James B. Torrance, that I owe the greatest debt of gratitude. For it was at his invitation that I began this study and with his encouragement that it has now reached completion in this form.

Finally, I am grateful for permission to quote at length material previously published by T&T Clark Ltd. (Karl Barth, *Church Dogmatics*, 4 vols. in 13 pts. Edinburgh: T&T Clark, 1958–81. Reprinted by permission of the publisher. All rights reserved. Use of copyrighted material in any electronic form is not permitted.)

Advent, 1998   Gary W. Deddo
Cranbury, New Jersey

Preface

The aim of this present book is three-fold: First, we intend to make a detailed study of how Karl Barth, in his *Church Dogmatics*, comprehended the close interconnections between the Christian doctrine of God, the doctrine of humanity and Christian ethics. In short, the nature of the eternal trinitarian relations within God, revealed through the Incarnation of the Son of God in Jesus Christ, sheds light upon the true nature of humanity and so upon the nature of right relationships between persons. Taken together these three doctrines form what we call Karl Barth's theology of relations. Second, we examine his section on "Parents and Children" to show, by way of this specific example, how Barth's theology of relations provides the foundation for his special ethics generally. Third, we demonstrate the relevance of Barth's theology of relations. We show that it is fruitful for critiquing both Christian/theological and non-theological approaches to understanding the parent-child relationship. And we demonstrate its potential by using it to investigate some of the profound implications of Barth's trinitarian and Christological theology for contemporary issues facing the American family in particular.

Why Karl Barth and the *Church Dogmatics*?

Karl Barth has had his critics from early on. He has also had avid promoters from the beginning of his career. On the one hand many have noted the unusual insight Barth actually provided in his sections on ethics in the *Church Dogmatics*. Paradoxically there have been those who, concentrating on his theology proper, could not see how Barth could sustain a convincing ethic on that theological basis. However, beyond the initial prognosis, not much detailed work has been done on his theological anthropology, especially as it is so intrinsically connected to his trinitarian and incarnational theology and provides the basis for his theological ethics. This book aims at filling in that gap and answering his critics along the way.

The theological developments with which we are concerned occupy a place roughly in the middle of the *Church Dogmatics* and appeared sixteen and nineteen years after Barth had begun this work and eight years before the publication of the last complete volume. Barth's general ethics appeared somewhat earlier in his *Kirchliche Dogmatik*, Vol. II/2 in 1942 with the English translation coming out in 1957. His major anthropological section was originally published in German (Vol. III/2) in 1948 with the English translation completed in 1960. Barth produced his special ethics in Vol. III/4 appearing in German in 1951 and in English in 1961. These volumes provoked a wide variety of responses.[1] But many astute observers took note of Barth's unique contribution

---

[1] For an overview of these varied responses in the English-speaking world see Richard H. Roberts, "The reception of the theology of Karl Barth in the Anglo-Saxon world: history, typology and prospect" in *Karl Barth: Centenary Essays*, ed. S.W. Sykes (Cambridge, New York, Melbourne: Cambridge University Press, 1989). For a survey of responses to Barth within "American Evangelicalism" and an analysis of Barth's

in the areas of ethics and theological anthropology when these volumes were published, some suggesting that these aspects were among the most important Barth had to offer. However, others neglected or offered radical criticisms of them.

One of Barth's earlier and more insightful interpreters, the Roman Catholic, Hans Urs von Balthasar, highlighted the fact that he found in his ethics "a glimpse of the creative spark" which matched the genius of his original theological point of departure in the earlier volumes of the *Dogmatics*.[2]

One of Barth's English-speaking interpreters, Herbert Hartwell, regarded Barth's anthropology as "the most powerful and most timely prophetic message of his theology." Concerning his ethics Hartwell observed: "In making this freedom [of his anthropology] the foundation of his theological ethics Barth has thereby opened up a new vista in this field of dogmatics which will prove fruitful in future studies of this subject-matter."[3] Hartwell had also to acknowledge that "in the Anglo-Saxon countries, at least in the past, no continental theologian has been more widely misunderstood and misinterpreted than Karl Barth."[4] A particular point of misunderstanding, Hartwell charged, occurred over the crucial relationship Barth had forged between anthropology and ethics. Barth's teaching on freedom as the foundation for theological ethics

> should be viewed together with his teaching on humanity as co-humanity in order that the full implications of these two basic principles of his theology may be grasped. Again, the conception of the freedom into which man is called by God in Jesus Christ and the manner in which this concept has been worked out in the special ethics of the command of God the Creator prove, together with the concept of the humanity as co-humanity and with Barth's teaching on the church and its mission in the world, that the criticism of the remoteness of his theology from the world in which we live is unjustified.[5]

A number of years later, after Barth's ethical and anthropological teaching had some considerable exposure, even on the American theological scene,

---

relation to it see Gregory Bolich, *Karl Barth & Evangelicalism* (Downers Grove, Illinois: InterVarsity Press, 1980). For an insightful reflection on Barth's methodology and it's potential contribution to "evangelical theology" from the perspective of an American Baptist systematic theologian see Bernard Ramm, *After Fundamentalism. The Future of Evangelical Theology* (San Francisco: Harper & Row, Publishers, 1983).

[2] Hans Urs von Balthasar, *The Theology of Karl Barth*, trans. John Drury (New York, Chicago, San Francisco: Holt, Rinehart and Winston, 1971) p. 36 (orig. German edit.: 1951). (Hereafter, *TB*)

[3] Herbert Hartwell, *The Theology of Karl Barth: An Introduction* (London: Gerald Duckworth & Co. Ltd., 1964) pp. 182-183. (Hereafter, *TBI*)

[4] *Ibid.*, p. vii.

[5] *Ibid.*, p. 183.

Thomas Oden argued the thesis that "Barth holds special promise for us today precisely at the point at which he is most frequently dismissed, i.e. his ethics, his understanding of the Christian life, Christian freedom and ethical responsibility." He went on to note more specifically that "Barth may have profound promise [for] the question of man, the definition of man, true humanism, a truly hopeful understanding of man..."[6]

More recently Stuart McLean, one of the few who have recently taken up the task to expound Barth's theological anthropology, avers that "Barth's discussion of humanity is among the most profound in Western literature." He goes on to lament of the "distortions" and "caricatures" of Barth, based on second-hand knowledge or incomplete study of the Barth corpus, which have persisted. He makes it his aim to rectify these "distorted images of Barth's theology."[7]

It is our aim as well to take up, as Hartwell recommended, the challenge to examine Barth's unique contribution to theological anthropology and ethics, especially in their relationship to one another. We will attempt to make explicit this vital connection in terms of understanding the parent-child relationship as Barth presents it in the second of three sections of his part on "Freedom for Fellowship" in Vol. III/4. It is our hope as well that certain criticisms against Barth's ethical relevance will be answered while we too will raise some criticisms.

We have selected to explore this section on "Parents and Children" for two reasons. First of all there is in the literature no extended treatment of this section. Yet, the relationship of parents and children comprises one third of Barth's consideration of humankind's being in freedom for fellowship. We contend that what Barth has to say here is as important as the first section on man and woman. It is perhaps the finest theological discussion of parenting available in the English language. Much attention and much controversy has been given to the preceding section on "Man and Woman." However, the following two sections on the parent and child and the near and distant neighbors form a whole piece. Interpretation of the man and woman section has suffered through its being disconnected from the following sections. Each part should be interpreted in the light of the other two sections.

Secondly, while there has been acknowledged for decades, if not longer, that there are undesirable changes occurring in the American family, and there have been innumerable books written on the subject, there remains a decisive lack of sound theological reflection on parenting and the American family.[8] The

---

[6] Thomas Oden, *The Promise of Barth* (Philadelphia: J.B. Lippincott Co., 1969), pp. 36, 41. (Hereafter, *PB*)

[7] Stuart McLean, *Humanity in the Thought of Karl Barth* (Edinburgh: T & T Clark Ltd., 1981) p. vii. (Hereafter, *HTB*)

[8] This fact is pointed out in the most recent and perhaps most theologically comprehensive approach to the family *On Being Family*, by Ray S. Anderson and Dennis Guernsey, (Grand Rapids: Eerdmans, 1985). (Hereafter, *OBF*)

problems and issues facing parents in relation to their children in the United States provides a test case to see if Barth's theological grounding can offer an adequate framework for interpreting the contemporary situation and a foundation on which to build a meaningful response.

It has been the contention of a number of respected Barth interpreters that the misunderstanding and misinterpretation of him, at least in part, has been due to a failure on two counts: 1) to interpret the part in terms of the whole of Barth's work and 2) to pay attention to the details of what Barth has said. The co-editor and translator of the *Church Dogmatics*, Geoffrey Bromiley, has made the observation that "Many of the studies which presuppose a knowledge of the text show no great evidence of a full acquaintance with it."[9] Years earlier John McConnachie had pointed out the same problem in the work on Barth after only Volume I had been published.[10] Of course Barth himself in his "Forward to the English Edition" in Arthur Cochrane's 1952 translation of Otto Weber's *Karl Barth's Church Dogmatics. An Introductory Report on Volumes I:1 to III/4*, complained that in the Anglo-saxon world:

> I have the impression that there I exist in the phantasy of far too many—even of the best men—mainly only in the form of certain, for the most part hoary, summations; of certain pictures hastily dashed off by some person at some time, and for the sake of convenience, just as hastily accepted, and then copied endlessly, and which, of course can easily be dismissed. However, I could hardly recognize in them anything else than my own ghost!

Barth noted this about the particular criticisms that his ethics are "impossible," preaching involves an "otherworldly Biblicism and an inactive quietism," that for him creation was "non-existent" and that "culture and civilization are damned." He then requested that he be read calmly and in some measure completely if he was to be critiqued.[11]

Almost three decades later Bromiley had to make the same observation concerning even "well-trained scholars." "A failure to read and digest the *Dogmatics* has produced an enormous quantity of high-sounding and influential nonsense. This being the case, the need for a plain exposition needs no further justification."[12]

---

[9] Geoffrey W. Bromiley, *Introduction to the Theology of Karl Barth* (Grand Rapids: Eerdmans, 1979) p. xi. (Hereafter, *ITKB*)

[10] Speaking of one interpreter in particular but giving a more general warning to other critics he said "Many supposed objections to Barth's views lie not in the views themselves but in partial or complete misunderstanding of them." In *The Significance of Karl Barth* (London: Hodder and Stoughton Limited, 1931) p. 272. (Hereafter, *SB*)

[11] In Otto Weber, trans. Arthur C. Cochrane, *Karl Barth's Church Dogmatics: An Introductory Report on Volumes I:1 to III/4* (London: Lutterworth Press, 1953) p. 7. (Hereafter, *BCD*)

[12] *ITKB*, p. xii.

Not all the trouble lies with the interpreters of Barth. Barth could refer to his monumental work as having the appearance (in the white German edition) of Moby Dick, the white whale. The sheer size of the *Dogmatics* is daunting; complete reading much less comprehension is a monumental task. Additionally, as McConnachie noted early on "Barth is not easy to grasp, his style weighted and involved, and his thought intricate and sometimes obscure."[13] The length of the *Dogmatics* and difficulty of style is not altogether due to an idiosyncrasy of Barth himself. T.F. Torrance notes that the content of his message and the corresponding methodology of his presentation call for such a presentation.

> At every step forward in his *Church Dogmatics* Barth probes ruthlessly into the subject from different angles, going round and round the same point at different levels with different series of questions until he can see and understand the truth in its own reality and wholeness and then he set himself to find a way of expressing it, in ways that are adequate and appropriate and faithful to the whole truth in its objectivity, in its manifoldness and in its native force.[14]

The subject matter itself, as Barth saw it, required intense observation and listening from many angles, before one faithfully could say much about it. Barth's presentations follow along this pattern of making multifaceted observations as he attempts to grasp and convey the whole message and meaning. Barth's presentation involves a kind of circularity of lengthy observation which only then leads to his concluding statements. His is not a theology which begins with axioms or definitions which are then merely to be followed out logically. Barth's approach demands our having a panoramic perspective before we can see what he is saying and make any suggestions of our own.

But even more demanding of the reader than the length of presentation and the need for comprehensive reading is the task of re-categorization to which Barth's observations and conclusion lead. Listening to T.F. Torrance again:

> Barth was engaging in a terrific struggle with theological and philosophical language....every language...has its own web of meaning, its own network of coventions and its communal qualities.

---

[13]*SB*, p. 272.

[14]Thomas F. Torrance, *Karl Barth: An Introduction to his Early Theology, 1910–1931* (London: SCM Press Ltd., 1962) pp. 20-21. (Hereafter, *BET*) Eberhard Jüngel similarly attributes the length and difficulty of style to two factors: Barth sought always to begin at the beginning. His sense of theological development required him to constantly re-evaluate and qualify his theology even if this meant modifying its direction. But he could do this only by way of renewed fidelity to the ultimate Christian foundation in God's self-revelation mediated to us through Scripture, not by leaving this indispensable source behind. In this way Barth was "from the beginning an avowed enemy of systems" (*BTL*, p. 27). Jüngel cites Barth's *Evangelical Theology: An Introduction*, p. 165, where

Any use of words involves in some measure or other a compromise with, or a manipulation of, the communal meaning in which they share, and must therefore come to terms with the culture or the philosophy or the traditions from which they derive and into which they quickly and easily slip back. Thus any attempt to break a way through into a new direction of thought, or any attempt to set our thought on a new basis, involves a passionate and creative effort to wrest the words we use from their original meaning, and then great power of concentration to hold them in their new context until they become sufficiently assimilated to the new direction to be habituated to it.[15]

Barth's thinking then requires this transformation of meanings if he is to be comprehended. This is why numerous interpreters have called his thinking revolutionary; involving reversions or reversals.[16]

Such a history of the interpretation of Barth in the English-speaking world guides us in our task. We will want to pay particular attention to the details of what Barth says. Consequently a significant part of this thesis will be comprised of plain exposition and extensive quotations. We run the risk of making too many and too long citations, but given our desire to be faithful to Barth we would prefer to err on this side rather than the other.

On the other hand it is our intention to demonstrate *the interrelations* of his anthropology and the special ethic of the parent and child relationship and their grounding in Barth's Christology and trinitarian theology. This demands a more comprehensive understanding of the *Church Dogmatics* and calls for an attempt to see the part in light of the whole. In this way we hope to bring out 'the full implications' of Barth's understanding of parents and children in relationship.

Garret E. Paul has noted that Eberhard Jüngel's interpretation of Barth had much in common with Barth's own handling of the Apostle Paul's writings. This involves a desire to see things *with* the writer and to identify with the author's intention.[17] We too, to the limit that we are capable, will attempt such an interpretation of Barth. This approach may be mistaken for a lack of "critical distance" on our part. Let us say that given the difficulty of the material at hand, the fact of the history of misunderstanding of Barth, and that much of what Barth is doing is re-conceptualizing theology, it was judged that this approach,

---

Barth says, "In theological study, continuation always means 'beginning once again at the beginning.'"

[15] *BET*, p. 88.

[16] So Herbert Hartwell calls Barth's anthropology "the most consistent one of its kind and revolutionary in content....The traditional dogmatic way of thinking is here once more radically reversed" (*TBI*, p. 123).

[17] Eberhard Jüngel, *Karl Barth: A Theological Legacy*, trans. Garret E. Paul (Philadelphia: The Westminster Press, 1982) from the "Translator's Preface" (p. 7). (Hereafter, *BTL*)

as a point of departure for our own consideration, would best serve us, Barth, the academic theological community and the Church of Jesus Christ.

We do this with full awareness of the numerous criticisms and even wholesale dismissal of Barth, especially in the English-speaking world. We acknowledge many of the criticisms and difficulties which Barth presents in the accompanying notes. There we will regard it as our first task to point out possible misinterpretations of Barth in these criticisms, not in order to dismiss them, but in order to hold off prejudices which might prematurely bias us until more of the whole picture has been explored. It is our conviction, along with many of his interpreters, that the value and significance of Barth's contribution can only be recognized from a panoramic view of his work along with detailed study. Consequently, our own final criticism of Barth and evaluation of that of others are for the most part reserved for the concluding chapter.

Two more things need to be said in this preface. Our own approach to the subject matter follows along the lines of Barth's. We do not propose to begin with definitions of terms or axioms to interpret Barth. Barth explores a given theological terrain in order to end with a summary or something like a definition. We want to build up a picture of a theological landscape and then place the parent-child relationship in the foreground as Barth sees it. This means that the definitions and relationships of terms will become apparent only as the discussion develops. This also means that the force of argument and clarity of vision will arise out of the accumulated series of observations from various vantage points taken as a whole. Without this comprehensive "stereoscopic" perspective we would miss getting at the "heart" of what Barth has to say and to that extent we would be unable to make appropriate responses to Barth, make corrections, or build on what he has provided.

Finally, as Barth himself repeatedly acknowledged and as numerous of his interpreters have recognized, Barth intended to ground his exposition on the exegesis of the whole of the Biblical witness.[18] Despite the continuing controversy about how exegesis is to be done (not to mention its place in dogmatics itself) we are in substantial agreement with Barth that the single most important and indispensable criterion of theological adequacy is its faithfulness to the biblical witness to revelation: Jesus Christ. Consequently a sub-theme of our thesis will consist of pointing out (primarily in the notes) Barth's usage of

---

[18] So Arthur Cochrane in his "Translator's Preface" says that "No theologian in the history of the Church has so thoroughly and painstakingly grounded his theology in Holy Scripture....It is my conviction that the greatness of Karl Barth consists as much in being an expositor of Holy Writ as in being a systematic theologian" (in Weber, *BCD*, p. 13). Eberhard Jüngel points out that for Barth "it was the Bible that provided the decisive impetus for a proper theological beginning, in the sense of concrete biblical exegesis..." (*BTL*, p. 32). We also have Barth's well known lament: "If only we had returned to the Bible earlier, then we would have firm ground under our feet" in Barth's letter to Thurneysen, dated Nov. 11, 1918, cited in Eberhard Busch, *Karl Barth. His Life from Letters and Autobiographical Texts* (Philadelphia: Fortress Press, 1976) p. 106. (Hereafter, *KBL*)

biblical passages in his presentations and also of our own commenting on additional relevant biblical themes or passages which may bolster or call into question Barth's theological observations and conclusions.

It is our conviction, even though it is not our purpose to substantiate it here, that if those of Reformed/Evangelical commitment (especially in Britain, the United States and Canada) who have been suspicious of Barth's view of Scripture were to note carefully how he actually *uses* Scripture they would find in Barth a very helpful friend rather than a foe.

The theses of this book

So, in the light of both Barth's detractors and his supporters we want to put forth our own theses:

First we hold that the comprehension of Barth's special ethic of the parent-child relationship requires its interpretation in terms of his grounding it in his christological and so trinitarian anthropology. Second, we hold that the key, for Barth, to the interconnection between theology and ethics lies in comprehending the character of *the relations* in his doctrine of the *analogia relationis*. Third, we intend to show and make explicit the nature, or better, the "grammar" of his theology of relations which arises in his Christology, is central to his anthropology, is founded in his doctrine of the Trinity and which grounds his special ethics as illustrated in the section on "Parents and Children." Fourth, we contend that, in light of the grammar of personal relations, Barth's special ethic of parents and children, while not beyond criticism, is both relevant and fruitful for the Church's addressing many of the issues facing the contemporary American family.

Introduction

Today there is great concern over our human relations, whether in regard to the relations of men and women, parents and children, or among the peoples of the world's cultures and nations. What has become obviously problematic is the basis upon which to discern the shape of right relationship, that is, ethics. Whatever consensus there was in the West (and there was considerable agreement, even if it never was monolithic) is rapidly deteriorating. The effects of this erosion even upon the Christian Church have been evident for some time.

There are many new efforts to reestablish a basis for our human relations, that is, a basis for ethical discernment. Some have focused on the problem of the foundations for a non-religious public ethic in a pluralist society. Some have a concern for religiously based ethical reflections which arise out of particular traditions. Yet others are attempting to find how a particular religious foundation might nevertheless inform a public ethic.

Karl Barth (1886–1968), the eminent Swiss theologian, pursued his ethical explorations along the lines of this latter approach. The majority of his effort throughout his life focused on working out the essential Christian theological insights, a task he regarded as needing much revision in his day, and as inherently never beyond reformulation. However, his theological reflections were never done in a vacuum sealed off from ethical reflection.

This was due in part to his sensitivity and concern for his own historical situation. His thought took place in the context of the outbreak of World War I, the rise of Democratic Socialism throughout Europe, the rise of German National Socialism and the outbreak and resolution of World War II. But deeper than that, the connection discerned between theological truth and human relations he found to be intrinsic to Christianity. The study of the God of Christianity, the God present, active and revealed in Jesus Christ, demanded a theology which was inherently relational. A philosophy or theology uncritically adopted whose ontology was inherently non-relational Barth found to be woefully inadequate to the task of speaking faithfully concerning the object of Christian worship, the Triune God.

Of course, ethics rooted in the Christian tradition was the standard throughout Europe in Barth's day. However, in his view, the religious mindset of his day had reduced theology to anthropology and ethics. The failure of such a reduction had become manifest to him in Nazi Germany and in the unpreparedness of the Church to discern the nature of its threat to humanity and its own failure to establish a wide-spread and theologically informed resistance. Having seen this failure, the challenge fell to him to properly reconnect theology and ethics, faith and obedience. In fact, Barth's lifework can be regarded as a major reworking of how theology and ethics are interrelated.[1]

Barth's awareness of the intrinsic and thus unavoidable connection between theological faith and ethical obedience is evident throughout his writings. His first attempt systematically to develop a Christian ethic is found in his lectures on ethics at Münster for the summer semesters of 1928 and 1930.[2] The outline for these lectures is quite evident in the structure of the ethical sections proposed and written out in his later *Church Dogmatics*. While Barth significantly reworked the content, only the category of "orders of creation" was rejected outright for use in the *Church Dogmatics*.

In this present book we propose to investigate in depth and detail Karl Barth's theological grounding for his ethics as we find it in his *Church Dogmatics*. We explore and show how Barth saw the nature of the covenantal relationship between God and humanity revealed and actualized in Jesus Christ to be grounded in the trinitarian relations of Father, Son and Spirit. The relational nature of humanity and of the command of God to humanity are, in turn, found to be grounded by grace upon this Christological and trinitarian basis. There is, according to Barth, an *analogia relationis*, an analogy of relations. Beginning with the triune relations, there is a correspondence between them and the covenantal relationship established *ad extra* with creation and humanity in the person of Jesus Christ. Under the gracious command of God there is to be a further reflection or correspondence to the trinitarian and Christological relations in all our relations carried out "horizontally" within the creaturely realm. All these relations can be spoken of analogically as relations of covenantal love.

Barth's treatment is not meant to be speculative, but Christian. Thus, he regards himself as responsible for being faithful to Jesus Christ himself as attested to in the biblical witness. Barth's grasp of the theology of relations can be regarded as his attempt to draw together and understand the biblical witness to the reality and interconnection of the trinitarian, Christological, and human relations as they are embodied in Jesus Christ. In words attributed to Jesus Christ himself by the biblical authors, the Gospels attest to the analogy of these three relations. Jesus says, "As the Father has loved me, so I have loved you" (Jn 15:9).[3] Later, Jesus says, "...love one another as I have loved you" (Jn 15:12).

---

[1] John Webster, in his book, *Barth's Ethics of Reconciliation* (Cambridge: Cambridge University Press, 1995) clearly sets out the connection and proper relationship between Barth's doctrine of God, of humanity, and of the ethical nature of the covenantal relationship between God and humanity.

[2] Karl Barth's notes for these courses were collected and edited by Geoffrey W. Bromiley and published in English as *Ethics* (New York: The Seabury Press, 1981, second printing).

[3] Cf. John 16:27, "for the Father himself loves you, because you have loved me and have believed that I came from God."

Barth's theology of relations can be said to be "merely" theological reflections on the truth and reality to which Jesus in word and being bears witness.[4]

Despite all the differences, there is to be a correspondence, an analogy, between our human relations, God's relation to us in Jesus Christ, and the triune relations. Crucially, it should be noted that for Barth there is an irreversible direction for comparison. The triune relations provide the ontological and ethical grounding for our grasping and living out our relationship to God through Christ and then, in turn, for our relations with each other in the creaturely sphere. God's own triune love is the source and norm for our creaturely love. It is on that basis that we judge our human love. Although we inevitably begin with our own conceptions, we do not set them up as independent criteria by which to discern and judge God or humanity. Discerning the truth and reality of right relationship will call for *metanoia*, a repentance of mind as well as of action under the Word of God.

We attempt to show how Barth's theology of relations can, with careful qualification, be formulated in terms of a six-fold grammar of personal or covenantal relations. This grammar points to the "overlap" of the similarities among the relations, despite all the differences. Of course, the relations cannot be reduced to each other or to the formulation itself (the terms of comparison). The grammar is a (hopefully faithful) abstraction gained by theological reflection on the relations themselves as embodied in Jesus the living Word as attested to in the written Word. As such, the theological formulation is meant to serve the Word by assisting us in our preparation to live out our lives in right relationship to God through Christ and with each other.

There are those who charge that Barth's biblical and theological approach is necessarily ethically barren. We attempt to refute this in three ways. Taking a particular human relationship, we first show how incisively his trinitarian theology of relations informs what Barth calls his "special ethics of the parent-child relationship." Then, the fruitfulness of Barth's approach for enriching and critiquing both Christian and non-religious approaches to family relations is demonstrated by way of comparison with those formulated by F. D. Maurice, Ross Bender, Ray Anderson and Dennis Guernsey, James Dobson, Salvador Minuchen and Rudolph Dreikurs. Finally, the value of Barth's theology of relations is shown through some preliminary investigations into nine issues facing the family among which are procreation, adoption, and child rearing.

The study of Barth's theology requires a synthetic approach. All too often sections of Barth's work are considered in relative isolation. The result, often, has been a truncated interpretation and skewed critique. Barth's notion of analogy has been discussed at length in the literature. This discussion, however, needs to be enriched by Barth's grasp of relation. What he intended by the

---

[4]Cf. John 13:34, "I give you a new commandment, that you love one another. Just as I have loved you, you also should love one another."

concept of analogy cannot be grasped apart from what he saw to be analogous, namely, the relations. "Relation" is the subject, "analogous" is the predicate for Barth, not the other way around. In fact, his understanding of relations qualifies his entire theology and so, in turn, his ontology, anthropology and ethics. His ontology, theology and ethics are all relational. However, to merely note that Barth's theology is "relational" is only a start. How exactly did Barth construe these relations?

Barth himself never did synthesize into one section a comprehensive treatment of relationality. Perhaps surprisingly, Barth does not give us his most thorough treatment of relations within his doctrine of the Triunity of God. His most in-depth understanding of relation appears in his anthropology and in his presentation of the ethic of freedom for fellowship, parallel to it. Here one can see, in some of the most compressed theology to be found in the *Dogmatics*, that his ethical insight was rooted in his contemplation of the triune relations. The tree planted early on in the *Church Dogmatics* bears fruit in his anthropology and ethics.

But even bringing together the sections on the doctrines of the Trinity and humanity does not give us the most comprehensive view of relations. For Barth, the act and being of God are inseparably intertwined. Consequently, a consideration of the character or perfections of God, as manifested in the act of God *ad intra* within the triune life and *ad extra* towards creation, must also be taken into account. For Barth, relationality is not an abstract attribute of God's being. Rather, relationality involves being and act, form and content, living and doing. The trinitarian, Christological and human relations require a grasp of the shape of the relations as well as the interactions within the relations. Each qualifies the other. It is on the basis of this large and comprehensive theological understanding that Barth develops his view of the relational nature of humanity in being (ontology) and act (ethics).

The very structure, or what has been referred to as the architectonics, of the *Church Dogmatics* confirms this approach to understanding Barth. His ethical treatments always fall within the context of a theological grasp of the act and being of humanity which is placed in the more comprehensive context of the act and being of God in Jesus Christ, which is finally located within the most comprehensive context of the act and being of the Triune God. This is evident, for instance, if we consider the ethical section on the relationship of parents and children and see, first of all, how Barth refers back, explicitly and implicitly, to previous theological themes, and then note the structural context in which Barth has put this particular ethic.

Barth sets forth his special ethics of the parent-child relationship in *Church Dogmatics* III/4, Chapter XII, §54, part 2. This part volume comprises a single chapter entitled "The Command of the Creator." The section titles in this chapter are, in order after the introductory section, §53 Freedom Before God, §54 Freedom in Fellowship, §55 Freedom for Life, and §56 Freedom in Limitation.

Here we see humanity described in terms of acting in relation to others within the creaturely realm.

However, we find four sections exactly parallel to these earlier in Chapter X, "The Creature" in *Church Dogmatics* III/2. The titles of these sections are in order, omitting the introductory section, §44 Man as the Creature of God, §45 Man in His Determination as the Covenant-Partner of God, §46 Man as Soul and Body, and §47 Man in His Time. Here we see humanity described in terms of his being in relation—being in relation first to God, then to others, then within himself, and then to time. Chapter X provides the most immediate context within which to interpret Chapter XII. Taking these two chapters together, seeing humanity as both being and acting in relation, we have Barth's essential theological anthropology.

But we must point out that, within Chapter X on the creature, each of the four sections opens with a part devoted to discerning the true nature of humanity in terms of Jesus Christ. So, we find these headings at the beginning of each section: §44.1 Jesus, Man for God, §45.1 Jesus, Man for other Men, §46.1 Jesus, Whole Man, §47.1 Jesus, Lord of Time. Jesus Christ not only reveals to us God, but humanity as well. Not humanity apart from God, for there is no such thing, but humanity in right relation to God. So at the heart of his anthropology is Christology, properly distinguished and related to it. The Christological relation sheds light and gives life to humanity in its relationships, first with God and then with others. Humanity is given its existence in being and act by God through Jesus Christ. In freedom we live out our lives in being and act in correspondence to the essential relations in which we live and move and have our being.

The more immediate context for Barth's anthropology and the most comprehensive context for his special ethics ultimately reaches back to his consideration of "The Triunity of God" in Chapter II, "The Revelation of God," *Church Dogmatics*, I/1. The emphasis in this chapter is on the being of God as Father, Son and Holy Spirit, the Trinity in Unity and Unity in Trinity. This development, of course, does not exclude reference to God's act, Jesus Christ incarnate, or humanity. The emphasis here, however, is upon the revelatory act of the Triune God.

Barth's doctrine of God, however, cannot be comprehended apart from its subsequent explication with its emphasis on God's being in action considered in *Church Dogmatics*, II/1, Chapter VI, "The Reality of God" under four sections: §28 "The Being of God as the One Who Loves in Freedom," §29 "The Perfections of God," §30 "The Perfections of the Divine Loving" and §31 "The Perfections of the Divine Freedom." Barth's understanding of the triune relations cannot be fully appreciated until the content, that is, the action within the relations as we find it in these sections, is given full consideration.

Any approach to God's being without reference to God's acts is indeed merely abstract theological speculation. So much consideration of the doctrine of the Trinity, including that given to Barth's treatment, has focused on the description of the being, that is, the form or shape of the relations. In Barth's view, we can be faithful to the revelation of God only when we see that there is no "slippage" between the being and action of God. God is true to his being in his action.

Consequently, the perfections of God's being, as the one who loves in freedom, provides the actual content by which to interpret the triune being of God. The begetting, being begotten and the procession of Father, Son, and Holy Spirit are the internal and eternal expressions of the Being of God in Loving Freedom. God's own being exists as a being in holy triune love. Who God is antecedently within the triune relations, (*ad intra*) is manifested externally (*ad extra*) in and through Creation, Reconciliation, and Redemption. Consequently, the truth of this reality is reflected in the being and proscribed action of humanity with its origin, norm and end being found in Jesus Christ.

Thus, all of Barth's ethical reflections are essentially grounded in this ultimate context of the revelation of the Triune God in act and being through the covenant relationship established with humanity in Jesus Christ. Thus, being, act, and relation are, for Barth, all drawn together as essential to the existence of God and so, in its own creaturely way, essential to the existence of humanity.

Barth, in his general ethics (II/2) and again at the beginning of his special ethics (III/4), argues for the interconnection of theology and ethics. This unity is grounded theologically in his understanding of God as revealed in Jesus Christ. The Triune God revealed in Jesus Christ is the God who has his being in acting in relation. Following the internal pattern, the God who acts in relation to us by creating, reconciling and redeeming us at the deepest levels of our being is the same God who commands us to action in our relations.

Barth's intention from the outset is to develop a theological ethic. Ethics then is essentially regarded as a matter of the command of God to us, an expression of God's proper relationship to us. Accordingly, each volume of the *Church Dogmatics* begins with a lengthy theological presentation and concludes with a chapter on the relevant command of God. His discussion of theological ethics, in general, concludes his volume (II) on "The Doctrine of God." As we pointed out earlier, his chapter on special ethics, "The Command of God the Creator," concludes the volume (III) on "The Doctrine of Creation" in strict parallel with his development of his doctrine of humanity two chapters earlier in the same volume.

The very structure of the *Dogmatics* communicates volumes as to how Barth saw theology proper connected intrinsically to ethical reflection because God's own existence and ours in turn are essentially relational, involving act and being. However, the content of the various sections carries this through in great detail with persistent force.

Within the section on "Parents and Children" Barth does explicitly refer both to his anthropology and to its theological grounding. However, the references there are not exhaustive. The force and fullness of his explication of that relationship cannot be fully appreciated except in the context of the more comprehensive development of both his anthropology and its theological framework.

One can readily see in the "Parents and Children" section reference to the more comprehensive theological grounding. It is most evident where Barth refers to the purpose of parenting. He observes that the command of God regarding the relationship of parents and their children is rooted in the fact that "parents have a Godward aspect, and are for them God's primary and natural representatives."[5] Their "mission" (*Auftrag*) is "the correspondence of their parenthood to the being and action of God."[6] Later, Barth indicates that parents are to be a "pale reflection" (*trüber Abglanz*)[7] of the truth that God Himself is, and so are to be "ambassadors" (*Beauftragte*) of God.[8]

A full comprehension of what this mission of representation might mean for Barth depends on his understanding of God. For Barth this is not merely a matter of definition, because according to the biblical witness "No human father, but God alone is properly, truly, and primarily Father."[9] He explains this by saying that the Father is the Father of the Son and that, by grace, in correspondence (*in Entsprechung*) to His own, there should be a human fatherhood as well. Thus, human parenting exists on the basis of the Father-Son relationship as a human creaturely counterpart.[10] Again, to comprehend fully what this entails one must refer to Barth's understanding of the Father-Son relationship previously developed.

Awareness of the theological grounding is no less necessary when Barth describes the nature of the parent-child relationship. Following the biblical imperatives, Barth maintains that children are to honor and be subordinate to their parents. They are to be under their parents' discipline. Parents are to love their children and not provoke them to anger. If these and other characteristics of the parent-child relationship are to be understood theologically, as Barth would have us do, then his discussion of God's relationship with His people and the Son's relationship to the Father are essential for comprehending the parent-child

---

[5] *Church Dogmatics*, III/4, p. 245. (Hereafter, *CD*) "...*in der Blickrichtung auf Gott hin stehen und und ihnen gegenüber Gottes erste, für sie seine natürlich Repräsentanten sind*" (*Kirchliche Dogmatik*, p. 274). Page references for the *Kirchliche Dogmatik* (hereafter *KD*) will usually be given only for phrases or longer citations. The volume and part volume designations are identical for English and German editions.

[6] *Ibid.* "...*der Entsprechung ihrer Elternschaft zum Sein und Handeln Gottes*" (*KD*, p. 274).

[7] *Ibid.*, p. 247.

[8] *Ibid.*, p. 256.

[9] *Ibid.*, p. 245. Barth refers us to Eph. 3:15; Is. 63:16; Mt. 23:9; Is. 49:15; Ps. 27:10 and Is. 45:10 for some of the biblical grounding of this understanding of fatherhood. All Biblical quotations taken from secondary sources will be shown in single quotation marks, all other biblical references will be in double-quotation marks and will be taken from the Revised Standard Version (RSV) by the National Council of the Churches of Christ (1951).

[10] *Ibid.*

relationship. While Barth does expand somewhat on the grounding for his notions of the mission and the nature of the parental relationship, his discussion is limited because it assumes his previous theological discussion of humankind and God.

It should now be apparent why great attention must be given to Barth's understanding of relations to grasp not only his understanding of ethics, but also why it is essential for any understanding of his doctrine of God, Christology and humanity. The divine being in act of the God revealed in Jesus Christ is inherently relational, that is, is loving in freedom. In a corresponding creaturely way, our being in act is also inherently relational, first in connection with God and correspondingly with each other and with all of creation. We were created, reconciled and redeemed for giving glory to God by having our being in relation reflect God's own character of being in loving communion.

The structure of our own book then follows from this. The first part consists of three chapters on Barth's theological foundations. In the first chapter we will briefly explore Barth's Christological starting point for developing his theology of relations. In the second chapter we gather Barth's insights into the trinitarian relations. In the third chapter we consider Barth's anthropology, in which we see how Barth regarded true humanity, as revealed in Jesus Christ, essentially to be in covenantal relation with the Triune God, his Creator, Reconciler and Redeemer.

In the second part, beginning with the fourth chapter, we investigate how, through Jesus Christ, Barth understood our true humanity to be essentially relational in our communion with others. In the fifth chapter we attempt to draw our conclusions as to how Barth grasped the essential nature of relations as it pertains first to the Triune God, then to God's relation to us and our relation to God in Christ, and finally how it analogically pertains to humanity in its creaturely relations. We put forth a six-fold theological grammar of relations in an attempt to characterize the shape and content, our being, and act, in right covenant relationship.

In the third part of this work we explore, in three chapters, Barth's treatment of the special ethics of the parent-child relationship to see if our characterization fits and illuminates what Barth was thinking.

In the last part we attempt to make use of Barth's theology of relations and his special ethics of parents and children to work out some implications beyond what Barth developed. In Chapter 9 we demonstrate how Barth's theology of relations and special ethics are helpful for enriching and critiquing both Christian and non-religious approaches to family relations. In Chapter 10, we explore the implications of Barth's theology of relations for nine issues facing the contemporary family in the United States. These issues range from establishing the purpose and goals of the family, to the potential for new models of the family, and the meaning of procreation, adoption, child rearing and children and family in the Church.

Part One

Barth's Theological Grounding of Anthropology and Ethics

Chapter 1

The Christological Starting Point for a Theology of Relations

To begin, we will point out how Barth understands the theological task and what in general he intends by pursuing a theological anthropology.[1] We will see that for him the norm of all theology is the Word because the Word of God reveals both God and humankind and also establishes their actual being in relationship, and that humanity is created in such a way through the Word that it images the Triune God.

The Theological Task: Faith Seeking Understanding of the Word of God

The task that Karl Barth saw set before himself was to "interpret"[2] the Word of God as revealed in Jesus Christ; that Word to which the Bible is the unique witness. Faith in that Word carries within it the impetus to pursue the understanding of that Word. Theology has the task of thinking in a way that corresponds to and so is ordered by that Word of Revelation. The theological task Barth had before him was not to discover God, or to defend belief in God, or even expand our knowledge of God, but to unfold faithfully the knowledge of the God who is given to us in Jesus Christ. Theology is done by the Church in faith for the sake of faith. For Barth the object of faith determines the motive and contour of reflection upon it. We could say that Barth regards it as his task to interpret the Word as it is given to him by that Word. Faithfulness to the givenness of the Word provides the reason why Barth attempts to make his anthropology and ethics theological from start to finish.[3]

The Theological Source: The Word Revealing the Knowledge of God and the Knowledge of Humanity

How does Barth see the relationship between anthropology and a theology founded upon the Word of God? He perhaps puts it most simply: "Man is made an object of theological knowledge by the fact that his relationship to God is

---

[1] It should be noted that we will not attempt to explore the validity of Barth's grounding anthropology in the Word nor critique his decision to do so. Our aim is not to explore why he did so but how he carried out his theological anthropology and what results he achieved.

[2] Barth also uses the words "analyze" (*Analyze*), "translates" (*übersetzt*), and "exegetes" (*exegesiert*), to describe his theological task. See *CD,* I/1, p. 308; *KD,* p. 325.

[3] His wrestling with the issues and the development of the nature of this faith orientation to the dogmatic task are unfolded in his discussion on prolegomena in *CD,* I/1, §1.

revealed to us in the Word of God."[4] A true knowledge of humankind,[5] like our knowledge of God, is not gained through an autonomous human quest. It is a given, it is a made known truth. The point at which this true knowledge of human being is given is the same point at which we come to faith in God: Jesus Christ. Jesus Christ, as the object of our knowledge of God, is also the object of our knowledge of mankind. The same faith that leads to reflection on God leads to reflection on man. The God-man Jesus Christ is the object of our faith and the object of our anthropological (and subsequently ethical) inquiry. The contours of our investigation are determined by the object of our faith. Thus, reflection upon humankind, too, is an act of faith; an act of faithfulness to its source and object.

Since formulating a theological anthropology is an act of faith, this means that even the questions to be asked are critiqued by this faith. Faith must remain faith if it is to have faithful and so theological knowledge of humankind. So Barth comments:

> [Theological] anthropology confines its inquiry to the human creatureliness presupposed in this relationship [between God and man] and made known by it, i.e. by its revelation and biblical attestation. It asks what kind of a being it is which stands in this relationship with God. Its attention is wholly concentrated *on the relationship.*[6]

For Barth, the biblical witness directs us to understand humankind in terms of its *relationship (Verhältnis)* with God.

---

[4] *CD*, III/2, p. 19. The word Barth used, which is translated "man" or "mankind," almost invariably is *Mensch*, It has no exact English equivalent, but it certainly has an inclusive connotation since it refers to the whole of humanity. The English "man" is perhaps closer to the German *Mann*, especially if its inclusive sense is questioned, which can be translated "male." *Der Mensch* can be translated "humanity." However, this is a translation which, in the *Church Dogmatics*, is reserved for the words *Menschlichkeit* or *Humanität*. When quoting Barth we have stayed with the standard English translation. So, it is important to remember the German behind it. In this book we have attempted to accommodate our usage out of a concern for inclusivity. For the most part we have used "humankind" or "humanity" instead of "man" or "mankind" without too much awkwardness. However, given the complexity of the topic itself plus the interaction of the two languages, for reasons of style or clarity it is at times best to use "mankind" interchangeably with "humankind" or "humanity." This occurs especially when Barth is speaking of the particular character of the humanity (*Menschlichkeit* or *Humanität*) of all mankind (*Der Mensch*).

[5] Barth recognizes that human existence may be considered at various levels. His presentation is shaped by the way he understands the biblical witness to regard the whole of human existence. As he works it out he comes to hold that there is a determinative factor, namely, our acknowledged or unacknowledged relationship to Jesus Christ. All other factors of human existence, then, are relative to this. Thus, all knowledge about any aspect of human existence will be seen in its true sense only when comprehended in terms of this determinative factor. See Barth's discussion of this in "The Phenomena of the Human" in *CD*, III/2.

[6] *CD*, III/2, p. 19. My emphasis.

The knowledge of God revealed in Jesus Christ is the knowledge of the God of mankind. The knowledge of humanity revealed in Jesus Christ is the knowledge of the humanity of God. The God to whom we refer in our inquiry is none other than the God of humanity. Who else is this humanity but the humanity of this God? Thus, our inquiry, if it is to be faithful to what it seeks to know, must be directed to the God of this humanity and the humanity of this God. So Barth observes: "In the Bible revelation is always a history between God and certain men."[7] This relationship determines humanity's essential identity.

Thus, faithful reflection upon the Word—which is ordered by that Word, reveals both God and humankind because in the person of Jesus Christ we encounter the relationship of God and mankind. A theological anthropology and ethic is one grounded in the incarnate Word of God.

The foundations for such an approach were of course laid much earlier in the *Church Dogmatics* than III/2. It lies at the root of his consideration of the Word of God in *CD*, I/1. Christian faith, at its most basic point, the point of revelation, has to do both with God and with man. For there to be a Word of God, that is a revelation at all, implies One who speaks and the one to whom the Word is spoken. Faith itself implies a relation between the God who reveals and the one who receives the revelation. This is developed as early as *CD*, I/1 in sections such as "Dogmatics as an Act of Faith" (pp. 17ff.), "The Word of God Revealed" (pp. 111ff.) and "The Knowability of the Word of God" (pp. 187ff.)[8]

---

[7] *CD*, I/1, p. 298.

[8] We must guard ourselves at this point and not be misled. The points which Barth lays down earlier in the *Church Dogmatics* do not function as principles or axioms which then control all later expositions. The earlier conclusions do not control in this way the later conclusions. Barth is not developing a systematic theology by way of logical deduction. Thus he says that his work is not "...a self-contained and fully established coherence of principles and deductions, constructed on the basis of the presuppositions of a certain fundamental perspective and with the rise of certain sources of knowledge and axioms" (*CD*, I/2, p. 861). For further discussion see Geoffrey Bromiley, *Introduction to the Theology of Karl Barth* (Wm. B. Eerdmans Publishing Co.: Grand Rapids, 1979) pp. x–xi; Colin Gunton, "Karl Barth and the Development of Christian Doctrine," *Scottish Journal of Theology*, Vol. 22 (1972) p. 173; W. A. Whitehouse, "The Christian View of Man. An Examination of Karl Barth's Doctrine," *Scottish Journal of Theology*, Vol. 2 (1949) (Hereafter, *SJT*), p. 58.

Often, what is said at one place in the *Dogmatics* is actually a more complete explication of a certain aspect of the one whole truth left rather undeveloped previously when considering another aspect of it. However, in some sections the full explication will be referred to in a shorthand way assuming familiarity with it while developing another related point. The way Barth's thought develops perhaps can be likened to circumnavigating a fixed center point. The Word of God, Jesus Christ stands at the center. It is the object of our inquiry and subsequent interpretation. The circumference of the circle around the center represents the many points of Barth's theological explication. A particular point is both a place to stand to interpret the Word and is the subsequent doctrinal point explicated from that

Thus, the Word considered both as Incarnate and as Revelation indicates a relationship of God with humankind. A theology of the Word of God in Jesus Christ carries within it an anthropology, an anthropology that is grounded in a particular relationship. It is Barth's task then to allow this Word to order his interpretation of humankind.[9] We might say that for Barth the Word is God's

---

position. Barth begins by standing at one point on the circle and interprets the Word from this particular place. From this one place he must "assume" what has been said at other places in order to assist in critiquing the one place where he is now standing. Of course the place in which he stands is no *tabula rasa*. He may begin with certain definitions and understandings and questions, however these are all to be questioned in the light of the living center point. The other points on the circumference do not serve as axioms, but are referred to by way of correlation. They serve as secondary points of confirmation of one's interpretation from the present angle of consideration. What develops at one point may serve to send one back to other points to re-evaluate them. The other points may serve to call for further evaluation and development of the issue presently concerned. There is thus an ongoing dialogue around the perimeter concerning the primary conversation with its living center. The aim of such Church dogmatics is a discernment of the Word spoken being confirmed from numerous angles around the center. Eventually all points could be developed and critiqued but this cannot be done for all points at once. What this means is that at no point is faith in its one object, Jesus Christ, dismissed. Doing this would altogether eliminate the primary object of investigation at the center of the circle around which the theologian moves. The object of Christian faith at its center cannot be confused with its own linguistic and human creations on the perimeter. Jesus Christ Himself is never just another theological point on circumference of the theological circle.

At this point we may note the affinity Barth has with Dietrich Bonhoeffer's understanding of the theological task as indicated in his *Christ the Center*, new translation, Edwin H. Robinson (New York, Hagerstown, San Francisco, London: Harper and Row Publishers, 1978), published in England under the title *Christology*. Theological science is always Church dogmatics, by faith for faith. But all points of it may come under scrutiny at one time or another that every point of explication may be faithful to its source, the revelation in Jesus Christ and the Scripture which bears witness to Him. As T. F. Torrance and others have noted, this approach has methodological parallels with contemporary science as set forth most explicitly by Michael Polanyi and others such as Albert Einstein and James Clerk Maxwell. See Thomas F. Torrance, *Transformation & Convergence in the Frame of Knowledge: Explorations in the Interrelations of Scientific and Theological Enterprise* (Grand Rapids: William B. Eerdmans Publishing Co., 1984); *Theological Science* (Oxford, London, New York: Oxford University Press, 1978), and Michael Polanyi, *Personal Knowledge* (New York: Harper, 1964).

[9]It is not the syntactical relations of language which ground Barth's understanding of the Word as revelation, as he goes to great lengths to explain (*CD*, I/1, p. 296). The words Revealer, Revelation, and Revealedness do act linguistically as subject, predicate and object. His most basic affirmation of the whole of the *Dogmatics* "God reveals Himself as Lord" exhibits the same syntactical relations. But the grammatical logic does not form the weight of his argument. The logic and the grammar of the God of Jesus Christ are found in the *event* of the revelation, which then one may express, inadequately but approximately and faithfully, in a linguistic

own interpretation of mankind to which we in our theological reflection must attempt to be faithful. What is essentially revealed in this Word is that humankind cannot be understood apart from its relationship with its God, nor is God to be understood apart from humankind. By this we cannot mean "God" in a general way, or "humankind" in a general way. Both are to be interpreted in light

---

form which does happen to bring with it a logic of its own. However this secondary logicality cannot become a criterion for theology and so it may be finally "left behind" (*CD*, I/1 p. 361). Timothy Bradshaw, *Trinity and Ontology. A Comparative Study of the Theologies of Karl Barth and Wolfhart Pannenberg* (Edinburgh: Rutherford House Books, 1988), pp. 79–82, completely misses this point when he cites Wolfhart Pannenberg, *Grundfragen Systematischer Theologie*. Gessamelt Aufsatze Band 2, (Göttingen: Vandenhoeck und Ruprecht, 1980) pp. 101–102, who accuses Barth of "speculative" arguments for the Trinity from "the inner logic of the concept of revelation in which subject, predicate and object...have to be differentiated" rather than on the more legitimate basis of exegesis and the historical relation of Jesus to the Father. According to Pannenberg, Barth remained ironically "addicted" to Hegelianism. The trinitarian definitions are "only confirmed after being derived from the sentence, 'God reveals Himself as Lord'..." Whatever Barth's relationship to Hegelianism, the logic of the language had no *normative* influence on his definitions of the Trinity. Bradshaw's thesis, that Barth's relation to Hegelianism is helpful in understanding him [Barth], is misleading. It gives the impression that the structure of Barth's thinking was somehow necessarily and normatively shaped by the parameters of Hegelian thought. While Barth could admit to utilizing certain philosophical thought patterns, the question as to whether these thought patterns had a normative influence and whether they undergo critical transformation when utilized by Barth in the service of the Word, are crucial questions. The order of dependency is of ultimate importance for Barth, as we shall see. The inner logic that Barth is working with is not determined by a given system of thought or grammar. The Word contains its own inner logic. (For a discussion of the inner logic, i.e. the theo-logic, see Ray S. Anderson, *Historical Transcendence and the Reality of God* (London: Geoffrey Chapman Publishers, 1975), pp. 103–227.) While Barth may admit to a certain correspondence of the structure of his thought and that of Hegelianism, it would be truer to say, following Barth, that the correlation came about in a purely secondary way as Barth sought to correlate his theology with the Word. Barth certainly considered himself under no obligation to correlate his conclusions with any part of Hegelianism. His intention was to overthrow Hegelianism as a controlling conceptual structure. If it does correspond to his thought at points it is all but purely accidental in regard to the ultimate concerns Barth had. This is not to deny a certain correlation. But it raises the question of discerning the ultimate grounds for there arising such a correspondence and deciding which perspective is the more comprehensive. Is Barth's thought finally under the constraint of being conditioned by the authority of the Word or by Hegelianism? To deny that the former is a possibility and affirm that language and predetermined concepts preeminently condition all our thoughts is to succumb to Arianism all over again. Given the fact that Bradshaw does not believe that Hegel's conception of God is a more adequate interpretation than Barth's, but the opposite, then in the final analysis it would perhaps be more accurate to say that by understanding Barth, in the light of the Word, we have gained great assistance in understanding Hegel, rather than *vice versa*.

of the Word itself, Jesus Christ. This is Barth's theological anthropology of the Word. It is a Christological anthropology which asks who God and mankind are and answers that they are who they are and are truly known only in this relationship. Thus, it is their being in this relationship which constitutes the content of the revelation of God and humankind.

Yet this does not mean that his anthropology results in an improper Christocentrism which neglects the Father and Spirit in favor of the Son.[10] Jesus reveals to us Himself *in relationship* to His Father in the Spirit. Jesus introduces us to the Triune God who exists in eternal relations and has established with us a gracious relationship by which we may participate in the triune life. Thus, the Christological relation *reveals the trinitarian relations.*

Furthermore, it is self-evident that ethics is concerned with human relationships. A theological ethic, grounded in the Word and so the triune life of God, does not obliterate the human sphere. The Triune God, who has revealed himself in the Word, is the commanding God. For Barth, the commands of God call persons in their human relationships to correspond in their being and action to his. Persons are created, reconciled and redeemed to become in their persons those who are like Jesus Christ, the Word Incarnate. Our relationships with one another are to become analogous to the Christological relationship of God with humankind and so become analogous also to the triune relationships, albeit in a further removed way. It is through the Word that we have the warrant to consider each relation, trinitarian, Christological and human, to be constituted in its own way as a form of covenantal love.

In exactly what way this is so will require much more explicit development. For now, by way of anticipation, we can only say that it is on the basis of the Word of God that Barth attempts to understand the triune relations. And that in the light of that same Word he demonstrates in his anthropology how the relationships among the Triune Persons, between God and His people, and in all our human relations, for all their differences, are to be comparable, that is, are "analogous." Thus, his doctrine of *analogia relationis* finds its source in the Word of God, living and so written.

The Shape of our Relations: The *Analogia Relationis*

While much attention has been given to Barth's understanding of analogy, we want to explore the nature of *the relationships* which Barth indicates are analogous. The term *analogia relationis* does not occur until Barth considers the Christological grounding for anthropology. This makes perfect sense in that there would be no sense of speaking of some kind of comparison until the second term of comparison is brought to the foreground, in this case our human relations to God and then with each other. However, since Barth ultimately sees

---

[10]See *CD*, I/1, p. 395, for one of Barth's earlier expressions of the need to avoid an improper "Christocentrism," as held within Pietism, as well as an equally improper one-sided belief in God the Father.

human existence to be grounded in the triune life of God, a detailed study of the nature of the triune relationships is required for us to recognize in what way the relationships in the spheres of Christology, anthropology and special ethics are indeed analogous. We will do just that shortly.

Before we move on to the trinitarian relations, we should note an important way Barth comprehends relations. In his discussion of the *analogia relationis,* Barth, without much explanation, expounds his understanding of the nature of relationships using two mutually related terms: "form" or "structure" and "material content" or "action." For Barth, relations can be grasped in terms of form and content, or structure and action. These terms cannot be separated from one another. Each interprets the other. The basis for this categorization is not any commitment to Platonism or Idealism, even if this terminology is found there, too. For Barth, while the categories of form and content may be borrowed, they must be critiqued and filled out theologically. These terms reflect Barth's understanding that the God revealed in the Word is united in being and action.[11] The Word concretely and particularly reveals God as united in being and act. Barth interprets form as pointing to the being/character of the one in a relation and interprets the content, even more unusually, as the action which corresponds to the being in relation. Through Jesus Christ, God is true to his being—true to his character, in his acts of creation, reconciliation and redemption. His actions are actually revelatory of Who God is. In Jesus Christ, the *self*-revelation of God, the act and being of God in person are co-incident. Jesus says, 'He who has seen me has seen the Father" (John 14:9). And in another context he says, "I only do what I see the Father doing" (John 5:19). In Jesus Christ, God himself is present (Immanuel) in the act of his revelation and salvation. Jesus' identity, who he is, is entirely wrapped up in what he does. He is what he does, he does what he is. He is Lord and Savior because by his Lordship he reconciles and redeems. The form and content of his relation with God and with us are in complete correspondence. So, for Barth, all relations can be comprehended in terms of the theologically defined categories of form and content. The trinitarian, Christological and human relations can be said to be analogical in the sense that each in its own way involves inseparably act and being, content and form.

This much is clear and easily discerned in Barth's work. However, how exactly he characterizes the relations under each of these two foundational categories is, at first glance, not obvious. He nowhere explicitly sets out his full grasp of relations. In Barth's anthropology of *CD,* II/2 the characterizations, which are many, seem fluid since he seems to interchange different word/concepts to point to the same dimension of relationality. He characterizes relations as a whole sometimes in terms of two categories (form and content), sometimes in terms of four categories, and most often in terms of six categories.

---

[11] This theme is especially developed much earlier in *CD,* II/1, §28, "The Being of God as the One Who Loves in Freedom."

There is not perfect consistency in the structure and language of his thought. But clearly he is filling out the shape and content of his grasp of relations.

This study is an attempt to draw together and synthesize Barth's thought on a theology of relations. Indeed, careful study of Barth's treatment of relations in all three spheres, the trinitarian, Christological and anthropological, which Barth himself said were analogical, comparable, and an in-depth study of the Scriptural basis for his thought, to which Barth understood himself to be ultimately accountable, led to a clear and coherent grasp of how Barth sees covenantal relations and why he then asserts that they are analogical.

We intend to make explicit how Barth comprehended the nature of the relations first within the triune life, then Christologically, and then in our human relationships, devoting a chapter to each sphere of relation. However, by way of anticipation, it might be helpful to present here the basic outline of our conclusions. When taken altogether as Barth understood them, and in accordance with the biblical witness, the pattern of relationship which is analogous among all these relationships can be formulated in terms of a six-fold "grammar" of relations. This grammar can be subdivided into the two major categories of the Form of the Relations and the Content or Action in the Relations as Barth theologically defined them. As a title we have chosen to identify this formulation as our "Personal-Covenantal Being-in-Relationship." We will contend that the grammar of being-in-relationship involves these six characteristics under two headings:

OUR PERSONAL-COVENANTAL BEING-IN-RELATION

The Form of our Being-in-Relations
1) A unity of persons or subjects
2) A distinction of persons
3) A co-ordination or correspondence of persons

The Content or Action in our Relations
4) A personal-loving communion/fellowship of interaction between persons
5) A dynamic of becoming persons in the process of being in covenant relationships
6) An extension of persons to others to include them in covenantal relationship

It is this grammar of relations which will be more explicitly developed as we follow Barth from his doctrine of the Trinity, through his Christology and anthropology and on to his special ethics of parents and children.

Chapter 2

The Trinitarian Relations: Son, Father and Holy Spirit

What we propose to do in this part is to survey Barth's discussion of the Triunity of God in Vol. 1 of the *Church Dogmatics* and make more explicit the nature of the internal relations revealed in Jesus Christ as Barth draws them out. Barth's perspective on the triune relations as set forth in this volume is confirmed again and again for him as he considers them from different perspectives throughout the *Church Dogmatics*. In this volume he focuses specifically on the action of God's self-revelation which attests *who* God is as Father, Son, and Spirit.

On the basis of the revelation of God, Barth rejected the traditional Scholastic scheme of asking in order: How do we know God? Does God exist? What is God? "and only last of all: Who is our God?"[1] For Barth, the biblical witness sets the priority for our question and bears witness to the answer as to who this God of Jesus Christ is. We must begin with the question of Who and on that basis we may come to know the God who has revealed himself. In Christ we see that who God is, is the Triune God: Father, Son, and Holy Spirit. Thus, Barth begins his *Dogmatics* proper with the doctrine of the Trinity. Barth's discussion in this section (I/1, Chap. II "The Revelation of God") focuses on what he occasionally calls the structure or form of these internal triune relations. Later he fills out the content (by this Barth means the action which takes place in the relations) which characterizes these specific triune relations (II/1, "The Reality of God").[2] For Barth, who God is revealed to be is One who exists in triune relations.

---

[1] *CD*, I/1, pp. 297–303. The significance of this insight and "methodology" cannot be over-stressed. It has ramifications throughout Barth's works. We will find it playing an important role in his anthropology and ethics.

[2] See *CD*, I/1, p. 363, *KD*, p. 383 for his designations: "*den inhaltlichen Verscheidenheiten*" = material differences and "*die formalen Eigentümlichkeiten*" = formal distinctions. Barth will come to use, in III/2 (See pp. 142, 145; *KD*, pp. 170, 173), the terminology of the "form" (*Form*) or "structure" and "material content" (*inhaltliche Füllung*) for describing the whole reality (ontology) of being in relationship. These terms have unique meanings for Barth. What Barth means by structure or form has to do with the contours of being, the nature of being in relationship. The material content of the relationship denotes the interaction which occurs in the relationship. For Barth these two can never be separated. Being in relationship manifests itself in action and action confirms or is a participation in the structure of being in relationship. See Stuart McLean, *Humanity in the Thought of Karl Barth* (Edinburgh: T&T Clark Ltd., 1981) pp. 25–30 (Hereafter, *HTB*) for a helpful discussion of this. It will become clearer what exactly Barth means by structure and content as we follow along. It seems that it is somewhat confusing for him to use these terms in the way he does. Each content has a form which can also have a content itself and even though action takes form Barth usually discusses form

The Shape of Relation in God's Self-Revelation

For Barth, the knowledge of the Triune God, and so faith in God, has come about through the Triune God's own initiative and presence in Jesus Christ. His *Church Dogmatics* begins with an analysis of the Word of God. This Word is a Word of Revelation which turns out to have a threefold shape itself. There is the Subject of revelation (Revealer), there is the action of the revelation (Revelation), and there is the accomplishment of the revelation (Revealedness) in the object of the revelation. Thus, Barth speaks of the threefold Word as the Revealer, Revelation, and Revealedness of the Triune God. Though the Word of Revelation is threefold, there is a certain kind of priority among the three "modes" of God's Word. The "innermost circle" of this threefold yet one Word is the Word become flesh, Immanuel, God with us.[3] God's action in His revelation, the Word Incarnate, is primary because it leads us to the other aspects of His revelation.[4]

The biblical witness considered as a whole presents us with the question of a threefoldness of Revealer, Revelation, and Revealedness. Yahweh is the one who has revealed himself as Lord of man. Yet, if we follow the biblical witness, we must in some way distinguish among the Revealer, the Revelation and the being revealed. Nevertheless, the fact that this knowledge of God is accomplished by the initiative and action of the Revealer and the fact that He reveals *Himself*, so that there is an actual knowledge of Him, point to a kind of identity among the elements of the threefoldness. This question of the identity and yet distinction in God's revealing Himself as Lord, as posed in the Biblical witness and not by the "logic" of the syntax of language, is answered in Jesus Christ the Son of God.[5]

In the person of Jesus Christ we meet with the embodiment of and so also the source of our knowledge of the unity and distinctions of God. In Him we come to know God in His internal relations as Father, Son and Holy Spirit. It is this relational reality which stands ontologically prior to God's being Revealer, Revelation, and Revealedness. God is the one who as *One God* reveals Himself. However this revelation involves three ways of being revealed. Revelation demonstrates that there is both a unity and a differentiation in God. However, it

---

first and then the action taking form. We will follow his usage for the time being and allow him to re-define these terms for us.

[3] *CD*, I/1, p. 119.

[4] "...biblical revelation has on the one side a specific historical centre and the doctrine of the Trinity has on the other side a specific historical occasion in biblical revelation. Historically considered and stated, the three questions answered in the Bible, that of revealer, revelation and being revealed, do not have the same importance. The true theme of the biblical witness is the second of the concepts, God's action in His revelation, revelation in answer to the question what God does, and therefore the predicate in our statement. Within this theme the two other questions, materially no less important are answered" (*Ibid.*, pp. 314–315).

[5] See *CD*, I/1, pp. 298–299.

is only when we see in the Word that this corresponds to God's triune being in relationship as Father, Son and Spirit that we come to comprehend that the true nature and source of the unity and distinctions arise in the life of God.

Consequently, for theology, for faith which seeks understanding, there is a Christological concentration of our knowledge of God because God concentrated His self-revelation as the Lord of man in Jesus Christ. In the order of knowing we must begin with God where God has begun with us: with the Word of God. However, in and through that Word we know God as one who exists eternally and internally in relationships of unity and differentiation as Father, Son, and Spirit. Consequently, we see a confirmation and correspondence of that in the three-fold structure of his revelation.

Knowledge of God in Christ, i.e. by revelation, leads to a knowledge of God as triune: Father, Son and Holy Spirit. "The doctrine of the Trinity is nothing else than the unfolding of the knowledge that Jesus is the Christ or the Lord....It can proceed from nowhere else."[6] This historical event, the fullness of time, in "the existence of the man Jesus of Nazareth"[7] provides the noetic ground for our knowledge of God.

But, in this event of revelation we encounter an ontological reality. In Jesus God is who He is. "He acts towards us [in Christ] as the same Triune God that He is in Himself..."[8] There is no detriment to the knowledge of God Himself in His revelation.[9] In the revelation of Jesus we have the revelation of God: Father, Son and Spirit, because we have the actual presence of the Triune God in the form of the humanity of Jesus.[10] And what we find present there in Jesus is the prior ontological reality which is the ground for the revelation of Jesus.[11]

So while Christology is the noetic ground for knowledge of the Triune God, the triune Being of God is the ontological reality giving rise to the revelation and the ontological presence in the revelation of God in Jesus of Nazareth.[12]

---

[6] *CD*, I/1, [p. 384] p. 334. Square brackets indicate the quotation is taken from the earlier Thomson translation of *CD*, I/1, *The Doctrine of the Word of God Prolegomena to Church Dogmatics, Vol. 1/1*. Translated by G. T. Thomson, (Edinburgh: T&T Clark, 1936), the page number following indicates the page in the Bromiley/Torrance translation.

[7] *Ibid.*, [p. 365] p. 318.

[8] *CD*, II/1, p. 51.

[9] *Ibid.*, p. 315.

[10] "He is already what corresponds thereto, antecedently in Himself, namely in His relation to him by whom He becomes manifest, hence in His relation to Jesus..." (*CD*, I/1, [p. 449] p. 391).

[11] "Only by proceeding downwards from the triune existence of God can we understand how God stands before us, how in His revelation He gives us Himself to be known and is known by us" (*CD*, II/1, p. 51).

[12] *CD*, II/1, p. 51. Cf. "Revelation in the Bible does not mean a minus, a something other over against God. It means the equal of God, a repetition of God. Revelation is of course the predicate of God, but in such a way that this predicate coincides exactly with God himself" (*CD*, I/1, [p. 343] p. 299). Thus in dealing with Barth's

The Trinitarian Relations

Thus, Barth understands the biblical witness to indicate that what God is antecedently in Himself He is in His revelation in Jesus. We know God and that our knowledge of Him is actual and real because God knows Himself and has come to know himself in a human way in Jesus. This becomes clearer when we consider the Triunity of the God made known in Jesus Christ.

> If it is true that God stands before man, that He gives Himself to be known and is known by man, it is true only because and in the fact that God is the triune God, God the Father, the Son and the Holy Spirit. And first of all in the heart of the truth in which we know God, God knows Himself; the Father knows the Son and the Son the Father in the unity of the Holy Spirit. This occurrence in God Himself is the essence and strength of our knowledge of God. It is not an occurrence unknown to us; rather it is made known to us through His Word; but it is certainly a hidden occurrence. That is to say, it is an occurrence in which man as such is not a participant, but in which He becomes a participant through God's revelation and thus in a way inconceivable to himself.[13]

Although Barth is not explicit here, he is saying that, in the Word, God establishes a relationship with humankind, reveals that relationship, and reveals

---

theological methodology we must wrestle with the fact that there is a noetic order and an ontic order. Barth, and Christian theology in general, may follow the order of knowing or the order of being in explicating its doctrine. However, in the final analysis the ontological priority must be acknowledged as the final ground of our reflection upon the Word. The ontic priority must come to play its foundational role as the ontological ground for the noetic order. Noetically Jesus Christ interprets Himself ontologically as the Son, and also interprets the Father and the Spirit. Ontologically this is so because of the oneness of Father, Son and Spirit in Jesus and because the "man Jesus is included in the inner circle of the Triune life." We could also say that the knowledge of God in His revelation *ad extra* gives us knowledge of God *ad intra* and also the *ad extra* knowledge of God is a knowledge of God's true being, i.e. is ontological, because the one God, *ad intra*, is actually present in His revelation *ad extra*. While we may begin at the point at which we come to know God, in His Revelation, we come to see that such a knowledge is ontologically grounded. This contribution of Barth's is perhaps the most significant of all. It suggests a radical realism which corrects the vast majority of the whole of the Western theological tradition. It represents an overthrow of Platonic and Kantian dualisms between God and human knowledge of God, the undoing of Medieval and Reformation Scholasticism (and its vestiges even in the Reformers) with its separation between intuitive and immediate knowledge of God Himself and abstract indirect knowledge of God. For an exhaustive and illuminating exposition of this theme see Eberhard Jüngel, trans. Darrell L. Guder, *God as the Mystery of the World. On the Foundation of the Theology of the Crucified One in the dispute between Theism and Atheism.* (Grand Rapids: William B. Eerdmans, 1983). (Hereafter, *GMW*) See *CD*, III/2, p. 65.

[13] *CD*, II/1, pp. 48–49.

the eternal triune relations which constitute the Word itself. Furthermore, these relations are characterized as being relations which involve a unity and a distinction. Barth is demonstrating that God reveals Himself through the establishment of a relationship (in the Word) and what is revealed is that God in Himself is One whose being is in relationship: Father, Son and Spirit.

The Christological Knowledge of God in Himself

Our human knowing of God is actual because we share, by sharing in the humanity of Jesus Christ and knowing Him, in the Son's own relationship of knowing the Father which is God's own eternal knowing of Himself. Our knowledge is a participation in the knowledge of God's own self-knowledge of the Father by the Son in the Spirit.[14]

And, of course, it is not merely a matter of knowing God abstractly in Jesus Christ. It is a concrete knowing because it is a self-revelation of God, the actual presence of God Himself in creaturely form available for our knowing God himself, concretely. Our knowing is concrete because the relationship established between God and man in Jesus Christ is concrete, actual, in our time and space. It is also a concrete knowing because the relation of the Son's sonship is not something that takes place for the first time in the revelation.[15]

The Shape of Relations in God's Triunity

Barth's most comprehensive statements regarding the internal relations is found in his section on the Triunity of God. In summary we may say that God's triunity indicates the oneness of God, not a plurality of gods nor a plurality of parts in God.[16] "The name of Father, Son and Spirit means that God is the one God in threefold repetition, and this in such a way that the repetition itself is grounded in His Godhead..."[17] Each is equally God, God in three modes or ways. This unity is unique to God, it is a unity of neither singularity nor isolation.

The concept of the revealed unity of the revealed God, then, does not exclude but rather includes a distinction (*distinctio* or *discretio*) or order (*dispositio* or *oeconomia*) in the essence of God.[18]

For Barth, there is no way to either reduce the three in their distinctions or to disintegrate the one God into three separate individuals. The unity and the

---

[14] "We receive a share in the truth of His knowledge of Himself....in this share we have the reality of the true knowledge of Himself" (*CD*, II/1, p. 51).

[15] "He does not first become God's Son or Word in the event of revelation. On the contrary, the event of revelation possesses divine truth and reality because in it the specific nature of God becomes manifest, because Jesus Christ reveals himself as the person he already is antecedently, even apart from this event, actually in himself....Jesus Christ, the Son of God, is God Himself, as God his Father is God himself" (*CD*, I/1, [p. 474] p. 414).

[16] *CD*, I/1, p. 350.

[17] *Ibid.*

[18] *CD*, I/1, p. 355.

distinction are each unimpaired by the other. In fact the differentiations confirm the unity and the unity confirms the differentiations. Consequently, Barth speaks of the threefold repetition of God, God three times God, and all this eternally. This is the repetition *aeternitatis in aeternitate*.

Three Modes (Ways) of God's Being God: The Personal and Relational Nature of God

At this point most theological discussion has inevitably proposed the question: Three and one of what? *quid tres*? Barth gives considerable discussion to this as it relates to the history of the development of the doctrine of the Trinity in terms of three "persons."

For Barth, the terminology of "persons" is problematic because, by analogy with human persons, it can have connotations of tritheism, especially given the modern (19th Century to the present) stress on self-consciousness and personality as individual, isolated centers of consciousness. Barth also notes that the underlying key insight in the trinitarian discussions of the Church fathers came to be focused on relations rather than on persons (as *personae*, ὑποστάσεις or πρόσωπον).[19] Barth also backs away from considering the "what" of God in terms of an essence or a rational nature. Barth prefers "modes of being" or "ways of being" as more adequate for indicating "what three." He is not inventing a term but using a rendering of the τροπος ὑπαρχεως which reaches back to the Nicene Fathers' designation.[20] He summarizes his point:

> The statement that God is One in three ways of being, Father, Son and Holy Ghost, means, therefore that the one God, i.e. the one Lord, the one personal God, is what He is not just in one mode but—we appeal in support simply to the result of our analysis of the biblical concept of revelation—in the mode of the Father, in the mode of the Son, and in the mode of the Holy Ghost.[21]

These modes of being God are not to be exchanged or confounded or reduced. They are essential to God. God would not be the One God were He not God in these three distinct ways essential in Himself and in His relation to the world and mankind.[22] Consequently, what is three cannot be taken either as attributes or acts of God. For these designations apply to each—Father, Son and Spirit—and therefore do not distinguish them at all. Even the fact of the differing actions of revelation does not tell of the actual distinctions between those modes of God's being, for these are also unified in their variety.

For whether it be a matter of the inner property or the outer form of

---

[19] *Ibid.*, p. 359.
[20] *Ibid.*, pp. 355–361.
[21] *Ibid.*, p. 359.
[22] *Ibid.*, p. 360.

God's essence, all that is to be said can and must finally be said in the same way of Father, Son and Spirit. No attribute, no act of God is not in the same way the attribute or act of the Father, the Son and the Spirit.[23]

He comes finally to affirm that the three distinctions, the three ways of being, are the distinctive genetic *relations* one to another—the fatherhood, the sonship, and the spirithood of God also understood as paternity, filiation and spiration. These are the characteristics of God which are due to their distinctive relations to one another. Thus, following the Name given us in the New Testament witness to the revelation of the One and the same God, Barth says:

> in this one God there is primarily...let us put it cautiously, something like fatherhood and sonship, and therefore something like begetting and being begotten, and then a third thing common to both, which is not a being begotten, nor a proceeding merely from the begetter, but, to put it generally, a bringing forth which originates in concert in both begetter and begotten.[24]

These relations of origin occur in God Himself: an origin and two different issues also within the origin. He is, as God: Giver (Father), Receiver and Giver (Son), and Receiver (Spirit). For these relations of origin there is no analogy.[25] Consequently, Barth, along with many Church theologians, acknowledges the inadequacy of words in light of the reality to which they point.[26]

---

[23] *Ibid.*, p. 362.
[24] *Ibid.*
[25] *Ibid.*, p. 364.
[26] Alan Torrance's important book, *Persons in Communion. Trinitarian Description and Human Participation* (Edinburgh: T&T Clark, 1996), hereafter *Persons,* critiques Barth at this point by arguing that Barth, in *CD* I/1 did not trust in his own theological methodology at this crucial point and so declined to refer to the triune hypostases as "persons." Barth recognized that all terms must be borrowed then redefined, even in the context of cultural inertia. This is done in terms of an *a posteriori* and analogical consideration of the revelation of God who commandeers our language. However, in this case, Barth judged that the general connotation of human "individuals" could not be overcome and so preferred the term "modes" or "ways" of being. Torrance finds the notion of "mode" (*Seinweise*) far less adequate than "person" because it tends to undermine the mutual interrelations of the Father, Son and Spirit rendering the relations in functional terms. We concur with Torrance that Barth's alternative is even more problematic. However, it is not clear that Barth's choice of terminology indicates a problematic grasp of the reality even if it obscures it. Did Barth in fact have an non-personal and non-relational understanding of the Trinity even in CD I/1? In our estimation Barth's description of the Triune loving in freedom in CD II/1, §28 and in his approach to human personhood as co-humanity in terms of its analogical correspondence to the triune relations revealed Christologically in *CD* III/2 and III/4 indicate that despite his misleading terminology in I/1, Barth did conceive of the triune hypostases in terms

Triunity: Perichoretic Fellowship

Barth sums up his exposition by showing that we must say both that God is "unity in trinity" and "trinity in unity" and that the designation "triunity" indicates a conflation of the two. But even this term cannot be regarded as a perfect synthesis into one formula.

> In practice, however, this concept of "triunity" can never be more than the dialectical union and distinction in the mutual relation between the two formulae that are one-sided and inadequate in themselves.[27]

Furthermore, the Triunity indicates a dynamic of relations. For Barth the designation Triunity "indicates that we are concerned here, not just about unity, but about the unity of a being one which is always also a becoming one."[28] Thus, what is indicated in the two formulae is a movement, a dynamic which occurs in the internal, eternal, and original relations of the Triune God.

Here we have the root of Barth's later insistence that human persons also are involved in a dynamic becoming similar to God's own becoming. This forms part of Barth's essential understanding of being-in-relationship.

The single concept that comes closest to coordinating the dynamic of the relations captured in the two statements is the doctrine of *perichoresis* or *circumincessio*. Barth leads up to his discussion of this term by saying:

> The triunity of God obviously implies, then, the unity of Father, Son and Spirit among themselves. God's essence is indeed one, and even the different relations of origin do not entail separations. They rather imply—for where there is difference there is also fellowship—a definite participation of each mode of being in the other modes of being, and indeed, since the modes of being are in fact identical with the relations of origin, a complete participation of each mode of being in the other modes of being. Just as in revelation, according to the biblical witness, the one God may be known only in the Three and the Three only as the

---

of personal communion! For in those sections his explication of triune relations is not restricted to modes of origin or function. Rather, the emphasis is that personhood, divine and human, each in their own way, is constituted by communion. The action of love constitutes the being of God and humanity. We conclude that Barth's terminology in I/1 was the result of Barth's failure to trust in his theological methodology, not of a basic misapprehension of the triune nature of God. Personal relationality seems to be present from the beginning of Barth's *Church Dogmatics*, even if this does not become clear until later on. His objection to calling the divine hypostases "persons" was not, then, theological but practical.

[27] *CD*, I/1, p. 369.
[28] *Ibid.*

one God, so none of the Three may be known without the other Two but each of the Three only with the other Two.[29]

The *perichoresis* and *circumincessio* indicate that there is both distinction and complete unity or communion. They indicate that each "inexists" in the others, that there is a "co-existence" of each with the others, that there is an "involution and a convolution" of each in the other and over against the other. The three modes involve a mutual indwelling of each in the other.[30] This is the relational dynamic of God's being God in Himself. Eberhard Jüngel interprets Barth as saying that "this being is a being structured as a relationship."[31] And with this we have the culmination and most comprehensive consideration of Who this God revealed in Jesus Christ is.

In this discussion of the perichoretic nature of God's triune relations we have the roots of Barth's understanding of being in relationship involving loving communion or even covenantal fellowship, and the fact that true relationship involves a going out in order to include the other within that communion. This forms another essential dimension of what we have called Barth's grammar of personal being in relationship.

Ambiguity in *CD* I/1?

Some have argued that the aspect of intra-trinitarian communion as developed in CD I/1 is undermined by Barth's rendering of the divine oneness and his refusal to designate the Father, Son, and Spirit as persons. Although Barth does say that God is indeed personal he is suspected of giving the oneness of God a priority over the threeness, of finding the unity of God in the notion of a singular I-subject. While most conceed that Barth has not fallen into a form of modalism, he seems to some to avoid it mostly by raw qualification.[32]

In response to this I would have to say that in CD I/1 there is an unresolved tension and so an ambiguity in Barth's doctrine of the Trinity. His exposition of the perichoretic communion of Father, Son and Spirit, taken alone, does not fall under the condemnation of his critics. Here the unity in triune personal communion seems to be evident. In fact, it seems to be somewhat in tension with his treatment of the unity of God and his argument for his preference for "mode of being" over "person" previously developed.

However, later on, when Barth is not explicitly guarding against the misuse of the word "person" and the actual character of the relations are in view and the

---

[29] *Ibid.*, p. 370.

[30] *Ibid.*, pp. 370–371.

[31] Eberhard Jüngel, trans. Horton Harris, *The Doctrine of the Trinity. God's Being is in Becoming* (Edinburgh & London: Scottish Academic Press, 1976), p. 25. (Hereafter, *Trinity*)

[32] See for example, Jürgen Moltmann, *The Trinity and the Kingdom* (San Francisco: Harper and Row, 1981) and Catherine LaCugna, *God for Us* (San Francisco: Harper Collins, 1991).

being-constituting character of relations is in focus Barth's explicit rejection of the term seems to have little affect. This will become apparent when we consider Barth's treatment of the Divine Perfections in *CD* II/1 and his Christological anthropology (III/2) and ethics (III/4). His rejection of the term in I/1 did not prevent him from discerning the unifying and person-constituting nature of the relations considered elsewhere. Consequently, Barth's doctrine of the Trinity as developed in I/1 can only be considered a root. It reaches a more coherent and more satisfying development only later on in the *Church Dogmatics*.

Christological (Human) Knowing of Father, Son and Spirit *ad extra* as a Relational Reality of Unity and Distinction

Barth goes on to unfold the nature of our knowledge of the Triune God. He argues that our knowledge of God as Father, Son, and Spirit reflects the reality of God's own being in Himself. Thus, our triune knowledge is a real knowledge of God. We cannot trace out his entire discussion here, but Barth demonstrates how it is that knowledge of God in Christ, that is in God's action towards us *ad extra*, is a triune revelation of God in Himself as Father, Son and Holy Spirit, distinguished and becoming united in perichoretic communion.

This concludes Barth's consideration of the triune and so relational form of the being of God. In our final section on Barth's trinitarian doctrine, we must consider some themes he develops in his section on the Doctrine of God in which he considers the nature or character and the attributes of the Triune God. This constitutes the content of the relations in the being of God.

The Content of Relation is God's Loving Freedom

Perhaps the most comprehensive formulation of the reality of God which Barth makes is in the title of II/1, §28, "The Being of God as the One Who Loves in Freedom." It encapsulates the character of the relations God has with His creation and the internal triune relations as well. We will follow along with Barth's unfolding of this title identifying his major themes.

The being of God is a being in event and act because this God is the Living God. What Barth means by this is that God, as He is known in His revelation, is the event and act in the coming, living, dying, and rising of Jesus Christ. Moreover, in this event we come to see the interrelations of God as Father, Son and Spirit, in Himself and in His internal perichoretic life. He is *in Himself* living and acting and the event of interrelating.

This act and event and life of God cannot be understood as pure spirit or as creation. A unique "nature" of the action and life of God is affirmed in the revelation of Jesus Christ. We can only indicate Barth's conclusion here: the unique nature of God is a unique divine "being in person."[33] "The particularity

---

[33] *CD*, II/1, p. 268.

of the divine event, act and life is the particularity of the being of a person."[34] Barth continues and further defines the unique personhood of God.

> What is meant is certainly not personified being, but the being that in the reality of its person realizes and unites in itself the fullness of all being. In its person means in its unity of spirit and nature. For in this unity, in the due superiority of its spirituality, in the due inferiority of its naturalness, it is not an "It," nor is it a "He" like a created person. It is genuinely (and therefore also for a genuine understanding) always an "I." It is the I who knows about Himself, who Himself wills, Himself disposes and distinguishes, and in this very act of His omnipotence is wholly self-sufficient.[35]

This, says Barth, is another way to indicate the triune being of God, Father, Son and Spirit. God is the being who "knows, wills, and decides of itself, and is moved by itself."[36] In this God is unique for only God so self-disposes of Himself.

> Now if the being of a person is a being in act, and if, in the strict and proper sense, being in act can be ascribed only to God, then it follows that by the concept of the being of a person, in the strict and proper sense we can understand only the being of God....The real person is not man but God. It is not God who is a person by extension, but we.[37]

The Triune God: Being-in-Becoming and Creating Loving Fellowship

1. Fellowship of Love

Barth then takes a further step in coming to terms with the being-in-person of God in triune willing, deciding, and acting in Himself and towards us. What is the distinctive character of this divine nature and spirit in a personal union? This God in Himself and towards us is fellowship creating and so loving. And this is the one thing that God is and does. We will quote at length this very significant passage, for here we also have the root of his theological anthropology.

> God is He who, without having to do so, seeks and creates fellowship between Himself and us....It implies so to speak an overflow of His essence that He turns to us....God is He who...seeks and creates fellowship with us, and who (because His revelation is also His self-revelation) does this in Himself and in His eternal essence....He wills to be ours, and he wills that we should be His. He wills to belong to us and He wills that we should belong to Him. He does not will to be

---

[34] *Ibid.*, p. 267.
[35] *Ibid.*, p. 268.
[36] *Ibid.*
[37] *Ibid.*, pp. 271–272.

without us, and He does not will that we should be without Him. He wills certainly to be God and He does not will that we should be God. But He does not will to be God for Himself nor as God to be alone with Himself. He wills as God to be for us and with us who are not God...He places Himself in this relation to us. He does not will to be Himself in any other way than He is in this relationship. His life, that is His life in Himself...leans towards this unity with our life....God seeks and creates fellowship...God wills and does nothing different, but only one thing—this one thing. And this one thing that He wills and does is the blessing of God, that which distinguishes His act as divine, and therefore also His person as divine....That is to say, we shall find in God Himself, in His eternal being, nothing other than this one thing. As and before God seeks and creates fellowship with us, He wills and completes this fellowship in Himself. In Himself He does not will to exist for Himself, to exist alone. On the contrary, He is Father, Son and Holy Spirit and therefore alive in His unique being with and for and in another....He does not exist in solitude but in fellowship. Therefore what He seeks and creates between Himself and us is in fact nothing else but what He wills and completes and therefore is in Himself. It therefore follows that as He receives us through His Son into His fellowship with Himself, this is the one necessity, salvation and blessing for us, than which there is no greater blessing—no greater, because God has nothing higher than this to give, namely Himself; because in giving us Himself, he has given us every blessing. We recognize and appreciate this blessing when we describe God's being more specifically in the statement that He is the One who loves. That He is God—the Godhead of God—consists in the fact that He loves, and it is the expression of His loving that He seeks and creates fellowship with us.[38]

2. Loving Fellowship

Of course this loving of God is unique and so cannot be derived from other common notions of love. Barth develops this uniqueness in four points. We will take out excerpts without further explanation.

a) Sole Good—"God's loving is concerned with the seeking and creation of fellowship for its own sake." God is triune loving in Himself and so is Himself the loving into which He takes us. The fellowship we share in is itself God's own being as a loving fellowship. "Loving us, God does not give us something, but Himself and giving us Himself, giving us His only Son, He gives us everything." This participation in the fellowship of loving that God is, is our total blessing, without remainder.

b) Sole Ground—"God's loving is concerned with a seeking and creation of fellowship without any reference to an existing aptitude or worthiness on the

---

[38] *Ibid.*, pp. 273–275.

part of the loved. God's love is not merely not conditioned by any reciprocity of love. It is also not conditioned by any worthiness to be loved on the part of the loved, by any existing capacity for union or fellowship on his side."

c) Sole Aim—"God's loving is an end in itself. All the purposes that are willed and achieved in Him are contained and explained in this end, and therefore in this loving in itself and as such....Certainly in loving us God wills His own glory and our salvation. But He does not love us because He wills this. He wills it for the sake of His love. God loves in realizing these purposes. But God loves because He loves."

d) Sole Blessedness—"God's loving is necessary, for it is the being, the essence and the nature of God. But for this very reason it is also free from every necessity in respect of its object....His love for us is His eternal love, and our being loved by Him is our being taken up into the fellowship of His eternal love, in which He is Himself for ever and ever. All the same it is a 'being taken up.' It is not part of God's being and action that as love it must have an object in another who is different from Him. God is sufficient in Himself as object and therefore as object of His love....In the fact that He determines to love such another His love overflows. But it is not exhausted in it nor confined by the fact that although it could satisfy itself, it has no satisfaction in this self-satisfaction, but as love for another it can and will be more than that which could satisfy itself. While God is everything for Himself, he wills again not to be everything merely for Himself, but for this other."[39]

The Triune God: Personifying Person

Barth then comes back again to develop his definition of "person" in the light of this understanding of God's loving. God in His loving shows us what a person is in His own knowing, willing and acting as a person. This means that:

> Man is not a person, but he becomes one on the basis that he is loved by God and can love God in return. Man finds what a person is when he finds it in the person of God and his own being as a person in the gift of fellowship afforded him by God in person. He is then (in his own way as creature) a person wholly and exclusively in the fellowship of Him who (in His way as Creator) is it in Himself. Therefore to be a person means really and fundamentally to be what God is, to be, that is, the one who loves in God's way. Not we but God is I. For He alone is the One who loves without any other good, without any other ground, without any other aim, without any other blessedness than what He has in Himself and who as He does so is Himself and as such can confront another, a Thou.[40]

---

[39]*Ibid.*, pp. 276–281.
[40]*Ibid.*, p. 284.

Since personhood is originally proper to God and our own becoming persons is founded in being taken up into his loving fellowship, Barth goes on to make a contrast between this and any anthropomorphizing of God as person.

> God is a person in this way and He alone is a person in this way. He is the real person and not merely the ideal. He is not the personified but the personifying person, the person on the basis of whose prior existence alone we can speak (hypothetically) of other persons different from Him.[41]

Thus, to be a person is "to know, to will, and to act like God as the One who loves in Himself and in His relationship to His creation."[42] And where we can know this love in a human way and can be taken up into this loving can only be in Jesus Christ. In Him we see "in person" the knowing, willing, acting and so loving of God in the creaturely sphere loving us that we might be taken up into His loving fellowship and become persons in His own likeness.

In his conclusion of this section Barth indicates that while he dropped the term person to indicate the ways of God's being, there is nevertheless a place for it in the doctrine of the Trinity.

> What we can describe as personality is indeed the whole divine Trinity as such, in the unity of the Father, Son and Holy Spirit in God Himself and in His work—not the individual aspects by themselves in which God is and which He has. Not threefold [Person], but thrice [Person]...in their being with each other and for each other and in each other, in their succession one to another—the one triune God is the one who lives and loves, and therefore One, the One, and therefore, if we want to call it so, personality...The one God is revealed to us absolutely in Jesus Christ. He is absolutely the same God in Himself. This one God as the Triune is—let us say it then—the personal God.[43]

The Triune God: Lovingly Free

In the final part of this section of the *Church Dogmatics*, Barth considers the being of God in freedom. He has already touched on this in his consideration of God's loving. Here what Barth emphasizes is that God's freedom is a "determination" (*Bestimmung*) of His unique loving. God is free to love. He is self-moved and self-determined to love. His Lordship is one of love. His sovereignty is a sovereignty of love. We have here no abstract notion of freedom as arbitrariness. God's freedom is the exercise of his triune life of perichoretic love. God loves in freedom and is free in His love. God is free to love in

---

[41] *Ibid.*, p. 285.
[42] *Ibid.*, p. 286.
[43] *Ibid.*, p. 297.

Himself and is freely loving in relation to His creation. Barth concludes his section:

> It is not that God first lives and then also loves. But God loves, and in this act lives. If we have interpreted the divinity of His act, or the divinity of God, as freedom, we could not and cannot mean by this notion of freedom anything different from Himself as the One who loves. We cannot mean a "universal" in which he merely participates as the One who loves. We can mean and characterize only the manner, the utterly unique manner of his love. His loving is, as we have seen, utterly free, grounded in itself, needing no other and yet also not lacking in another, but in sovereign transcendence giving, communicating itself to the other. In this freedom it is the divine loving. But we must also say, conversely, that only in this divine loving is the freedom described by us divine freedom. If we abstract the love of God and therefore the purpose of God...we describe only a world-principle. Therefore we must not think away the love or the person of God for a single moment if we wish to think rightly and truly of God's divinity. God is free. Because this is the case, we must say expressly in conclusion that the freedom of God is the freedom which consists and fulfils itself in His Son Jesus Christ. In Him God has loved Himself from all eternity. In Him He has loved the world. He has done so in Him, in the freedom which renders His life divine, and therefore glorious, triumphant, and strong to save.[44]

This understanding of freedom and love will find its way into the heart of his anthropology and so inform his ethic as well.

The Triune God: Freely Loving in all His Ways

In addition to this we have only one further thing to add. It should be obvious that in Barth's consideration of the attributes of God he does nothing else but interpret them in the light of God's loving freedom. He classifies them under two heads: "The Perfections of the Divine Loving" and "The Perfections of the Divine Freedom," coordinating each with the other. It is under these more comprehensive categories that Barth interprets all God's attributes. His loving then is His Grace and Holiness, His Mercy and Righteousness, His Patience and Wisdom. The divine freedoms are His Unity and Omnipresence, His Constancy and Omnipotence, and His Eternity and Glory.

While we cannot draw these out now, in these further conceptions there are implications for understanding human attributes in the likeness of God's. This is especially true in regard to notions of human authority and power. We will have to break here, although at a later point in our discussion of his theological anthropology, we will have to return to Barth's crucial interpretation of God's

---

[44]*Ibid.*, p. 321.

perfections in terms of His triune, free, loving, personal and perichoretic fellowship.

Summary

To summarize our section on the content or action of God's being-in-relation, internally and externally, we have seen how God is He who acts to form and sustain a communion or a fellowship of love. This communion-creating action results in a becoming within God and for humankind. It is the action of a love of God's free unconditional self-giving for the sake of love itself, which God is in Himself, that others might be included in His love. By way of this love God creates creatures who are to become persons in His image, that is those who may also enter into loving communion with others. God's loving is unconditioned, it is free, it is unbounded. It is purely loving. God is He whose freedom is to love in a myriad of ways which all express his freedom in love. In all these ways we may say that God is He who has His being in personal loving dynamic relations of communion. These are the characteristics of the relational action of God within and external to the triune life of God.

The "Theo-logic" of Barth's Trinitarian Grammar

Our intention in making such a detailed survey of Barth's theology of the Trinity is to make explicit the nature of the relations he envisions. Barth interpreted the triune relations in terms of Revelation, in terms of the trinitarian internal relations of origin, and in terms of his triune relations with his creation. As a kind of shorthand we propose to encapsulate all that Barth has said regarding the triune relations into six formulae which, as inadequate as they are to the reality depicted, may nevertheless be used to refer to Barth's entire exposition and the triune reality beyond it.

Inasmuch as Barth intended to establish a theological anthropology and because Christology necessarily leads us to the Triune God both in Himself and towards us, we hope to show how these trinitarian relations are analogous to those he develops in his anthropology and which finally informs his understanding of the command of God for parents and children. In the doctrine of the Trinity we have the foundation for the basic grammar[45] of being-in-relationship.

---

[45] The concept of "grammar" for use in this way was originally suggested by the lectures on Christology given by Prof. James B. Torrance, Costa Mesa, CA, in the summer extension course of Fuller Seminary, 1987. The characterization of an attempt to uncover theologically a structure or grammar (στοιχείωσιν) within the Gospel can be traced back to Athanasius' work (*De Inc.* 56). By grammar we are suggesting that what Barth has provided is not so much a vocabulary by which to consider the Triunity and reality of God, but a grammar which coordinates and "makes sense" of the reality and the vocabulary used. As such it is a kind of logic oriented to its object, the revelation of Jesus Christ. In this sense we may call his grammar a Christo-logic. What is clear is that if what Barth is trying to say is evaluated on the basis of a logic alien to the object of his inquiry, then there is

Our formulation of this basic grammar of relations as we have found it in Barth's doctrine of the Trinity is as follows:

BARTH'S "GRAMMAR" OF THE INTRA-TRINITARIAN PERSONAL RELATIONS

The Living, Personal, and Loving Being of the Triune God is:

A Personal Relational Being-in-Triune-Fellowship (Form) which is:
1) a fellowship of unity in differentiation,
2) a differentiation in unity,
3) a correspondence of "persons" in succession and ordering of origination, being begotten and procession.

A Being in Personal Loving Action (Content) which is:
4) a free and reciprocal interaction of glorification, loving and blessing,
5) a dynamic action of being-in-becoming,
6) which is extensive and so inclusive of the other in itself.

We propose that these six characteristics under these two headings describe the major features of Barth's presentation of the form and content of the trinitarian relations which arise out of his Christology.[46] In the following

---

hopeless confusion. A vocabulary and a grammar must be native to one another for there to be "sense." Much misunderstanding arises when Barth or others interpreting Christian truth are understood to be offering a particular vocabulary for fitting into some assumed logic or grammar. Of course on this basis the new vocabulary seems woefully inadequate. However, if Barth and others are also providing an alternative grammar (and thereby critiquing other grammars as inadequate) they must be understood in terms of this contribution or they will not be understood at all, much less will evaluation of them be helpful. Indeed this thesis is designed to highlight Barth's contribution as one of a Christological grammar and to interpret his anthropology in this light, a light native to it.

It is not our primary concern to evaluate how the features of Barth's "grammar" critiques or coordinates with the logic of other philosophical frameworks. This has been done by others such such as T. F. Torrance in most of his works, but especially in this connection see T. F. Torrance, *The Ground and Grammar of Theology* (Belfast, Dublin, Ottawa: Christian Journals Limited, 1980); Lesslie Newbigin, *Foolishness to the Greeks* (London: SPCK, 1988); John D. Zizioulas, *Being as Communion* (New York: St. Vladamir's Seminary Press, 1985) and Eberhard Jüngel, *God as the Mystery of the World*. For additional consideration on this theme see also Carver Yu, *Being and Relation. A Theological Critique of Western Dualism and Individualism* (Edinburgh: Scottish Academic Press, 1987) and Michael Polanyi, *Personal Knowledge* and Thomas S. Kuhn, *The Structure of Scientific Revolutions* 2nd Ed. (Chicago: University of Chicago Press, 1970).

[46]Admittedly, at this point the depth of exploration into Christology as a basis for his doctrine of the Trinity to a large degree has been limited to a consideration of Revelation in its threefold form. However there are hints here in Barth that indicate

chapters we will come to see how they also provide the basis for his theological anthropology and, in turn, ethics.

---

greater depths. We will return again to his Christology as it appears at the beginning of his anthropology and see much more specifically how his Christology has these same eight characteristics and again how this is ontologically grounded in the trinitarian life. It will become more evident as we follow along that Barth's doctrine of the Trinity is not merely the result of an analysis of the linguistic grammar of subject, predicate and object of revelation, but is, as Barth claims, far more a development out of the depths of the revelation of God in Jesus Christ.

Chapter 3

The Christological Relation: Humankind as Being-Covenant-Partner with God

We have seen in the previous part of this chapter how in the Word we have been given the revelation of the Triune God. This is a revelation of the internal and eternal triune relations of Father and Son, in the Spirit and the revelation and actualization of analogous relations with creation through that same Word incarnate in Jesus Christ. We have attempted to state in six formulae under two headings the characteristics of these relations as Barth has presented them so far. We will go on to show that these characteristics, present in his doctrine of the Trinity, will also be found more explicitly developed in the Christology provided for his anthropology, and manifested in his special ethics.

We must now explore how Barth makes the transition from his trinitarian theology to his anthropology. This begins to occur early on in the *Church Dogmatics* and so we will begin there as well.

The Relationship of Christology and Anthropology: Barth's General Orientation in *Church Dogmatics* I/1 through III/1

1. Humankind in Light of our Knowledge of the Triune God: Creature, Reconciled Sinner, Redeemed Child

In the revelation by the Son of the Father through the Spirit we come to recognize the activity of the one God apportioned to each person of the Trinity. The Father is the Creator, the Lord of life; the Son is the Reconciler, the renewer of life; the Spirit is the Redeemer, the giver, the conveyor of this life which is given, sustained and renewed.

In this threefold knowledge of God we see in each a man-ward reference. The Father-Creator is the Creator of the creature, humankind. The Son-Reconciler is the Reconciler of us sinners. The Spirit-Redeemer is the Redeemer of humankind with new life eternal. Thus, in our knowledge of the Triune God in Christ we already begin to see who mankind is: the creature of God, the reconciled sinner against God, the one redeemed by grace to be a child of God. Furthermore,

> this Lord can be our God, He can meet us and unite us to Himself, because He is God in these three modes of existence as Father, Son, and Spirit because creation, reconciliation, redemption, the entire being, language and action in which He wills to be our God is grounded and typified in His own essence, in His Godness itself. As Father, Son and Spirit God is, so to speak, ours in advance.[1]

---

[1] *CD*, I/1, [p. 440] p. 383.

This threefold relationship of God to humankind is what we must keep in mind whenever reference is made to the Christological, trinitarian, or theological foundations of Barth's anthropology or ethics.

2. The Humanity of the Incarnate, Crucified, Resurrected Jesus Christ: Noetic Source and Ontological Determination of Humankind

For Barth this threefold relationship of God with humankind constitutes a determination (*Bestimmung*)[2] of human existence. This means that the pattern, meaning, purpose and destiny of the whole of human existence is established through God's relationship to humankind in these ways. It refers to the unchangeable sphere of relationship in which, for which, and through which humankind may live and move and have being. This sphere *includes* the freedom of persons to confirm the reality of this determination and the consequences for refusing to confirm it. Barth holds that such a sphere exists on the basis of the reality of God and mankind being together in relationship in Jesus Christ. In this reality of who He is we have a true image of the nature of all human reality.[3]

---

[2] This is a difficult word. It can be translated 'determination,' 'destination,' 'destiny,' 'statement' or 'definition.' It should be remembered first that Barth empties it of any connotations of a mechanical cause-effect relationship especially as grounded in some divine exercise of raw power over persons. It qualifies our existence in relationship to God, it is an onto-relational term. This word gathers together the notions of purpose, meaning, destiny, definition and design. It denotes the givenness of the character of our being-in-relationship with God which is inviolable. Perhaps the closest alternative English word is designation. We have been designated by God to be who we are in relationship to Him. We will occasionally use this word as a synonym for what Barth means by *die Bestimmung*.

[3] Such a determination or designation applies to all persons. God upholds all persons in the gracious gift of their humanity given to them by virtue of creation preventing them from becoming inhuman through their sin and rebellion. This is the gift of creation-grace through Jesus Christ, the Word through whom all things are created. Such a determination has a positive orientation towards God, not a neutral one towards God or others. We are *with* God and *with* others. Yet this positive orientation is neither a saving one, nor one with a power to prevent us from falling into sin. It is the gift of his humanity maintained by God by grace. Thus while not all persons are "in Christ" they are all "in relationship with Christ" which from God's perspective is entirely positive, aimed at the completion and perfection of humanity, or rather at persons' participation by the Spirit in the humanity perfected for them in Christ. Thus not all are Christians, not all are filled with and respond to the Spirit. But God's intention for them is maintained objectively in his maintaining their humanity for their participation in Christ's humanity. As we will come to see, this determination, designation, is actual and real for all persons. Barth does not regard this as a potential. Their purpose, meaning, design, destiny and definition of who they are is established. The question is whether persons will participate in this truth of who they are. Their human nature, upheld by grace, points towards the One upholding them. But only in responding to the Spirit who says Yes to him a second time in a second way for his redemption into life in God does one enter into Christ, become a member of his Body. Our determination is God's first Yes of grace said in creation and maintained in the face of sin. Our salvation is participation in our redemption, God's second Yes to us in Christ Incarnate,

Christology and Anthropology in *Church Dogmatics* III/2

Thus, when we come to *Church Dogmatics* III/2, we do not come to something entirely new or distinct, but to the particular development and unfolding of one aspect of Christian doctrine with the previous explications serving as counterparts.

Before we deal with specific points of his theological anthropology we will survey Barth's more general way of articulating the relation of Christology to anthropology and how the overall structure and themes of this part of the *Church Dogmatics* reflect this relationship.

1. The Christological Grounding of Anthropology: General Statements

Barth makes quite apparent the Christological orientation of our knowledge of humankind by way of numerous general statements in III/2. Barth's argument, from within faith, is simply that in Jesus Christ God, without ceasing to be God, has also become essentially human and has done so for our sakes at an ontological level, that is, in terms of who we, as subjects, are.[4]

The priority of the Who question, established in the section on the Doctrine of God, is maintained in the anthropological sphere. Who we are is for Barth relationally understood. In Jesus, God himself has renewed all humanity to be in right relationship with Him and so, into a relationship in which we are to participate.[5] In Him we see who we are purposed to be.[6] Thus, anthropology must be *founded* on Christology.

> If we rightly consider the special difficulty of a theological anthropology, there can be no question of any other point of departure. But the choice of this point of departure means nothing more nor less than the founding of anthropology on Christology.[7]

2. Christological Grounding: The Structure of Church Dogmatics III/2

The centrality of the Word made flesh for understanding mankind is also apparent in the structure of Barth's treatment. There are four headings under which Barth unfolds his anthropology: "Man as the Creature of God," "Man in His Determination as the Covenant-partner of God," "Man as Soul and Body,"

Crucified and glorified, which is not a determination but our echoing of God's second gracious act in his Word aimed at having us be not only with Him but *within* Him by the Spirit. God is with and for all in Christ. But God is with and for us so that we also may be taken up to be within the Triune communion in Christ. See especially *CD*, III/2, pp. 274–285 for Barth's discussion of this difficult distinction between Christian and non-Christian.

[4] *CD*, III/2, p. 13.

[5] *CD*, III/2, p. 3. All page references in this chapter will refer to *Church Dogmatics* III/2, unless otherwise noted.

[6] "The nature of the man Jesus alone is the key to the problem of human nature. This man is man" (*CD*, III/2, p. 43).

[7] *CD*, III/2, p. 44.

and "Man in his Time." Under each of these headings the first section to be developed concerns Jesus, who is the "norm"[8] and "archetype"[9] of man. These sections are titled: "Jesus, Man for God," "Jesus, Man for other Men," "Jesus, Whole Man," and "Jesus, Lord of Time." The humanity of Jesus Christ, first of all, and then for all others, is understood in terms of four all-encompassing relationships: The God-man relationship, the man-man relationship, the relationship to oneself (as soul and body), the relationship to time. For Barth, following the dictates of the nature of the object of our faith, man as the creature of God can only be rightly understood in these four comprehensive dimensions of his creaturely existence in the light of Jesus Christ's own relationship within them. Barth traces out the nature of the relationships in each of these spheres in his anthropology and shows how they are similar and dissimilar. We have already seen him trace out the nature of the triune relationships. Now we want to follow his development of the "grammar" of two other relationships which apply to his ethics, *viz.* the God-man relationship and the man-man relationship in this part on "the Creature of God."

The Trinitarian Grounding of Anthropology

We must also, at this point, take note of the trinitarian reference Barth makes in his introductory statements to his anthropology. Creation and so the creature itself has a purpose and meaning which has to do with God *in Himself.*

> [God] is concerned about the whole meaning and purpose of His work. In this, which would not be without Him, His will and therefore His own innermost being is manifested. In its existence He responds to and reveals Himself. In creating it, He bound it to Himself. If it pleased the Creator to associate and co-ordinate the creature with Himself it also pleased Him to associate and co-ordinate Himself with the creature. Creation is the divine distinction of the creature. The doctrine of the creature is the doctrine of that which God distinguished by the very fact that He created it.[10]

What Barth means by this will unfold in the following pages. For now what we can anticipate is that through the Word of God true humanity is revealed to be in the *image* of the *Triune* God, that is God in Himself as Father, Son and Holy Spirit. The relationship into which mankind is determined and called is one of being an image. But, according to the New Testament witness, individual humans are not in themselves the image. Rather, Jesus Christ himself is the

---

[8] Barth encapsulates his point in saying, "the individual man with the name of Jesus Christ is the norm and measure to which every human being is subjected. Knowing him we know who man really is." This appears in perhaps Barth's most succinct presentation of his anthropology, trans. F. L. Herzog "The New Humanism and the Humanism of God," *Theology Today*, Vol. 8 (May, 1951), pp. 160–161.

[9] *CD*, III/2, p. 144. Cf. III/1, p. 28: "Here is Son of Man. Here is humanity..."

[10] *Ibid.*, p. 3.

original image, the true Adam, and so we are created to image the Image. In other words our lives are to correspond by grace to the the life of Jesus, especially in his relationship to the Father and in the Spirit. This is the way Barth sees anthropology as it is grounded in Christology.

What we now propose to do is to follow along with Barth and take up the first two of the four main headings in *CD*, III/2, and note the theological, that is both the Christological and trinitarian, grounding for Barth's anthropological conclusions.[11] What will emerge is a perspective on the life of humanity, the triune life of God, and the relationship of the two.

The Obstacles to non-Christological Approaches to Anthropology and the Adequacy of the Revelation in Jesus Christ

Before we develop the Christological grounding for our understanding of humanity within these four relationships we must mention Barth's considerable discussion of the question: How is it that the particular man Jesus may have such determinative significance for understanding humankind? In summary we can say that because of the uniqueness of the person of Jesus Christ and our sinfulness there can be no equation of Christology and anthropology. Jesus has a unique uncreated relationship with God and lived a sinless human life. Nevertheless there are significant similarities. His humanity is of the same constitution as ours even if not of the same status. He too lived in our time and space as we do. The relationship we have with God is the same relationship even if it is a creaturely one established by grace. The particular similarities and dissimilarities between Christ and the rest of humanity are exactly what allow Him to be the source and norm of our true understanding of all of humanity.

Moreover, all other sources for a true knowledge of humankind fail to be comprehensive or universal, argues Barth. They cannot comprehend the uniqueness of Christ nor can they consider anything more than particulars. Since humanity is created in Christ we have in Him a particular who encompasses the essential universal truth of the whole of human existence. Other sources do provide us with information, describe the phenomenon, and depict true

---

[11] In the structure of the *Church Dogmatics,* the four sections of his anthropology in III/2 correlate with the four sections of the special ethics of the Command of God as Creator in III/4.

Man as the Creature of God	: Freedom Before God
Man as the Covenant Partner with God	: Freedom in Fellowship
Man as Soul and Body	: Freedom for Life
Man in His Time	: Freedom in Limitation

We chose to develop only the first two of the four sections ("Man as the Creature of God" and "Man in his Determination as the Covenant-Partner of God") because these two most particularly relate to the special ethics of "Freedom in Fellowship" which includes our central concern, the part on "Parents and Children." The other two sections ("Man as Soul and Body" and "Man in His Time") relate most directly to the special ethics of the command of God in "Freedom for Life" and "Freedom in Limitation," respectively, which follow after the section of our central concern and so are not essential for our presentation.

"symptoms" of the human life but cannot uncover the wholeness and determinative aspect of human existence. Rather, their input may be truly helpful when interpreted in the light of the truth of humanity revealed in Christ.[12]

The Seven Spheres of Relation

We should indicate here one more preliminary issue. For Barth there are actually a total of seven spheres of relations which must be considered in the development of a complete theological anthropology. They are as follows:

THE SEVEN SPHERES OF BEING-IN-RELATION

1) Intra-Trinitarian Life: Son to Father in the Spirit
2) Jesus to the Father in the Spirit
3) Humankind to God through Jesus
4) Jesus to other humans
5) Humankind: one to another
6) Body to Soul
7) Eternity to Time

These seven spheres of relation provide the overall context of Barth's theological anthropology. The first sphere is initially considered in his doctrine of the Trinity. The next six spheres are addressed in his doctrine of the Creation, *CD*, III/2, Chapter 10, The Creature, that is, in his anthropology. Section 44 covers the relational spheres 2 and 3. Section 45, spheres 4 and 5. Sections 46 and 47 cover relations 6 and 7 respectively.

For Barth, all of these relations have the same formal structure. However, only the first five relations are personal. So their contents, the action within the relation, uniquely have direct implications for our personal relations, for theological ethics in the realm of interpersonal relations. Thus, Barth develops his special ethics in direct parallel to these two anthropological sections in Chapter 12, "The Command of God the Creator," under two corresponding sections: §53 "Freedom Before God," (the "vertical" dimension) and §54 "Freedom in Fellowship" (the "horizontal" relations). It is in this last section that we find Barth's consideration of the relations of parents and children. Consequently, of these seven spheres we will consider only the first five.

In the two sections of his anthropology to which we now turn, beginning Christologically, Barth brings out the essentially relational nature of our existence and the contours of those relationships. Altogether, he explores four different sets of relationships for his understanding of humanity. In §44 "Man as

---

[12] We should point out that it is not our purpose in this book, as important as it is, to defend the adequacy of Barth's method of grounding anthropology on Christology. For our purposes we are assuming that they are largely adequate. Our task is to trace out the results of his anthropology for ethics as it works itself out in the *Dogmatics*.

the Creature of God" Barth considers the "vertical" dimension of Jesus' human relationship with the Father and the Father's relation to humanity in Jesus. This is followed by a consideration of all others' relationship with God. Then in §45 "Man as the Covenant Partner of God" the "horizontal" dimension of Jesus' relationship with others is considered followed by that of all other persons' relations to other persons. It is in the midst of this discussion that he uncovers the *analogia relationis*. He will also link these relationships to the trinitarian relations he has already previously discussed.

Barth is not as explicit as might be helpful in bringing out some of the dimensions of the nature of these relationships, especially in connection with his understanding of the triune relations. He is most explicit in developing the Christological relationship. While Barth does not always make all the connections which are implicit in his presentation, we intend to gather up all the strands and make explicit the comprehensive picture of the "grammar" which comes to light in all these relationships.

We are not trying to establish certain pre-defined categories of our own or as given by others and then interpret Barth in terms of these by demonstrating a certain correspondence between Barth's categories and these others. Nor are we trying to systematize Barth's thought in a way alien to it.[13] We are attempting to bring out the kind of structure that Barth has seen which is due, as Barth sees it, to the faithfulness of God. The categories we use will be very similar to Barth's more explicit descriptions. However, we have seen fit to make more explicitly thematic two additional categories of relationship which remain implicit in Barth's presentation, although these implicit themes are pervasive throughout his *Dogmatics*.

Jesus Christ: The Revelation and Determination of Humankind as Being-in-Relation with God

We will now take up Barth's explicit anthropology developed in two sections in *CD*, III/2, §44 "Man as the Creature of God" and §45 "Man in His Determination as the Covenant-partner of God." The remainder of this chapter will be devoted to the first section, and the following chapter to the second section.

---

[13] Barth is clear about the kind of systematizing he is not doing: it is not "a self contained and fully established coherence of principles and deductions, constructed on the basis of the presuppositions of a certain fundamental perspective and with the rise of certain sources of knowledge and axioms" (*CD*, I/2, p. 861). On the positive side Barth explained in a short article "On Systematic Theology" *SJT*, 14 (1961), p. 226 that it involves this: "with all the previous course of Christian thinking and teaching fixed before ones eyes, to trace out the message of the Old and New Testaments, as analysed in its particulars by biblical-exegetical theology, in its unity and totality (and to that extent trace it out 'systematically')....In no sense has it to dominate this message. It has to serve it. It has to recount its utterance completely, coherently and consistently (and, again, to this extent 'systematically')."

As previously noted, the first part of each of these two sections is devoted to establishing the Christological foundation for his anthropology: §44.1 "Jesus, Man for God" and §45.1 "Jesus, Man for other Men." It is here in this Christological part of §44 that we find, for the first time, Barth explicitly characterizing the relations in terms of six criteria divided into the two major categories of being and act. The six-fold criteria are reiterated also in §44.2 "The Phenomena of the Human" where Barth explicitly correlates Jesus' humanity in relation with God as the criterion for understanding all of humanity's being constituted in relation to God. Here then is the root of our own synthesis of Barth's theology of relations. In the third part of this section Barth finally arrives at the heart of his theological anthropology, where he uses his six-part Christological criteria as a foundation for his final understanding "Real Man," in terms of Election. At this point, however, Barth leaves behind his strict six-fold description by compressing some of them and combining some, and expanding into further points on yet others. Despite the re-categorization, we can still see the correspondence to the foundational six Christological and anthropological categories.

In §45, "Man in His Determination as the Covenant-Partner of God," Barth uses this same six-part criteria in the first part of the section, "Jesus Man for Other Men," to describe the Christological relation of Jesus with others. However, within the six-fold structure Barth now engages in some re-categorization by integrating them with some of the compressed categories used in the last part of the former section. It is here that Barth introduces and develops his concept of *analogia relationis*. In line with this he also provides a reinterpretation of the *imago Dei*. He shows how Jesus' relation to God and our relation to God in him orients Jesus' relationship to others and our relationship to others. They are analogous.

In the second part, "The Basic Form of Humanity," Barth reinterprets the first three points of the form of interhuman relations in terms of three aspects of the I and Thou relation. The final three points of the actional content of the relations he re-conceptualizes in terms of what he calls the four elements in the history of encounter. Again, while there is significant re-categorization, Barth's intention for continuity is clear.

In the final part of §45, "Humanity as Likeness and Hope," Barth attempts to expound his theological anthropology by way of the *analogia relationis* and the *imago Dei*, as it is most simply, universally and concretely expressed in the marital covenant of man and woman. Here we find Barth's full blown theology of relations confirmed in a particular covenantal relationship.

We will now lay out in an anticipatory way our conclusions regarding the basic grammar of human being-in-relation with God and with others as Barth saw it. This will serve as a kind of map to assist the reader as we attempt to retrace our own steps through both sections of his anthropology. The content of these formulations will only become apparent once we survey all four relationships as Barth lays them out in these two sections of his anthropology.

What will also become apparent is that our tentative characterization of the trinitarian relations, never explicitly formulated by Barth, here explicitly grounds his anthropology. His doctrine of the Triunity is greatly clarified when it is considered in the light of his Christological anthropology, that is, in the light of his doctrine of the *analogia relationis*. In fact, considered independently, his doctrine of the Trinity, as we find it developed under the rubric of revelation and speech in *CD* I/1, is open to criticism. These sections provide a much needed corrective to what Barth has said there.[14]

What we find in his anthropology then can be formulated as follows:

BARTH'S RELATIONAL GRAMMAR OF HUMAN BEING-IN-RELATION

A. Humanity exists in a Relational Form involving:
  1) Unity (fellowship/communion) yet with differentiation
  2) Distinction yet in fellowship or communion
  3) An ordered correspondence/image/witness

B. Humanity exists through an Actional Content involving:
  4) Personal and Covenantal Loving
  5) Dynamic and Eschatological Becoming
  6) Extension for the sake of creating Communion with Others[15]

---

[14] Alan Torrance has written extensively of the inadequacies of Barth's treatment of the Trinity as found in *CD*, I/1. See his *Persons in Communion. Trinitarian Description and Human Participation*, (Edinburgh: T&T Clark, 1996). What Barth wrote in III/2 concerning the Trinitarian relations does not, in our estimation, exhibit the weaknesses and ambiguities Torrance points out in regard to I/1. In this later section Barth does not explicate the Trinity under the rubric of revelation. Here the personal and relational nature of the inner Triune Life is apparent. Here, Barth cannot be critiqued for emphasizing the doctrine of *De Deo Uno* over the *De Deo Trino*.

[15] We must caution the reader that while we have broken down the relationships into distinct formulae, and into two subsets, following Barth, the reality of being-in-personal-relations is inadequately so depicted. The formulae give the appearance of perhaps a greater and more rigid structure than intended. The formulae must be taken as a whole. So, for example, the form and content for Barth cannot be at all separated. Following Barth, the categories of "form" and "content" are used to delineate two interdependent aspects of human existence. The form refers to the structure and given context of human existence while the content refers to the appropriate and correlating action of human existing. For Barth the form of mankind's existence is that of having being by virtue of being in relationship, to God and to other human creatures. This form cannot be separated from its purposed action. Humankind exists as an act of being and as a being in action. This unity of being in form and action is similar to his understanding of the being of God. For Barth this unity of the relational form of being and actional content of human existence constitutes humankind as a personal being in the image of God. Thus humankind is personal being only in the unity of its relational form and actional

We will attempt to show that it is these two primary categories and six subcategories of the personal being of humankind which come into view more and more as we explore Barth's theological anthropology as he explicates it within four of his seven spheres of relational being. It is our contention that this relational grammar of humanity is grounded in what Barth had discovered in his explorations of Christology and the inner triune relations revealed there. In the light of those relations Barth has developed his anthropology. This in turn, we will come to see, underlies his special ethics in general and as exemplified in his section on "Parents and Children."

Barth's Foundational Christology

In a matter of a few pages (*CD*, III/2, pp. 55–68) Barth lays out in summary form, indicating its biblical sources, his essential Christology. It is on the basis of the New Testament witness to the Word that Barth develops his understanding of Jesus Christ as one who essentially has his being only by virtue of His relationship to God and in relationship to mankind. And this relationship is a particular relationship, it is exclusively the history (*Geschichte*) of a gracious, saving, covenantal relationship enacted in Him, both from God to man and, in response, from man to God. His Christology, as we might expect, finds the ontological grounding of his being-in-relationship in the inner triune life.[16] Here Barth shows how it provides the foundation for his anthropology. We will attempt to summarize the five points Barth makes to establish this foundation.

1. In the person of Jesus there is the co-incidence of act and being

The New Testament witness "says who He is by telling what He does."[17] The NT predicates for Jesus (e.g. from I Cor 1:30: "He is our wisdom, righteousness, sanctification, redemption.") all refer to the history of the accomplishment of the actions of Jesus. "He is what he is in these actions, in this history."[18] Jesus' own self-attestations, his ἐγώ εἰμι, point in the same direction: He is the Way, the Truth, the Life, the Light, the Door, the Bread, the Shepherd. "Hence in all these sentences 'I am' means that My being and nature, consists in what is suggested by all these words, concepts, titles and names. I

---

content. The form of relationship manifests itself in action and the action takes place in terms of the form of the relationship. Notwithstanding this explanation we must question whether the concepts of form and content are helpful at all, especially since what Barth means by content is action! We maintain the distinction for the moment only because it correlates with Barth's presentation of it. The divisions between the six formulae are fluid and cannot in real human living be isolated. They are distinguished for the sake of analysis but are intended to be thoroughly integrated in personal relationships.

[16] The terms Barth uses which we render "being-in-relationship" or "being with" is "*Zusammensein*" or "*zusammen*."

[17] *CD*, III/2, p. 58.

[18] *Ibid.*, p. 56.

am as I exist in the mode thus indicated."[19] The New Testament witness is almost exclusively occupied with presenting Jesus in terms of his being at work (εργαζόμενος) and any mention of what we might call some aspect of personality (being hungry, angry, tired, sleeping, resting, sorrowing) is always taken within the greater context of his working, never independently. Jesus is designated as the One who is coming, who has come, and who will come again, again indicating by a history and an action Who He is. Thus, "Jesus is wholly and utterly the Bearer of an office."[20] The New Testament witness assumes that Jesus was not converted into, was not equipped or subsequently appointed to his ministry and office.[21] His name, Ίησους, and his titles, Χριστός, Κύριος, indicate who he is by telling what he does: the Savior.[22] Who Jesus is, is identical with what he does and accomplishes.

In summarizing his discussion, Barth says that only of Jesus may it be said,

> that His work itself is one with His active person, and therefore that He the doer and His deed are indissolubly one....The point which interests us here is that we cannot separate His person from His work, if only for the reason that it is in His person, because He gives nothing more nor less than Himself, that He accomplishes His work....How could He be the Saviour accomplishing this work—the work of self-sacrifice with which He brings life and salvation to the world—if He existed otherwise than in His work, or where to be sought and found elsewhere than in His work?[23]

On this basis Barth finds his ultimate noetic ground for affirming that we should understand personal being as the unity of being and act. This is why Barth refuses to separate in his discussion of the Person of Jesus Christ and the nature of humankind, the form of personal existence from the content (action) of personal existence. In Christ we find the personal union of act and being.[24] So

---

[19] *Ibid.*

[20] *Ibid.*

[21] *Ibid.*, p. 57.

[22] *Ibid.*, p. 58.

[23] *Ibid.*, p. 61. See Barth's note here about his departure from much of orthodox theology which had the effect of dividing His Person and Office for more than the reason of mere exposition. This is one of Barth's significant contributions to Christology.

[24] This is the Christological confirmation of the two major categories of our formulae. However, it argues for a unity rather than a disjuction of the two. This does raise the question as to why there must be a distinction made here, then? We would venture to say, at this point, that by linguistic convention we denote a difference between a subject and its action. Barth is willing to go along with this formal distinction. Also such distinctions between the person and work of Christ, the being and action of God are a part of traditional theological discourse. Barth seems to enter the theological discussion assuming these formal distinctions but only in order to invalidate them for usage in any essential way. That leaves us with the question as to

too, we find here Barth's basis for considering the act and being of God to be in complete correspondence as developed in *CD*, II/1, §28, "The Being of God as the One Who Loves in Freedom."

2. This Jesus, in the unity of being and act, is a human person

Jesus in the unity of being and act is unreservedly a human person, a man. "There is no doubt that he is a real man."[25] This is certainly clear in the New Testament witness. "He is not a real man in spite but because of the fact that He is the Son of God and therefore acts as the Saviour. For this reason He remains a real man even in His resurrection and ascension and session at the right hand of God, and it is as real man that He will come again."[26] It is as man that He accomplishes his work and fulfills His office. Yet, "to be sure, it is as the Son of God that He is empowered to act in all this as the Saviour."[27] The Son of God has a human nature which is the same as ours, yet which cannot be measured by ours because it is original in Him. So, it reveals what our humanity truly is.

> It is not the case, however, that He must partake of humanity. On the contrary, humanity must partake of Him. It is not the case, then, that He is subject to these specific determinations and features of humanity. It is not that He is conditioned and limited by them, but in so far as humanity is His, it is He who transcends and therefore limits and conditions these features and determinations. As the nature of Jesus, human nature with all its possibilities is not a presupposition which is valid for Him too and controls and explains Him, but His being as a man is as such that which posits and therefore reveals and explains human nature with all its possibilities....It is to be explained by Him, not He by it. It is revealed in His light, and not *vice versa*. The nature of human possibilities rests upon and is knowable by the fact that they are realized in Him.[28]

---

if and when the distinctions themselves should be left behind altogether if clarity is to be gained and dogmatic discourse is allowed to develop further.

[25] *Ibid.*, p. 58. Jesus is "real man (*der wirchliche Mensch*)." It is not the case, as we shall come to see, that since Jesus is designated real all others are unreal. It is just the opposite. Our reality is established in Him. For Barth it is misleading to speak only of Jesus as true man, that is as an ideal, as a potential reality which may or may not become realized. There is only one reality of our humanity. It is that established in Jesus Christ. It is that reality in which we now live and move and have our being. The only question is whether we will live according to that reality or not. Not doing so does not establish a counter-reality, or a less than ideal reality, but constitutes a denial of the reality of who we actually/really are: those who have their being in relationship to God in Jesus Christ.

[26] *Ibid.*

[27] *Ibid.*

[28] *Ibid.*, p. 59.

Jesus has his being in real relation to humanity. In the unity of His person and work we can discern true humanity which is our humanity because of Jesus' complete union with humanity. The essential difference between the man Jesus and other human persons, *viz.* that the humanity belongs to *the Son of God*, does not threaten this relationship but is that which empowers Him to be and to reveal true humanity to and for us. Were He not the Son of God, but rather another human creature, we could not see nor enter into our true humanity. Because He has His humanity uniquely, He has our humanity for us in a way that even we, or any creature, in our own present experience, do not have it.

Thus, in this way Barth asserts that Jesus *can be* and *is* the revelation of humankind as *essentially* existing as a being-in-relation-with-God.[29] Jesus Christ is the original Adam through whom, to whom and for whom all human beings exist and through whom we are being renewed.[30]

3. The history, action, and work of the person of Jesus has no other reason for being except the Salvation of humankind

Jesus, according to Barth, *is* this history. "The work with which we have to do is the absolutely unique work of the Saviour, resolved and accomplished by Him alone. What Jesus does, and therefore is, is this work, which cannot be interchanged with any other, and can be His work alone."[31] Even His role as judge is to be interpreted as being within and under the work of Salvation. It is a necessary and temporary transition. "But the real purpose of His coming is not attained with this division."[32] The Scriptural witness to this over-arching office (Lk. 19:10; Jn. 10:10; Lk. 2:11; Phil. 3:20; Eph. 5:23; Jn. 12:46; Jn. 18:37; Mt. 10:34ff.; Lk. 12:51ff.), which is significant for Barth, consists of the titles given to Jesus (Jesus="Yahweh saves"), Messiah, Son of Man, Savior (Σωτήρ), and the statements of Jesus regarding his own purpose.

It is on this basis that Barth grounds his understanding of the content (actional dimension) of human existence as a participation in the history of God's action for his salvation and that of every man. We could also call this the history of God's covenant grace to humankind.

---

[29]For his most in-depth exegetical account of this understanding see Barth's, *Christ and Adam. Man and Humanity in Romans 5* (Edinburgh & London: Oliver and Boyd, 1963), Germ. edit. 1952. (Hereafter, *CA*). See also Philip Hughes, *The True Image. The Origin and Destiny of Man in Christ* (Grand Rapids: Eerdmans, 1989) who confirms Barth's point that Jesus Christ is the true image of God according to whom we were created and renewed.

[30]See Rom. 5:14; I Cor. 15:22,45; Rom. 11:36 and Col. 1:15–17; 3:10. We are renewed after the image of our Creator, God through Jesus Christ, who is the original Adam.

[31]*CD*, III/2, p. 60.

[32]*Ibid.*

The Christological Relation

4. The life and work of this man are identical with the life and work of God, yet in such a way that the real humanity of Jesus is confirmed and not subsumed

The New Testament witness is again clear for Barth. "God acts as Jesus acts."[33] "Only He who has created it can save that which is lost. When Jesus performs this work, God is revealed in Him....The divine work is accomplished in the work of this man. And the work of this man consists in the abandonment of all other work to do the work of God."[34] There is a complete correspondence between God and Jesus.

Barth's exposition of this theme is grounded in his concise survey of the Gospel of John where the Gospel writer himself testifies to this identity of His work with God's work and to Jesus's own testimony to that identity of workings. Commenting on 5:17–22: "the Son can do nothing of his own accord, but only what he sees the Father doing; for whatever he does, that the Son does likewise..." Barth says:

> The works done by the Son are those of the Father Himself, of the One who has sent Him, for the Father has given Him these works to accomplish in the Father's name and for the manifestation of this name....The converse is also true. Because the Father dwells in Him, the Son, it is the Father who performs the works through Him (14:10).[35]

Barth sees that there can be "no dualism" between the Father and the Son in terms of their working. However, there is also no ontological dualism: "to be one with God in the accomplishment of this work is the being of this man to the exclusion of all other being." This man Jesus is, in His being, what He does. So Jesus is united to the Father in his being as well as His doing. Jesus, in His own being, reveals the being of humankind essentially to be a being-in-relationship with God.[36]

However, this does not mean the loss of His person, the absorption of His humanity. He is and remains related, indeed united, to humanity in a saving, covenantal way. His unity does not dissolve the relationship by one collapsing into the other. The unity is of the sort that maintains an intimate relationship which may properly be called a oneness. This unity is one which calls for differentiation within it. It is a relational unity.[37]

---

[33] *Ibid.*, p. 62.

[34] *Ibid.*

[35] *Ibid.*, p. 63.

[36] Here we get the emphasis that reality is essentially personal and relational as we saw in his understanding of the Trinity being understood as personal and relational. We also see the relationship between Jesus and God being characterized as a unity of being and action.

[37] "Hence the fact that He does the work of God, and in so doing is one with God, does not mean that He Himself—the man as such—is subsumed in the process. On the

Barth grounds his understanding of the relational nature of unity which calls for a differentiation between the man Jesus and God, in part, on the exegesis of passages from the Gospel of John, especially Chapter 17. The Father has life in Himself and so gives life to the Son so that the Son has life in himself (5:26). The man Jesus has a will (5:21; 17:24; 21:22ff). Jesus is not "some sort of vacuum."[38] When we hear that the Father loves the Son (10:17; 15:9; 17:23, 24, 26) "He is already described as at least an object distinct from the Subject that loves." Yet it is just as obvious that this object is also a Subject who "exists independently as such, [and] is implicit in the fact that the Son also loves the Father in doing what the Father gives Him to do (14:31), and that he abides in His love (15:10) by keeping the Father's commandments."[39] Barth summarizes this by saying: "In no event which takes place between the Father and the Son is the Son merely an object."[40] This is especially true in the activity of Father and Son which is proper to their relationship only, namely, the mutual love and glorification (Jn. 7:18; 10:17; 12:16, 23, 28; 13:31, 32; 14:13, 31; 17:5, 18, 24). Each acts as a Subject initiating towards the other, who also acts as a recipient of the action of the other. The unity does not dissolve the relationship; the differentiation does not threaten to undo the relationship.

It is on this basis that Barth grounds his conception of the basic form (*Grundform*) of personal being as essentially existing only as a being-in-relationship-with-God which does not in the least threaten the creature as a creature but rather the opposite; it truly establishes it as distinct and in correspondence within that life-giving relationship.

5. The unity and continuing distinction between the man Jesus and God is ultimately grounded in the intra-triune relations of Father, Son and Spirit

The mutuality of relationship between Jesus and the Father (of indwelling, working, loving, glorifying, and finally, having an identity—"I and the Father are one" which establishes each so that there is no confusion or separation, but a continuing relationship of one with and in the other) is really the revelation externally of the intra-triune relations of the Father and the Son in the Spirit.[41]

---

contrary, it is in this way, in the doing of the work of God, and therefore in His oneness of being with God, that He is Himself, this man" (p. 64).

[38] *Ibid.*

[39] *Ibid.*

[40] *Ibid.*, p. 65.

[41] "It is clear that in this matter [of mutual glorification] that we have to do with a regular circle. It is the circle of the inner life of the Godhead. For the complete explanation of it we should have to return to the perception of the unity and trinity of God—to the Paraclete, too, there is ascribed His own δοξάζειν of the Son (14:6)—and therefore indeed to the...fine theologumenon of the *perichoresis* of the Father, Son and the Holy Ghost....according to the Fourth Gospel it is not merely the eternal but the incarnate Logos and therefore the man Jesus who is included in this circle" (*CD*, III/2, pp. 65–66).

In the humanity of Jesus, as he relates to the Father, we come to see the triune relations of Father and Son in the Spirit. But also in the relations of the man Jesus with other human persons are revealed the inner relations of the triune God. Barth explains this:

> in this Gospel the relation of Jesus with His disciples is described in the same categories as the relation between the Father and Himself, so that it is a revelation of the inner life of the Godhead in which Jesus shares. It is in the so-called high-priestly prayer (Jn. 17) that these correspondences are developed with particular fullness.[42]

The decisive point in demonstrating this in Jn. 17 is, for Barth, the saving work of Jesus in his self-giving, his laying down his life for his friends. For this self-giving of Jesus is the revelation of the mystery of love within the triune personal relations.[43]

It is on this basis that Barth affirms a correspondence (*Entsprechung*) (with all its dissimilarity and yet similarity) among a) the intra-trinitarian relations, b) the relation of the man Jesus and God, c) humankind's relationship to God d) the relationship of the man Jesus with other human beings and e) the personal relations among human beings.

Barth returns to a consideration of the ontological grounding of the Christological and human relations several times in these two anthropological sections. In fact his grasp here of the nature of the relations serves to qualify his previous explication of the Triunity of God in *CD,* I/1.

Six Characteristics of the Particular Humanity of Jesus Christ: Being-With-God

On the basis of his explorations in Christology Barth sums up his findings regarding the relationship of God to man and man to God as revealed in Jesus Christ in six characteristics of humankind in the light of this man, Jesus. Barth's fullest description of how the Christological relation illumines all of

---

[42]*Ibid.*, p. 66. We may attempt to indicate what Barth may have had in mind. The following phrases apply in Jn. 17 to *both* the relationships of Father and Son and also the relationship of Jesus to His disciples: give words, give life, are one, have joy, are sent into the world, are sanctified, being in each other and so being one, are loved, with each other, know each other. A direct comparison of the two relationships is also specifically indicated when Jesus prays, "for those who believe in me through their word, that they may all be one, even as Thou Father, art in me and I in thee, that they also may be in us" (v. 20–21). There is also to be a relationship of unity/oneness between the disciples and those who come to believe through their word which is directly compared to Jesus' relationship with the Father and His relationship with His disciples.

[43]"[The self-giving of Jesus is] the same thing, only in its aspect as self-revealing work, as is elsewhere (3:16) described as God's so loving the world that He gave His only begotten Son" (p. 66).

humanity's relation to God is found in the second part of §44.[44] Barth uses this six-fold description of relationship numerous times throughout his two anthropological sections, sometimes compressing it to a few words.[45] We will quote in full Barth's own summary of these six characteristics as we find it in the third part of this section.

> [1] We remember who and what the man Jesus is. As we have seen, He is the one creaturely being in whose existence we have to do immediately and directly with the being of God also. [2] Again, He is the creaturely being in whose existence God's act of deliverance has taken place for all other men. [3] He is the creaturely being in whom God the Saviour of all men also reveals and affirms His own glory as the Creator. [4] He is the creaturely being who as such embodies the sovereignty of God, or conversely the sovereignty of God which as such actualizes this creaturely being. [5] He is the creaturely being whose existence consists in His fulfillment of the will of God. [6] And finally He is the creaturely being who as such not only exists from God and in God but absolutely for God instead of for Himself.[46]

Taking into consideration this and Barth's other explications of the humanity of Jesus in relation to God, we will attempt to concisely formulate each of these six dimensions of real man, that is, our humanity in its relationship to God, as revealed in Jesus Christ.

We see in Jesus Christ that humankind exists as:

1) A being by virtue of God's being related to this man in such a way that God is present in this man (as a co-existence).

2) A being by virtue of necessarily actively participating in the saving action of God inaugurated for Him.

3) A being by virtue of living and having this personal existence only within the history of the sovereign love and so for the glory of God.

---

[44] *Ibid.*, pp. 73–74.

[45] See *CD*, III/2, p. 133 for Barth's very compressed one word or phrase summary.

[46] *Ibid.*, pp. 132–133. The enumeration is mine. This six-fold description Barth uses on a number of occasions without always explicitly indicating its repetition: see pp. 68–71 for Barth's first explication of the humankind's relationship to God in the humanity of Jesus; pp. 73–74 for the implications for the relationship of humanity in general to God (this six-fold description is captured in a series of phrases or even in six words in three other places, p. 95, 109, 121); on pp. 162–163 there is a partial recapitulation of humanity's relation with God; on pp. 214–221 he describes in parallel fashion Jesus' being-in-relationship with God and his being-in-relationship with man as a being "with," "from, "for" and "to" man. While he does not explicitly use this six-fold description for the person to person relationship it is implicit, as we will show later, in his explication of I-Thou relations and the corresponding four elements of persons-in-encounter.

4) A being who only lives by and under the Lordship of God, fulfilling through his obedience, the sovereign saving purpose of God.

5) A being whose purpose for existence (or orientation in existence) entirely consists in the totality and unity of his being and action corresponding to God's own being and action for man's salvation.

6) One who has being only by virtue of being-for-God, in the service of God.

These six points of Jesus' relation with God demonstrate that "Basically and comprehensively, therefore, to be a man is to be with God. What a man is in this Counterpart is obviously the basic and comprehensive determination of his true being."[47]

Christological and Trinitarian Being-in-Relationship

Barth variously labels and groups these six characteristics. He seems to understand these characterizations in ever more comprehensive concentric circles. Beginning with his initial Christological formulation and correlating it with other statements throughout these two sections, we observe that the first three are often referred to respectively as Jesus' being *from* God, *to* God, and *in* or *with* God. This last category (being *with* God) is the most comprehensive of the first set of three categories which constitute the form of the relationship. The second set of three categories is comprehensively spoken of (in the sixth category) as three ways Jesus is *for* God. This constitutes the content of the relationship.

This last category also seems to be the most comprehensive of all six categories. It denotes three aspects of Jesus' active participation in the reality of the "form" of the relationship established by the Father as described in the first three categories.[48] We could thus depict Barth's understanding as six concentric circles, the center being the first characteristic listed above with the sixth being the outermost and so most inclusive category. These circles are subdivided into two sets, the inner three designated by the third circle (being *with* God) and the outer three (which really includes the inner three as well) designated by the sixth circle (being *for* God). In his Christological section Barth identifies the first three as corresponding to the person of Christ and the second three (which are comprehensive of the first three) to the work of Christ.[49]

What we want to point out now is that these six Christological characteristics are indeed parallel to his trinitarian grammar. Barth explicitly indicates this in his Christological section, but does not spell it out. We propose

---

[47] *Ibid.*, p. 135.

[48] Stuart McLean has helpfully pointed out this dynamic of participation in these two sets of three. See *HTB*, pp. 26–28.

[49] In the Trinitarian discussion Barth has a similar two level structure but labels them the Being and Action of God. In his anthropological section we find a similar structure again but this time Barth speaks in terms of "form" and "content" and the "indicative" and "imperative" of Election.

to show this by correlating them both in our frame of two primary categories of "Personal Being-in-Relation."

Barth has also suggested two primary categories of being-in-relation: its form and its content. In the Christological terms as discussed above, the form of Jesus' being-in-relationship corresponds to the first three characteristics cited above: his being "from," "to" and "with" God. It provides a kind of description of the ontological "structure" of the relationship. We could also label these first three as the Person (or Being) of Jesus. The last three Christological characteristics Barth designates as Jesus' being "for" God. Note how this second set provides us with the characterization of the nature of the *interaction* between Jesus and the Father: obeying, fulfilling a purpose, serving. This content of the relation corresponds with the "work" of Jesus. For Barth, the person and work of Jesus are inextricably bound together. This implies that the latter three constitute the essential *establishment* of the form of the relationship and that the first three demand a certain working out in terms of specific active responses. This corresponds to Barth's insistence that the person and work of Jesus cannot be separated. His being is a being in action in relationship with His Father.

We can diagram all this as follows:

Being of God	**corresponds to**	Act of God
Form of the Relation		Content of Relation
Person of Christ (from, to, in God)		Work of Christ (for God)
Human Being With God		Human Being For God
Characteristics 1–3		Characteristics 4–6

Implications for Barth's Doctrine of the Trinity

Now Barth has explicitly indicated that Jesus' human relationship with God is a reflection of the Son's eternal relationship with the Father in the Spirit, i.e. is the outward expression of the intra-trinitarian relations. We want to suggest that Barth's categories of Christological characteristics correspond to Barth's indication that God's own triune being is a *relational* reality, a fellowship, and secondly that the relationship is characterized specifically as the *interaction* of love one for another. Taken together, this means that God is a relational being-in-action of loving fellowship in Himself and towards us in Christ.

We will attempt to draw out the parallels for all six of the particular characteristics. The first three characteristics describe the form of the relations, the second three the action within the relations.

THE CORRESPONDENCE OF THE TRINITARIAN AND CHRISTOLOGICAL RELATIONS

1) Jesus exists only in virtue of His union with or relationship to God and yet as a man is distinct from God—So, in the triune life there is a unity and a differentiation of the modes of God's own being in relation, Father and Son in the Spirit, and each would not be except in co-existence with the others.[50]

2) Jesus' existence is a co-ordination and participation in the relationship given Him, a corresponding response ordered to God's action towards him. He is the Image of God—thus in the Triune God the "Persons" are ordered according to their relations of origin, but in these very relations they reflect or image one another, the Father the Son, the Son the Father, and both the Spirit as the Spirit bears witness to them both.

3) Jesus' existence consists in a dynamic history of this interaction of corresponding action where Jesus sees what the Father is doing and hears the command of the Father and Jesus follows His Father's leading and will. Jesus, though distinct, has his being in a continual orientation to the will and working of his Father in the Spirit. Similarly there is a mutual involution and convolution, a history of being one in the Spirit, the bond of love through successive interaction. Reflecting their relations *ad intra* they are united in working together *ad extra sunt indivisa*.

4) Jesus' action must be characterized by the specific content of living in covenant relation under the blessed Lordship of His Father to the end of fulfilling and participating in His Father's (and His own) good and loving purpose for the salvation of all humankind. He is included in this purpose. He is not subsumed, but rather is established in it. Jesus lives in the light of confirming his election as man. He is for God as God is for him. Correspondingly, we saw that God in Himself is the accomplishment of a loving personal fellowship, a history of the loving unification of Father and Son in the Spirit. The perichoretic union is a covenant unity of blessedness.

5) Jesus' action in relationship is characterized as his realization of his purpose for existence, his being in becoming who He was Elect to be, the Savior of humankind. His being is one of a becoming Who He was intended to be in and through the history of his obedience to the Father. Correspondingly, we saw how Barth indicated a living dynamic of relation such that God's own being is a being in becoming united in a perichoretic fellowship, whereby the modes and ways of God's being continually are personally established and sustained. The being of God is a divine history.

6) Finally, His being in relation was a service not limited to himself but which *extended* in two directions to those who are other than himself. Jesus loves, first in service of God, and then (because God serves others, first in

---

[50] In traditional theological discussion this points to the enhypostatic nature of the humanity of Jesus.

Himself and then also towards others) in loving service to other persons. Thus, Jesus lives "For" God and likewise "For" humankind. We saw how, for Barth, the Triune God has "otherness" within Himself and that the love of Father and Son is a self-giving on behalf of the other so that there is an exchange of life one with the other. Furthermore, this self-giving in a free act of God's love 'overflows' out into the creation, reconciliation and redemption of creation.

This concludes our explication of the essential similarities of relations. The only difference, according to Barth, between Jesus' being in relation with God and the Son's eternal relation with the Father in the Spirit is that the former is the externalization of the latter under the conditions of creatureliness. There is no intrinsic distinction. There is complete harmony and one to one correspondence. So, here we see how the trinitarian and Christological relations are indeed analogous. This will not be so in the same way as we compare the other relationships—although they properly will be said to have the same six-fold determination.

We have now laid out the shape of Barth's theological anthropology in terms of the intra-triune Being of God and the corresponding (Christological) relation of Jesus, in his humanity, His being in relation *with* and *for* God. We must now go on to explore Barth's characterization of mankind's relationship with God for those other than Jesus. Here Barth makes the correspondence of our relationship to God with Jesus' relationship to the Father explicit.

Humankind as Being-in-Relation With God: Six Criteria

Barth, in the second part of this section, now turns to humankind in general, those other than Jesus. He wants to "define more precisely the criteria which must be used in any attempt to determine the nature of man."[51] Given the "similarity between Him and us in spite of all dissimilarity" there can be no direct restatement of the distinctives. There can be points which acknowledge the distinction and similarity and so correlate with the six points of his Christological investigation. He recapitulates the Christological characteristics of humanity and then states for each point the correlating criteria for humankind in general. We will quote the second half of the pair. On the basis of who Christ is:

1) "...every man is to be understood, at least mediately and indirectly, to the extent that he is conditioned by the priority of this man, in his relationship with God, i.e., in the light of the fact that he comes from God, and above all that God moves to him."

2) "...every man is a being which is conditioned by the fact that this deliverance is for him, that every man as such must exist and have his being in a history which stands in a clear and recognizable relationship to the divine deliverance enacted in the man Jesus."

---

[51] *CD*, III/2, p. 73.

3) "...the being of every man, in so far as this history [of God's acting in the man Jesus for humankind's salvation] essentially concerns it, is not an end in itself, but has its true determination in the glory of God (in the very fact that it can participate in that history)."

4) "...it must be said of every man that it is essential to him that as he exists God is over him as his Lord and he himself stands under the lordship of God the Lord. Whatever may be the meaning of his freedom, it cannot consist in freedom to escape the lordship of God."

5) "...the being of every man must consist in this history. Not only his actions but his being will consist in his participation in what God does and means for him. His freedom will be his freedom to decide for God; for what God wills to do and be for him in this history. The proper action of real man can then be understood only in the light of the fact that it may correspond to the divine action in his favour, doing justice to the grace addressed to him."

6) "...his existence too, as an active participation in what God does and means for him, is an event in which he renders God service, in which he for his part is for God, because God first willed to bind Himself to man, and in so doing has bound man to Himself."[52]

W. A. Whitehouse summarizes these six criteria in the following way: "man belongs to God, exists only in relation to God's act, exists for the glory of God, under His Lordship, [according to His purpose], and in His service."[53]

Having said all this, Barth indicates that he has not yet arrived at the theological concept of man, but has only indicated its criteria, limits and minimal requirements. Barth goes on in the following part of this section to distinguish these criteria for real man from numerous other proposed criteria.[54] These other options (referring to one or another of humanity's capacities or potentials) all miss out on the essential determination of humankind's existence. They fail to see that man's relationship to God is absolutely essential to his

---

[52] *Ibid.*, pp. 73–74.

[53] "The Christian View of Man," p. 21, in his *Creation, Science & Theology. Essays in Response to Karl Barth* (Grand Rapids: Eerdmans, 1981). He has inadvertently [?] left one of the criteria out in his brief encapsulation, which we have provided in brackets. He also notes that this is a crucial point of departure since it marks a radical departure from the way human existence has very often been designated. W. A. Whitehouse has identified Barth's attempt to move from Jesus Christ to an understanding of person instead of *vice versa* as a "break from the Aristotelian habit of pre-conceiving manhood as one among many fixed species which can be known in general, and which will be found exemplified in the "personality" behind this work and office [of Jesus]" (p. 20). He sees this also as a departure from Scholastic theology. "Scholastic theology is open to criticism in so far as it works with an *a priori* world-view, and knowledge of a relation of God and creatures to which the God-man relationship must conform...[which is] established in some independence of Jesus Christ" (p. 18).

[54] Barth regards non-Christological approaches as inadequate to the reality. See *CD*, III/2, pp. 19f. for his in depth discussion of both the limitations and relative value of non-theological approaches to anthropology.

existence. Any attempt to understand humankind apart from his actual relationship to God misses what is essential to man and even the framework within which to understand the less essential, which Barth calls the "phenomena" of the human, the "symptoms."[55] The emphasis Barth puts on this is due to his belief that the knowledge of human existence as grounded in Jesus Christ is also the ontological determination of its existence. Thus, there can be no true knowledge of humanity apart from the relationship by which it is ontologically determined.

In the revelation of the Word of God, in Jesus Christ, we see that man is essentially a being-in-relationship with and for God and with and for others. If persons were not in relationship with others they would not be persons. Relationship is not an attribute or one optional aspect of human existence. Rather, relationship is essential to the being of humankind. This is to say that humanity is actually constituted in its relationships.[56]

---

[55] *Ibid.*, p. 75.

[56] This is in distinct contrast to most of Western theology since the time of Boethius' and his definition of man as "an individual substance of a rational nature." The emphasis on analyzing human existence in terms of an irreducible individual and his substance subsequent to Boethius was taken up and further refined within the framework of Descartes' most basic dictum: "I think, therefore I am" and the correlative Newtonian physics of individual irreducible particles interacting according to laws of cause and effect. These orientations when applied to persons further emphasized human existence as substantival, individualistic and materialistic/mechanistic. Later concerns and developments in 19th and 20th century philosophy and the sociology and psychology built upon it led to a preoccupation with the individual independent of others in any essential way. Thus by the 19th century in Western culture a concern for "personality" could most often be characterized as an individualistic concern with an intensified focus on the internal and so subjective dimension of human existence such as consciousness or spirit. Along similar lines some existential philosophy has largely regarded persons as isolated individuals or even existing in antipathy with others (Sartre) with an emphasis on the inner life of willing, deciding and taking individual responsibility and creating one's own meaning.

One may see how Barth himself traced out this history of religious philosophy and anthropology in various sections of the *Church Dogmatics*. See for example: II/1, pp. 287–297. Barth's essay "Evangelical Theology in the 19th Century" trans. by Thomas Weiser, in (Atlanta: John Knox Press, 1974) pp. 11–33 and his book *Die Protestantische Theologie im 19. Jahrhundert* Zürich: Evangelischer Verlag A. G., Zollikon, 1952) also trace out this thesis regarding Western theology.

In contrast to this, Barth is proposing a radical departure. Colin Gunton in his *Becoming and Being: the Doctrine of God in Charles Hartshorne and Karl Barth.* (Oxford: Oxford University Press, 1978) (hereafter, *Becoming*) suggests that one of Barth's most significant contributions may be "a shift from static to dynamic terms, from a substance- to an event-conceptuality" (p. 142). He goes on to cite (p. 143) another astute interpreter of Barth, Eberhard Jüngel, from his book *Gottes Sein ist im Werden*, who indicates that Barth has reframed the categories for conceptualizing God as 'an essentially relational being' (p. 76). This is an 'elimination' of the old substantival categories following Plato, which excluded event from itself (*Gottes Sein*, p. 107).

Being-With-God: Humanity's Relational Form

In the third part of §44 "Real Man" Barth comes to the heart of his description of humanity. He reiterates in just a few sentences the six-fold Christological criteria and then indicates in what way the man Jesus is the determination of true humanity. He encapsulates it all by saying that humanity, at the root of its being, has its being by being essentially with God. He then draws out the ontological import of what it means for us to be with God. Following the explication of this definition of humanity, Barth then proceeds to give being-with-God its most concrete expression in terms of God's action. Humanity is with God in that humanity is elect, summoned by God through Christ for a life lived out in a response of gratitude and responsibility. The form of the relation is filled out in terms of the actional content.

We will first look at Barth's understanding of the ontological form of the relationship created in Jesus Christ.

1. Ontologically Determined and Revealed in the Word

For Barth, humankind is not only revealed in Jesus, but is determined to be what it is in Jesus and his relationship to God. That is, humankind is given its ontological status in and with the being-in-relationship of the man Jesus to God. All humanity stands in this history of relationship.[57]

Thus, Barth says that "The Word of God essentially encloses a specific view of man, an anthropology, an ontology of this particular creature."[58] In his six characteristics of the particular relationship of Jesus with God and the corresponding six criteria for the relationship of humankind in general to God,

---

For a study of this line of development in Western thought and theology see John Zizioulas, *Being as Communion*; Ray Anderson, *On Being Human* (Grand Rapids: Eerdmans Publishing Co.,1982); Helmut Thielicke, *Evangelical Theology*, Vol. 1 (Grand Rapids: Eerdmans, 1974); John Macmurray, in two volumes *Persons in Relation* and *The Self as Agent* (London: Faber and Faber limited, 1953), the Gifford Lectures, 1953–54, and T. F. Torrance *Theological Science and Transformation and Convergence in the Frame of Knowledge*. Michael Polanyi's *Personal Knowledge* is also instructive on this point. For an overview of sociological perspectives see Dietrich Bonhoeffer's analysis of sociology and psychology as grounded in individualistic, rationalistic and substantival categories in his *Sanctorum Communio*, trans. R. Gregor Smith (London: William Collins Sons & Co., 1963), especially Chapter I.

[57] "The ontological determination of humanity is grounded in the fact that one man among all others is the man Jesus. So long as we select any other starting point for our study, we shall reach only the phenomena of the human. We are condemned to abstractions so long as our attention is riveted as it were on other men, or rather on man in general, as if we could learn about real man from a study of man in general, and in abstraction from the fact that one man among all others is the man Jesus. In this case we miss the one Archimedian point given us beyond humanity, and therefore the one possibility of discovering the ontological determination of man" (*CD*, III/2, p. 132).

[58] *Ibid.*, p. 13.

Barth has attempted to articulate this ontological relational reality. In summary, Jesus is with God in each of these six ways. He shows us that to be man is essentially to be with God. But He does not show us something other than what He is and so actualizes. Jesus is with God unlike any other human being. He is with God in a way that he is the presence of God Himself. Consequently, it is just because Jesus is with God in this unique way that all other persons are thereby brought into the presence of God and so are with God themselves. No man would be with God were not Jesus with God in His own unique way. This being with God is not a general truth or static background reality. Because Jesus is with God immediately, when he entered our human sphere of time and space all other human persons were then brought into the mediate presence of God by and in the person of Jesus. All human reality is thus conditioned by this presence of God in Jesus in our human sphere. This changed and established in the most basic way (ontologically) who we, as humans, are.[59]

Barth sums up his point by saying that "Man is with God because he is with Jesus." Such a situation Barth terms "ontological" which he explains to mean that his being with God then is not "merely one of many determinations of our being, derivative and mutable, but the basic determination, original, and immutable."[60] In and through and with Jesus all humankind is co-ordinated with God in this relationship. Jesus is not an example of a human with God; he embodies and enacts the immediate presence of God so that all others, by His presence and saving activity, are with God. Human existence is determined in form and content by this Word of God.[61]

2. Humanity's Ontological Status in Light of its Denial

There are those who resist this truth of their being with God as Jesus is with humankind. These persons are living a lie which has no ontological basis. "Godlessness is not, therefore, a possibility, but an ontological impossibility for man."[62] "To be in sin, in godlessness, is a mode of being contrary to our humanity." [63] To live in this lie

> is an attack on the continuance of his own creatureliness: not a superficial, temporary or endurable attack, but a radical, central and fatal

---

[59] "It belongs to his human essence that Jesus too is man, and that in Him he has a human Neighbour, Companion and Brother" (*CD*, III/2, p. 133).

[60] *Ibid.*, p. 136.

[61] Several of Barth's interpreters have noted the ontological nature of relationships or the relational nature of human existence. T. F. Torrance characterizes this understanding as "the kind of relation subsisting between things which is an essential constituent of their being, and without which they would not be what they are. It is a being-constituting relation." See his *Reality and Evangelical Theology* (Philadelphia: The Westminster Press, 1982), pp. 42, 43.

[62] *CD*, III/2, p. 136.

[63] *Ibid.*

attack on its very foundation, and therefore its continuance. His very being as man is endangered by every surrender to sin.[64]

Human being is with God, and exists only in this relationship with God. This being with God, because with Jesus, means that man is a being who "derives" and is "dependent upon" God. The man Jesus has his being only from, to, with and for God and from, to, with and for man. Consequently, all other human creatures are also determined in their being to be from, to, with and for God.

3. Humankind: Utterly Dependent upon yet Distinct in its Relationship to God in Jesus Christ

And yet as radically as this "from, to, with and for" must be taken, it does not imply an identification. Humankind "is not identical with the being of God."[65] Humankind is distinct yet utterly dependent upon its relationship to God for its existence. It can only exist in this orientation of relationship. In that Jesus is not to be confused with or separated from the Father so too man in general in his own way is not to be confused or separated from the saving relationship with Jesus, and therefore with God.

> It is distinct from and to that extent independent of the being of God. But in this distinction and independence it does not exist without but only by the divine being. It is a being absolutely grounded in the latter and therefore absolutely determined and conditioned by it.[66]

Were man one in being with God, man would not be with God or in relationship with God. But mankind exists only in this relationship, with God, yet deriving from God, in an absolute way. This conception is crucial for comprehending Barth's grasp of the relationship. This is the form of the relationship. Man exists only in relationship with "this One as the Other indestructibly unlike for all His likeness."[67] Man exists in this confrontation. "What constitutes the being of man in this sphere is not a oneness of being but a genuine togetherness of being with God."[68]

This of course does not mean, as Barth is often accused of indicating, that man has no sphere or being of his own. Being itself is a relational reality. One has one's own being *in relationship*. It is true that mankind does not have its own being autonomously, out of relationship. There is no human existence at all in this configuration. But *in relationship* mankind has its being which is distinct yet inextricably bound to God in Jesus Christ. Relationship of this sort is not a threat to man, but the ground of his existence, the fulfillment of his

---

[64] *Ibid.*
[65] *Ibid.*, p. 140.
[66] *Ibid.*
[67] *Ibid.*, p. 141.
[68] *Ibid.*

being. Thus, Jesus' humanity is not extinguished by his unity with the Father but is in fact established all the more.[69]

Humanity: Essentially Being *With* and *For* God

We may summarize by relating this to our proposal regarding the basic grammar of Barth's Christology and trinitarian theology and say that the form of humankind as revealed and determined in the Word of God is that humankind essentially exists as a being-in-relationship. We may explicate this being-in-relationship in three ways.

First, this relationship in which he has his being is essentially one of being-together-with-God, his Creator, Reconciler, Redeemer. There is a communion, a unity even, of God with humankind established in Jesus Christ for its very existence, despite all the disparity.

Second, there is a likeness in the face of the much greater unlikeness of God and humankind. This essential likeness Barth will explore further. For now we can anticipate and say that it is that they both essentially have their being in the form of relationship whereby humankind's being is ordered as a copy of God's own being-in-relationship. God exists in His intra-trinitarian life of perichoretic communion and man exists by virtue of his communion with God and with fellow humans, and so there is a correspondence, an imaging and bearing witness of man to God.

Third, with the great disparity yet likeness between the two, God and humankind, there is an ongoing relationship. They remain distinct though united and so exist in a history of confirmation and confrontation according to the ordering of relationship. Humankind, although in a certain sense independent, is nevertheless dependent upon its God for its origin and continuing being. God is not so dependent upon humankind. Yet the life of God has within it the life of humanity and has been "affected" by it. Without ceasing to be God in Himself, God has also become mankind's God by the Word, Jesus Christ. Similarly, there is a history of the relations of the persons in the inner life of God such that each in-exists or co-exists in the other and would not be without the others.

Thus, in the form of humanity, of real man, we find the same grammar as Barth's characterization of the Christological and trinitarian being in relationship. We see also the fact that the relations between the relations also exhibit this grammar of unity without confusion yet distinctions without separation, and correspondence of likeness and dissimilarity.

---

[69] "As he dwells in this sphere, man is so 'with' God that he derives solely and exclusively from Him. Again, this does not mean any cancellation of his independence, selfhood and freedom. But it does mean that in his independence, selfhood and freedom, he belongs only to the One who comes to him as Lord. It means that it is only with Him and not without Him or against Him that he can exist, and think and speak, and work and rest, and rejoice and mourn, and live and die" (*CD*, III/2, p. 142).

Being *With* and *For* God through Election

Having described the form of the relationship as a being-with-God, Barth comes around again and explicates its content this time under four points. He now approaches humanity's relationship to God entirely in terms of God's own action towards humankind.[70] He sees that the action of God in Christ determines the form and constitutes the corresponding action (content) of the existence of humankind. God's relationship with man is established by His Election. Since we are most concretely "with" God through his act of Election, humanity has the form of being 1) a calling from and 2) a listening to or hearing God. The way we are "for" God has, then, the content of 3) a gratitude for grace and 4) a responsibility to God. These four elements are further subdivided and correlated by Barth. The first two, calling and hearing, take place within in a history of being summoned by God's grace. Responsibility involves a) a knowledge of God, b) an obedience to God, c) the invocation of God, and d) a freedom for God. This fourfold explication of God's election serves as a further development of what Barth means by being-with-God. It is the personal and relational grounding for Barth's later more comprehensive treatment of the doctrine of election.

Here Barth covers the same ground occupied by the six criteria he developed earlier, but now looking at it primarily from the angle of God's action. This, Barth says, is the true material content and concreteness of the relationship. With this description we have reached the core of his theological anthropology.

It is not too difficult to see the relationship between the various aspects of these two descriptions of humankind. The latter fills out exactly how humanity is from, to, with and for God. The gracious election by the Word of God understood as a calling, listening and the history of that dialogue taken all together describe the "form" or structure of human existence in relationship with God. The aspects of gratitude and responsibility describe the corresponding action of being-for-God which takes place in the given relationship.[71] The electing

---

[70] See pp. 142–198. Although Barth uses terms which could be characterized as Platonic, e.g. "form," "content" and "participation," the way Barth uses them is quite distinct. The form occurs *in the cosmos*, in Jesus Christ. The form is already actualized in Jesus and as such does not represent an otherworldly ideal, but an actuality. Participation is understood in terms of human action in the cosmos, and is not essentially something in the mind or Mind. In addition the form and content cannot be separated in any way. They are mutually conditioning in historical reality. Finally they are dynamically related, there is a becoming in the participation, and the result is the formation of personal beings in personal relationship with a personal God.

[71] Stuart McLean notes how crucial this is for following Barth. The formal is the relationship itself, the material content is the action of relating within the given relationship. For Barth the relationship itself is established by the action of God, so that the material content is, according to McLean, "superordinate to form (relationship) and defines relationship..." This puts Platonic categories on its head. The action of God gives rise to the form of relationship of God and mankind. Action defines being. See *HTB*, p. 50, n. 9.

action of God creates the form of man's relationship with God, that is, his being from God, to God and with God and God's relationship with man as his Creator, Reconciler and Redeemer. This form in turn calls for a corresponding response, a corresponding action. In election God is "for" man. In this act of God, man is determined to be "for" God, and so is summoned to actively live out being "for" God.

So, here again, Barth reiterates the basic two-fold structure of being in relationship and living out the relationship. The Calling *from* God gives rise to the listening *to* God and taken together this constitutes a being in a history of relationship in grace *with* God, a dialogue in which God and man by grace become correlated or coordinated. This is parallel to Jesus' being from, to and with God and humanity. This corresponds to our first three characterizations of humanity's being in relation.

Correlating Barth's understanding of the actional content of humanity's election with Barth's six-fold criteria and our last three characterizations of relations is a bit more involved.

Being grateful for the grace of election corresponds easily with our fourth characterization of humanity as being in personal covenantal relationship. While Barth does not, as he does elsewhere, explicitly make the connection with the dynamic of becoming in relation here, humanity's responsibility can be seen to correlate well with our fifth characterization of humanity's becoming in and through the relation. Humanity becomes what God purposes it to be in and through the participating responsibly, that is obediently, prayerfully and knowingly, in the graciously given relationship.[72]

What of our sixth category of relationality? If we treat the final of the four aspects of Barth's development of responsibility as a distinct point (freedom for the service and and sake of another, which Barth indicates is the most comprehensive category) then we can see the parallel between the last responsive aspect of humankind's extension to others in order to include them in fellowship and communion. True freedom is personal responsibility to determine to serve another for the sake of the Kingdom of God. Barth notes that in the response to the Word one is "called out of oneself and beyond oneself...a genuine summons outwards."[73] Freedom is a determination to go out beyond one's self to another, and to serve others for God's sake and their benefit.

It will become clearer how the concepts of covenantal, dynamic becoming, and of extensive and fellowship-creating action represent important categories for Barth's thought here also in his anthropology when we take up how he specifically understands gratitude, responsibility and freedom.

---

[72] Colin Gunton, (*Becoming*) and Eberhard Jüngel (*Trinity*) have made special note of the theme of becoming in Barth's *Dogmatics*. We are proposing the additional theme of "extension for inclusion" as a significant one for comprehending Barth.

[73] *CD*, III/2, p. 166.

Correlating the content of humanity's election with Barth's second three characterizations of Jesus' being for others and for God, we see that 1) man is *grateful for* his creation and election *under the Lordship* of God. He is a being in gratitude. 2) He is obedient to and *responsible for* his knowledge of and participation in the *purpose* given him for his existence. He is a being who *becomes* who he is in responsibility. 3) He is *joyfully free for* his participation in the history of his relationship with God in *service of God extended* to others. The content of man's relationship with God can be summarized by saying man is *"for* God."

As Barth indicated earlier, Jesus is *for* God in that He lives gladly under the Lordship of God, for the purpose of doing God's will and for the service of God and so of mankind. It is our participation in the form of relationship (from, with, to God) which is graciously established by God in his action for man. Thus, the action of man is a reflection of the action of God which creates, reconciles and redeems the form of man's relationship to God. Because God is for man in Christ, man in turn can now be for God in Christ.

There is, here, an asymmetrical relationship. God himself has triune form which shapes his own free and loving action towards creation. This action of His, however, is what gives form to the relationship humans have with God. Humankind does not determine the form of its relationship with God. Consequently, there are only certain human actions which may correspond and so participate in the form of the relationship given it. Thus, the form of humankind's *action* is also given. However, this does not mean that humankind does not actually take action. It has humanly already taken place in Jesus Christ. Thus, for us the form and content are both given to him (Jesus) so that he might indeed correspond to it in his own being. We will attempt to represent this diagrammatically:

HUMANITY AS DETERMINED BY GRACIOUS ELECTION

THE CREATED FORM (Indicative)	Calls for	CREATURELY RESPONSE (Imperative)
BEING-IN-RELATION		BEING-IN-ACTION
God **for** Man		Man **for** God
Election and its History as a	<—Corresponds—> to	Man's Response and his History of Participation as
1) Calling: **from** Word	<—>	4) Gratitude **for** relationship **from**
2) Listening: **to** Word	<—>	5) Responsibility **for** obedience **to**
3) History of Relationship **with** Word	<—>	6) Freedom **for** service/participation **with**

As noted, for Barth there are a number of quite fluid but recurring categories which describe active participation in the form of humankind's being in relationship with God.[74] The fourfold description of mankind's being Elect is

---

[74] The correlation of all the categories Barth uses is a difficult task. For one, he is not attempting to make a symmetrical structure and then fit his theology within it. However, since he is aiming at coherence, there is perhaps more structure than is obvious at first glance. In the diagram suggested we should note that Barth does not say directly that he is recapitulating the six Christological characteristics and corresponding criteria of 'real man' in relationship with God, but he does indicate significant continuity, and does utilize some of the same terminology in his describing a second time humankind's relationship with God. It is the content of the characteristics dealt with here that calls for the correlation of them with the Christological characteristics.

To relate Barth's six criteria to his four-part explication of humankind's election we have enumerated separately each of the two aspects Barth takes up independently, *viz.* the calling and hearing, but subsumes under the one enumerated term, the Election of God. Our distinguishing them seems neither an innovation nor an arbitrary step. Barth himself separates and correlates man's being "with" and "from" God with God's election and hearing (p. 157). Our somewhat bolder second adjustment is that we have taken the last subdivision of the topic of the responsibility of man and given it its own enumeration. This is not arbitrary, but is based on Barth's obvious emphasis that this final category is indeed somehow more comprehensive than all the other categories, even though he discusses it as a subsection of "Responsibility." See p. 192 where he says "Under this fourth heading [responsibility as freedom] we shall summarize all that has been said under the first three..." Cf. p. 218: "And now we must take a last and supreme step" in speaking of the freedom of God for man and so of man for God as the image of God as one of the six criteria of humanity. This way of handling the material does leave open the question as to why Barth didn't again use his six-fold pattern. There seems to be no

one set of categories he uses in his section on anthropology. There is a correspondence between them, however. This is especially apparent when we consider what his most comprehensive category is in each sphere of relationship. We have seen in his trinitarian section how God's action is most comprehensively understood as a personal loving freedom. In his Christological section the most comprehensive category is that of living in freedom to serve under the Lordship of God. In the section above the most comprehensive category (including within it gratitude and responsibility) is that of responding to the election of God with a freedom to serve. Here we can see the parallel to God's loving freedom to create fellowship with others and Christ's freedom under the Lordship of God. In each case Barth recognizes an active participation in the gracious fellowship created by God.

We have seen so far how Barth's understanding of the Christological and trinitarian relations corresponds to his somewhat different conceptualization of humanity's being in relation with God. In order to grasp how Barth understood the relations it is important to consider how he filled out each aspect of relation covered in this part. To that we now turn.

Humankind: Elected for Covenant Relation by the Initiative of God

With this first statement Barth reiterates in different words his two basic Christological categories of "real man" as having relational form and actional content, filling out the covenantal character of each in that both form and content arise from the one electing action of God towards man in Jesus Christ. First, in Jesus we see that "the being of man as a being with Jesus rests upon the election of God; and that it consists in the hearing of the Word of God."[75]

1. The Indicative of the Covenant Relationship

Jesus is the one man elected[76] by God and the one who has responded to this electing will of God affirmatively. Thus, in the man Jesus man's relationship with God is fulfilled according to the saving will of God, for His glory, under His Lordship, and in service to Him.[77]

Thus, humankind exists in a particular kind of relationship with God, it exists by the initiative of God in a covenant-relation whereby God has elected, chosen, and decided that humankind should exist under His loving Lordship established and revealed in the Word, Jesus Christ. This constitutes the indicative of man's existence. Humankind exists in covenant-relation with God. This is the

---

formal or material reason why he couldn't have, and so in favor of the content of Barth's presentation over the enumeration of it we have made these adjustments for the sake of comprehension of Barth's thought with the help of a diagram.

[75] *Ibid.*, p. 142. This corresponds with his basic grammar of form and content—the trinitarian being and action, and the Christological person and work of Jesus Christ.

[76] Election is defined by Barth as "a special decision with a special intention in relation to a special object" (*CD*, III/2, p. 142).

[77] *CD*, III/2, p. 142.

graciously "given" ontological reality of humanity, the form of humankind's situation established by God's own action.

This election and humankind's affirmation of God's election do not have to deal only or even "primarily" with sin. Man's being, by virtue of being created, is already God's election, God's choice. It is a decision against non-being. God affirms man's existence, not his non-existence in his creation of humankind. Man is saved primarily from non-being even as he is created and is sustained in existence by God. Sin is a denial of this election/choice/decision of God. Sin is the affirmation of what God negates: man's non-existence, his nothingness.[78] Thus, sin threatens man with his non-being. God's saving mankind from sin is the saving of him from nothingness, the nothingness over which God continues to sustain him to live in relationship with Him.[79] This intention was included in God's intention to create.[80]

---

[78]This is a significant contribution of Barth's. It provides grounds for a theology of creation itself in the unity of the Trinitarian life. Creation itself is the act of the same God by the same Word which reconciles and redeems. Creation is an act of sovereign free love. God's agenda for humankind is as constant as God is faithful. It is God's purpose that humankind exist in covenant-relation with Him by virtue of Creation, Reconciliation and Redemption. Thus Creation is understood as the action of the Triune God, (*opera Trinitatis ad extra sunt divisa*) and so creation is understood to have a definite purpose itself, not merely some potential or neutral orientation, which amounts to no real purpose at all. Barth's exegesis of Gen. 1 has given some difficulties. However, his exegesis and his theological conclusions are not grounded on one point or text. Barth takes the text concerning creation as God's negation of the non-being of chaos in the light of Creation's coming to be by the same Word as the Word of Reconciliation and in the light of biblical concerns for life with God being preserved.

Although we are not aware of a place where Barth makes an explicit connection, perhaps what Barth means concerning God's "No!" to non-being and chaos is best understood as God's "No!" to the second death. It is clear biblically that we are not rescued essentially from earthly death, for we are not so spared, but from the second, spiritual death (e.g. Rev. 2:11). Salvation is not essentially from physical death at all. Salvation from death, for Barth, must have to do with "another" death and so "another" life, everlasting life. Physical death is the *sign* of God's eternal judgment. Correspondingly eternal life is not the mere perpetuation of earthly life but a life in the eternal life in God Himself. See *CD*, III/2, pp. 587–640. It is on these more pervasive and broadly defined grounds that Barth argues that God's ultimate concern is not for the preservation of humankind from physical death. There seems to be no apparent reason why Barth could not ultimately identify this with the chaos (and terms also such as the "nothingness") and thereby remain more firmly on biblical grounds. We are preserved from "the second death."

[79]*Ibid.*, p. 143.

[80]"As the Creator, He did not will a threatened and lost creation, but a saved and preserved [one]. And for the fulfillment of this aim He bound Himself to His creation from the very act of creation. As the Creator, He knew its impotence to save and maintain itself. Thus the fall of man, while it formed no part of His intention, was not outside His foresight and plan. From the very first He was determined to be the Preserver of that which He created, of that which He separated as being from non-being. Hence this aim of His will, and His initiative in its realization, His mercy

So, humankind in general, by being constituted as a being *with* Jesus, is the one who exists in this same sphere as that of God's election, namely, Jesus Christ. "He is face to face with the actualization and revelation of the will to save in which the Creator determined to hasten to the help of His creature even as and before He created it..."[81] And so as humankind is with Jesus and in the same sphere as Jesus, he too is affected and elected. [82]

This then is one aspect of what we mean by the God-man relationship being covenantal. It is freely initiated on the part of one party to benefit, bless, bring or share life with the other. It is a freely initiated, salvific relationship of love. Barth immediately turns next to the implications this has for the response of mankind. For it is conditioned by God's gracious formation of the relationship.

2. The Imperative Contained in Covenantal Relationship

In Jesus, then, all other persons are "elected along with or into Jesus."[83] All others are with Jesus and so with God in the electing activity of this relationship which includes mankind. This election is not a hidden choice, a choice involving no announcement or recognition. This election is a calling, a summons, as well as an ontological determination. Jesus is the one elected and the one in whom God's election is actualized but He is also the announcement of that Election, He is the Word of God.[84]

In the being of Jesus Christ we have the personal coincidence of relational form and act. Jesus is not just the means or instrument by which God speaks to man. He Himself is this Word to man. "The man Jesus not only speaks but is Himself the divine speech....in Him the divine address and summons to each and every man is actualised."[85]

Thus, humankind does not first have a nature and then find itself subsequently summoned. Its nature is that of one elected and so summoned: "Summoned because chosen—here we have a first definition of real man."[86] The being of man is determined in this relationship from the very beginning, the relation of God's electing and so speaking and revealing to him his election.

---

towards His creatures, was something resolved from the very beginning, even before the foundation of the world" (*CD*, III/2, p. 144).

[81] *Ibid.*, p. 145.

[82] "Man as such, because he is the fellow of the man Jesus, is from the very first destined to share in the deliverance from evil effected in this one man, to participate in the conflict against the enemy of all creaturely being, to figure in the history of the victory over this enemy, to belong to the body of the Head in whom the triumph of the Creator has been achieved on behalf of the creature" (*CD*, III/2, p. 146).

[83] *Ibid.*, p. 147.

[84] *Ibid.*

[85] *Ibid.*, p. 148.

[86] *Ibid.*, p. 152.

Man does not become the being who is in relationship. He is always in this relationship. "Man *is* the being which is addressed in this way by God."[87]

This is the other aspect of what we mean by covenantal relationship. The loving initiative of God establishes a reality in which man may and must indeed freely participate (if his actions are not to violate and contradict who he is). It is a relationship which calls for a specific correlating response, and so is also to be a loving and free action on man's part. It is a gracious indicative which is itself a gracious imperative,[88] a call for response and participation in that gracious reality of relationship initiated and established by God.[89]

---

[87] *Ibid.*, p. 151. Here we have the Christological grounds for the development of Barth's ethics. The indicative is grounds for the imperative. We will further develop this theme.

[88] In a very comprehensive and informative article, "Being Precedes Act: Indicative and Imperative in Paul's Writing," *Evangelical Quarterly,* Vol. 88, No. 2 (1988), Michael Parsons provides a history of New Testament studies dealing with the relationship of the two "moods" in the Pauline corpus. He also exegetes Rom. 12:1–2; Phil. 2:12–13; Gal. 5:25 and I Cor. 6:12–20. He concludes after this thorough investigation: "It must be stated that the indicative and the imperative are closely linked yet distinct aspects of the apostle's thought and writing. The connection is indissoluble—they cannot be separated. This position seems warranted by Pauline usage and also strongly counters the possibilities of the fusion of the indicative and the imperative, on the one hand, and their virtual irrelation, on the other....The indicative speaks of that which has been accomplished by God in and through Christ—but does not denote simply the divine element as opposed to the human activity in fulfilling the imperative....Paul's ethical admonition is directed to and is determined by, the present redemptive-historical situation. The new age that dawned with Christ's resurrection and the coming of the Holy Spirit determined that this should be so. The Spirit, himself, is the link between the indicative and the imperative of Christian reality and existence. He is at once an element of the former and a constituent part of the latter. The imperative is grounded on the reality that has been given, appeals to it and is intended to bring it to full development (Phil. 2:12–13). The moral behavior of the believer is to reveal something of the character of the new life given by God. Therefore, the indicatives—past, present and eschatological—demand an application on the part of the recipients of Paul's correspondence; they are a motivating force in the apostle's *parenesis*; a corrective factor to misbehaviour, and a sanction to right living before the Lord" (pp. 126–127). He we have sound exegetical confirmation in a Trinitarian framework of one of the most crucial structural features of all of Barth's theology.

[89] Stuart McLean offers as one of his major contributions his notation of the distinction between Barth's view of the covenant as a "root metaphor" and those of a contractual or organic kind. He notes seven elements of the covenantal metaphor that distinguish it from contractual or organic metaphors. It is dyadic, interactional but not unilateral as a contract, has harmony and unity but also confrontation, struggle or conflict (unlike organic), involves unconditional forgiveness (unlike contractual), is eschatological, taking time seriously (unlike organic), its structure of relationship is necessary but subordinate to the purpose and dynamics of the relationship (unlike contract and to a certain degree organic), and finally, involves loyalty and the trust of persons in relation, unlike organic and (to some degree) contract (*HTB*, pp. 56–58).

Covenant Relationship as a History

The third aspect of the form of relationship established by God's election is that it creates an arena for the dynamic history of interaction. Thus, Barth indicates that man's being *is* a history. What Barth means by man's being a history is defined and determined by the existence of the man Jesus.[90]

This being as a history is in contrast to the concept of a state. It indicates a dynamic whereby a being is affected in itself, essentially, by something completely outside of itself. It is changed by this encounter to the extent that it is even enabled to transcend itself in a movement towards the one who encounters it.[91]

More specifically we can see this dynamic in the existence of the man Jesus. He was what he was, did what he did, and became what he was to become only in virtue of his continuing personal relationship with His Father.[92]

This is especially evident as we consider Jesus as man's Deliverer and Savior. Man cannot rescue himself. He must be rescued by another from outside himself and his sphere, and be rescued from out of his sphere. "Jesus exists only in this history, i.e., in this history of the covenant and salvation and revelation inaugurated by God in and with the act of creation. Jesus is, as this history takes place."[93]

Here we can see the convergence of the Christological and anthropological sub-themes we want to make explicit. In the history of this relationship there is a change, a real becoming something that humanity previously was not. Secondly, this occurs as there is an outbreaking from one sphere and an inbreaking into another sphere. God "transcends" himself, that is, goes out of

---

For an in-depth study of the biblical background to covenant and the historical confusion of covenant with contract (*Foedus naturale*) see the important article by James B. Torrance "Covenant or Contract?" *SJT*, Vol. 23, No. 1 (Feb., 1970) pp. 51–76 where he contends that the seventeenth century development of Federal Theology exchanged the notion of covenant for one of contract, making the benefits of God's work conditional upon fulfilling certain conditions. Because of the radical dichotomy between Grace and Nature in the Federal scheme this notion, much in use in the political and social issues of the day, dominated the understanding of humanity in general as being under one kind of contract and the elect as being under another kind, the so called Covenant (contract) of Grace.

[90]"...we prefer not to deduce this principle from those which immediately precede, but to go back to the starting-point. It is the existence of the man Jesus which teaches us that the being of man is a history. What happens in this existence, i.e., that the Creator shows His concern for His creation by Himself becoming a creature, is the fullness and sum of what we mean by talking about history. Here, if anywhere, the use of the term 'primal history' is perhaps appropriate" (p. 157).

[91]"The history of a being occurs when it is caught up in this movement, change and relation, when its circular movement [within itself] is broken from without by a movement towards it and the corresponding movement from it, when it is transcended from without so that it must and can transcend itself outwards" (p. 158).

[92]*Ibid.*, p. 159.

[93]*Ibid.*, p. 160.

himself, to reach humankind, so that humankind may transcend its isolation and be included in the divine fellowship. This provides the root of what we mean by Barth's understanding of personal being in relation to include a personal becoming and the action of extension for the inclusion of others.

Although Jesus alone is the man who is this history of relationship with God, "He alone is all this on behalf of all those whom He is like as man and who are like Him as men. The likeness between Him and them means that what He alone is, is valid for them too, that this is the light in which they not only stand outwardly but are inwardly and essentially."[94]

All human persons subsequently share in what Jesus originally and immediately is and in the history which he actualizes. The result of this is that human being in general has the character in a derivative and secondary way of being an integral part of Jesus' own history of relationship as a movement of God towards man and man towards God.[95]

What we want to note at this point is that the action of covenant relation is further defined as a correlation of persons which is dynamic and eschatological. Man is from, with, in and to God. He exists as a history by participating in Jesus' history of being-in-relationship with God. This is significant. It indicates that for Barth the ontological is not static or substantival. The relationship is active, a movement, an interaction. There is a future towards which man moves. Thus, this is a history of humankind's becoming, of coming to be united with God in the inner-divine life. As humankind participates in the form of relationship given by God's electing action humankind becomes what it is determined to be, a being-in-fellowship with God. The place reserved for humankind in the pre-incarnate Son who was internal to God became external in Jesus Christ so that we who are external to God might become united to him and participate internally in the divine life of God himself through Jesus Christ. This is the dynamic history of our becoming by our correlating participation in the gracious relationship given us in Jesus Christ.

The Trinitarian Grounding of Humankind in Covenantal Relationship

We have been tracing the Christological ground for the form and material content of this man's being in relationship to God. Barth also takes note of its grounding in the trinitarian life because of its grounding in the person of Jesus Christ.

As the Word of God to man, Jesus corresponds to the Logos in the triune life, so Barth explains:

> ...Jesus is the Word of God; that He is to the created world and therefore *ad extra* what the Son of God as the eternal Logos is within the triune being of God. If the eternal Logos is the Word in which God speaks

---
[94]*Ibid.*, pp. 160–161.
[95]*Ibid.*, pp. 161–162.

with Himself, thinks Himself and is conscious of Himself, then in its identity with the man Jesus it is the Word in which God thinks the cosmos, speaks with the cosmos and imparts to the cosmos the consciousness of its God.[96]

Here then we have Barth's explicit indication of his grounding his anthropology in Christology which also reveals the knowledge of the Triune God. They are all brought into actual relation by God's covenantal action in Jesus. However, does this mean that humankind in Jesus is somehow related to God before its appearance at the moment of creation? Barth's answer is, yes. In his discussion of man's creation out of nothing (*creatio ex nihilo*) Barth indicates that there is a real pre-existence of man in the triune life.

...namely, a pre-existence in the counsel of God, and to that extent, in God Himself, i.e., in the Son of God, in so far as the Son is the uncreated prototype of the humanity which is to be linked with God, man in his unity with God, and therefore "the firstborn of every creature" (Col. 1:15). As God Himself is mirrored in this image, He creates man as the one whom He summons into life.[97]

In Jesus, then, we come to recognize that humanity is not alien to God, even though it is not identical with God and is absolutely distinct from God. The Son existing in the eternal Triune life exists as the prototype of humankind maintaining a place for humankind from all eternity.[98] Thus, humanity is actually represented in God. Consequently Barth indicates that "Man can be godless. But God —and this is the decisive point—does not become 'man-less.' He is always the Creator and Lord of man."[99]

Barth regards the testimony of the Gospel of John to be quite explicit in this regard especially in connection with the mutual glorification of the Son by the Father and the Father by the Son (Jn. 13:31, 32) and the mutual indwelling of Father and Son (Jn. 17) as indicated by the man Jesus. Humanity and divinity are

---

[96] *Ibid.*, p. 147.

[97] *Ibid.*, p. 155. *Cf.* II/2, p. 96 where Barth calls the Logos the "*locum tenens*" of Jesus. See Eberhard Jüngel's *Trinity*, p. 80, for a discussion of the Logos as the eternal "placeholder" for all humanity.

[98] This is a difficult and controversial aspect of Barth's teaching. See John Thompson, "The Humanity of God in the Theology of Karl Barth," *SJT*, Vol. 29 (1976), pp. 249–269 for a helpful exploration of the issues. We cannot possibly resolve the issues here. What is salient for our discussion is that humanity is not alien to God and never has been any more than the Son who is the Image of the Father in whose image we are created. Our creation through the Word means that at least concurrent with God's (Father, Son and Spirit) intention to create humanity there was created a place for us in the life of God with the Son of God and that the intention to create arose out of who God is and so is not one alien to who He is in his Triune being. God is for man and man for God in the Word.

[99] *CD*, III/4, p. 625.

not antithetical. Jesus' humanity is dependent upon its [his] participation/ relationship in the divine life. And so, likewise, is our own humanity.[100]

This is another way of indicating that man's humanity is constituted by its relation to God. Without relation to God originally and continually there is no human being. And outside this relationship there will be no human being. But God has not determined the being-in-relationship of man as a determination of the past, but as a determination of eternity. So Barth declares: "God created man to lift him in His own Son into fellowship with Himself"[101] Man is not only coming from God and being with God but is also "going towards God"[102] and all this in Jesus Christ.

Thus, humanity is with God from eternity to eternity by the Son of God with the humanity of Jesus. This indicates that man is *for* God. Man is eternally elected to be human by becoming a participant in the inner life of the Triune God made possible by God himself acting in Jesus on the behalf of His creature. This is an act of God's grace and love. It is not predictable or automatic or given by virtue of God's act of creation.[103]

At this point Barth concludes with one of his most profound insights. Here he testifies that God in Himself is Loving, is the Covenant God, and that the Covenant he makes with humankind arises out of Himself, the essence of His being. The Father, Son and Spirit in-exist each other covenantally. The perichoresis of the inner-divine relations can be further defined as being covenantal in nature.[104]

We can now see how it is that Barth regards the Christological and therefore trinitarian grounding of the being of man as a being essentially and eternally in relation *from, with, for* and so *to* God as elected and summoned by the Word of God in Jesus Christ. The form and content of the being of man in relation to God is the result of an "overflowing" according to God's own triune perichoretic covenantal nature.

Correlating with the relationship of Jesus to God are the actional dimensions, on the part of man, of the interaction of God and man which Barth

---

[100]"Undoubtedly all these things describe the inner relations of the Godhead. But oddly enough this mystery of the participation of Jesus in the Godhead is not at all the dissolution but the very foundation of His true humanity" (p. 66). This of course raises the λογος ασάρχος issue. See E. Jüngel, for his discussion of this in Barth, *Trinity*, pp. 80–81. See II/2, pp. 96ff.

[101]*CD*, III/1, p. 376.

[102] "The New Humanism and the Humanism of God," *Theology Today*, 8 (May, 1951), p. 161.

[103]*CD*, III/2, p. 71.

[104]"He is in Himself the One who loves eternally, the One who is eternally loved and eternal love; and in this triunity He is the original and source of every I and thou...and it is this relationship in the inner divine being which is repeated and reflected in God's eternal covenant with man as revealed and operative in time in the humanity of Jesus" (*CD*, III/2, p. 218).

highlights. We may summarize and say that this relationship of electing and hearing the Word and living out a history of interaction with that Word is, first of all, a relationship of gratitude for God's grace. And second, it is a relationship of responsibility, a response and returning to the grace of God continually. According to Barth, this responsibility may be said to have the character of a) a knowledge of God, b) obedience to God, c) an invocation of God in humility, and d) a freedom which God imparts to man. We will now expand on these dimensions of the content of humankind's being in covenantal relationship. Taken all together this will describe humankind as a being-for-God.

Being-For-God: Covenant Relationship as Being-in-Gratitude

Mankind's existence is a dynamic history in which its being is affected in and by its interaction with the God who transcends him and enables him to transcend himself. The one word which sums this relation of historic dimension which comes from beyond mankind to lift mankind out of himself, is grace. This grace of God which comes from without is that which makes man man. Man is what he is in "virtue of this relation."[105] This relationship is one of grace, grace which alters the being of man. Grace is the essence of his election and the history of man in this relation through Jesus Christ. Again this grace is not merely a passive environment into which mankind is transferred. In the light of the Word, the being of man exists in its corresponding action.[106]

An important theme again comes into view here. The dynamic of the life of humanity is grounded in God's grace as actualized in Jesus. This indicative by its very dynamic, relational and historic nature is also an imperative. This indicative of the grace of God is the basis for the imperative. This imperative comes from beyond man and calls man into a new existence beyond himself. Grace is a summons. "To be summoned is to be called out of oneself and beyond oneself."[107]

This dynamic relationship of grace which calls and enables man to go out of himself to One who is other, the opening of man's being as "a being open to God"[108] sounds another theme that will appear again as we move through his anthropology: that the form of covenantal relationship is one of extending the covenantal relationship in order to include yet others within it.

The call of humankind by the grace of God which liberates him opens the way to a relationship of gratitude. Even the freedom to be grateful is of grace. Mankind is given the privilege to relate to God with gratitude. This is a closed circle of God and mankind in which only God deserves the thanks of mankind,

---

[105] *Ibid.*, p. 165.

[106] "The Word of God is obviously not only a communication but a challenge, not only an indicative but as such an imperative, because it is the Word of His grace....Hence it must be in obedience to this Word that its being and history is continued. Obedience means that this Word claims it" (*CD*, III/2, p. 165).

[107] *Ibid.*, p. 166.

[108] *Ibid.*, p. 167.

God can only be thanked by mankind, only as he thanks God does mankind fulfil his true being and only mankind must thank God in this way.[109]

Thus, we can see from the forgoing discussion Barth's unfolding the covenantal relationship as a history of being in God's grace that, within the threefold form of relationship, it has a content which is a) dynamic and not static relationship in which there is movement and change occurring in the history of relationship, and so there is a real non-predetermined interaction of persons concerning God's election of mankind. b) The covenantal relationship also has the character of a self-transcending extension of one to another, beginning with God's movement toward man to the end of inclusion or the internalization of relationship which we might call an eternal fellowship with God in Christ. c) There is also a proper becoming of humankind in this history of interaction with the Electing God. The interaction concerns the future of humankind, his determination of his being *to* God as well as from and for God. d) The givenness of the grace of God active in this relationship calls for gratitude on the part of humankind. The indicative carries within it the imperative.

Being-For-God: Covenant Relationship as Being-in-Responsibility and Freedom

At a deeper level this gratitude is a spontaneous responsibility. The fact that God is gracious and reveals to man that He is so, calls for a response, and enables the response of thanksgiving as a continual orientation of the being of humankind.

1. Responsible and Participatory Knowing of God and so of Man

In this responsibility to God there is a knowing of God and of man. By man's responding to the grace of God he corresponds to what God does and so participates in a knowing of God.[110]

In this movement of the knowledge of God by correspondence to the Word of God man also gains self-knowledge as a consequence. In the act of responsibility to God's grace in gratitude in the history of this relationship, man becomes aware of himself.[111]

Thus, self-knowledge is a derived indirect result of a true knowledge of God in the responsibility towards God of thanksgiving for His grace. On the basis of the affirmation that "God is" man may go on to say in a relative way that "I am." This "I am" means that "I am" as I am in this relationship of response of gratitude to God for His grace which created, sustains and gives me a future hope

---

[109] *Ibid.*, pp. 169–172.

[110] *Ibid.*, p. 177.

[111] In this relation of going out of himself in gratitude to God, man is himself and posits himself "he becomes an object to himself. In proportion as he takes this step, he moves Godward out of himself, thus detaching himself from himself, and like the God of grace from whom he comes and to whom he goes becoming to himself another....In this act [unlike God] he will find himself only as a relatively other" (*CD*, III/2, p. 178).

of life in this Word of grace and so with this God of grace. In so doing this man comes into his own, as it were; he becomes, relatively speaking, a subject as he is in relationship to God as his primary object.[112]

Thus, we see again in terms of the covenant relation of humankind to God as responsibility that it involves the loving initiative of God and the action of humankind. This action is responsible action as it correlates with God's electing action towards him. He is responsible as he is a being for God. Further, this responsibility is a responsibility of knowing God. This knowledge comes from outside, beyond humankind. It involves an extension of mankind beyond himself because God has extended Himself beyond Himself to us. It is a knowledge differentiated from humankind. It is graciously given to mankind. It calls for mankind's knowing and so becoming something other than he knew himself to be. It occurs in a history of relationship with God and so is a dynamic. Mankind comes to know himself as the one he is to become; one who lives in fellowship with God. And finally, mankind is not threatened by this but is all the more graciously differentiated by this fellowship and knowledge. Humankind comes to know itself as it actually is, as existing in this gracious covenantal relationship with God and determined for eternal participation in the very life of God.

2. The Responsibility of Obedience

This relationship of responsibility may further be understood as having the characteristic of obedience. Since the Word of God is "the action of God," knowledge of this Word and response to this Word cannot be only a matter of "acquaintance, insight and disposition."[113] This Word made known to man is a summons to him to "move out of itself as God the Creator has come forth from Himself, coming to man and therefore becoming the very foundation of his being."[114] Mankind can be only as he fulfills his knowledge of God and goes in obedience to God who summons him. The fact that "God is" leads further to both the relative affirmations that "I am" and "I will." This indicates that "I recognize the fact that my being is not simply a gift with which I am endowed but a task for which I am commissioned. Indeed, I affirm and grasp my being as my task, and treat it as such."[115]

Thus, the relative statement that "I am" is defined by both the terms "I will" and "I do." Responsibility towards God is embodied in action, in going out of one's self in giving one's self to God. This is an act of total and irreversible

---

[112]*Ibid.*, pp. 178–179.

[113]*Ibid.*, p. 179.

[114]*Ibid.*, pp. 179–180.

[115]*Ibid.*, p. 180. "I am, and I know that I am, as I choose the possibility prescribed and offered me in my knowledge of God. To will is to obey. I have only one possibility, and I do not discover this for myself, but it is prescribed and offered me in my knowledge of God. In it I affirm and grasp my being in the determination which it has not given itself but with which it was created. What lies before me is my way to God from whom I come, and this way has been determined by its origin and will never abandon the curve which it has begun to describe" (pp. 180–181).

commitment.[116] It means that there must be a correlation in each person of willing, deciding and acting.[117]

Thus, the fact of God's being a willing, deciding and so an electing, speaking, and a gracious acting towards mankind carries with it the summons for him to co-respond. The indicative of God towards humankind is also an imperative. This summons to action is not incidental or accidental to his existence. This willing and doing according to the being, willing and action of God's own self-giving involves mankind's *becoming*, his moving through history to leave himself behind only to enter into the new self that God graciously has determined for him, a being-in-relation from, to, with and for God. Man's being is in his becoming; in his doing according to the will of God. It is only in this way that mankind is truly, really, human, and so becomes a living subject: a being whose deciding and willing correspond, and whose being in action God corresponds with God's being-in-action towards him.[118]

Again, we can point out the themes of the covenantal relations (indicative-imperative), the dynamic and eschatological becoming, and the extensive self-transcending nature of the responsibility of obedience. It is also clear here and elsewhere that the form of the relationship as a unity, a differentiation and yet a correlation are foundational for making sense of how Barth understands the dynamics of the material action of man and God in relationship, especially in terms of responsibility as obedience.

3. *Responsibility as Invocation*

This being-in-responsibility to God has the character of an invocation to God for his mercy that we might come to God. There is "a supreme disparity between the coming of God and the going of man, between the objective and the subjective basis of human being."[119] God does not ask permission to transcend mankind within mankind's sphere. God does not come to humankind because He needs to do so. God does not put Himself at mankinds's mercy or need mankind. God could have remained Himself without humankind. There is no inner "pressure" for God to be gracious. It arises from his freedom and love to create, reconcile and redeem.[120]

From humanity's side coming to God is a response to God's own coming to him. Humankind comes out of its need for being maintained in existence, for

---

[116]*Ibid.*, pp. 181–182.

[117]*Ibid.*, p. 182.

[118]*Ibid.*

[119]*Ibid.*, p. 187.

[120]"If God comes to man in His divine Word, He does not do so because He needs man. God does not flee to man for refuge. He is not obliged to be the Creator, nor to be gracious to man. He is glorious in Himself. He could be content with that inner glory. The fact that He is the Creator of man and is gracious to man is a free overflowing of His glory. And so the objective foundation of human being is an act of divine majesty. But for this very reason it is also sure and certain, clear and consistent....This is how He transcends the limits of the creature" (*Ibid.*, p. 187).

being saved from sin and the threat of non-being; out of humility. It is a response—an invocation of prayer according to God's will.[121]

While there is a correspondence of action between God and humanity, humanity's action is a response made possible only by God. There is no identity of action, but humanity's action is in relation to, and so is relative to, God's action. Humanity's action remains humanity's action even as a response entirely dependent upon God's action.[122]

While there is a correspondence of God's being in his action of self-transcendence in self-giving to mankind's being in his action and self-transcendence in self-giving, there is also an ontological ordering. God's is original, primary, autonomous, and absolute while man's is derived, secondary, dependent and relative to God's. All our ways are to be understood as being-in-relation to God. There is nothing at all about humankind which can be taken as if it were not in actual ontological relation to God as creature to Creator.[123]

Here we find especially the themes of the covenantal initiative of God and the response of humankind and the theme of the extension and transcendence of humankind called for by the extension and transcendence of God. The formal theme of the differentiation and so ordering of the relationship by God is also clearly visible.

4. Responsibility as Freedom for God: A Being Personal

Finally, the being of man in responsible relation to God has the character of freedom which God gives him. Barth explains that this means that the "responsibility of man before God is a personal responsibility" and so "precludes any idea of it being a function of God Himself or a function or partial function of the divinely created cosmos. It is man himself who knows and obeys God and seeks God."[124] Here we see that there is a correspondence of God's own freedom and mankind's rendering each in relation to the other as self-existent and so as personal. It is ultimately the being of mankind in freedom, to the extent that it corresponds to God's, that refers to humankind's existence as a personal one.[125]

There is a correspondence to God's own freedom because mankind comes from God and is going to God and is responsible before God. This freedom of mankind to be a true subject in relation to God is the gift of God to mankind.

---

[121] "The Yes in which man answers the divine Yes, man's knowledge of God and obedience to Him, can never have more than the force and reach of an echo" (*CD*, III/2, p. 188).

[122] *Ibid.*

[123] "To offer himself and place himself at the disposal of God—it is to this that he is summoned and for this that he is strengthened and empowered. Doing this, he is established as a human subject, and posits himself as such. Failing to do it, he fails to realise himself as man" (*CD*, III/2, p. 189).

[124] *Ibid.*, pp. 192–193.

[125] "The fact that the self-existent God intervenes for man determines his own being as one which on its side too is self-existent....This selfhood of man is the character of his being as freedom" (*CD*, III/2, p. 193).

Summing all this up, we now affirm that in his knowledge, obedience and invocation man is himself and acts in freedom because God is first free in relation to him, Himself being the ultimate ground of all selfhood and as the Saviour and Keeper of His creature the ultimate ground of all personal responsibility.[126]

This freedom of course cannot then be understood autonomously. Mankind is mankind only as he is in relationship to God. His freedom is one from and with God. This is a gift which cannot be separated from its source. Mankind's relationship with God is a living thing and as such is a history of inter-relating. So too is his freedom. Consequently, he has no freedom except in relation to God. He is a subject **for** God. And no other "reality" can negate this for it is established and maintained by God himself. For mankind to attempt to use his freedom in disregard of God in an autonomous fashion is for him to reject his freedom and so personhood. He is denying his own being as mankind. His freedom can be only as it corresponds to God's freedom for him. This can only mean that mankind is not free in some neutral sense. He is not free to sin. He is not free to choose anything he will. He is free only in relation to God, only in his correspondence to God. "Even his sin cannot alter this fact. Sin means that he is lost to himself, but not to his Creator."[127]

With this Barth concludes that mankind is good in spite of his evil deeds. Mankind cannot undo God's good determination, God's taking responsibility for him. The humanity that exists before God is the humanity which is good, otherwise he would not and could not exist before God at all. His sin conceals who he really is but cannot change who he is.[128]

Here again we see the correlation but also the ordering and distinction between God's and mankind's freedom, goodness and so personhood. What has come into focus finally is what is designated by the word "person." To be a person is to be one who corresponds to God his Creator in a relationship of being with and from God in a history of interaction of gratitude to God for his grace, of response and responsibility to and so towards God which consists of a knowledge of God and so self, an obedience to God and so a being in becoming, an invocation of God's gracious judgment through self-giving and so self-establishment, and a freedom to be all this personally by God's own personal goodness. Thus, to man there

> belongs in a decisive and comprehensive way the freedom to be both from God and to Him, the endowment and adaptation to be the partner of God, the partner of *God* and not merely of an undefined transcendence, the *partner* of God and therefore not merely the sharer in a transcendence immanent in human existence itself. As man is, he is

---

[126]*Ibid.*, p. 193.

[127]*Ibid.*, p. 197.

[128]*Ibid.*, pp. 197–198.

endowed with reason to perceive God and responsibility to answer Him, he is capable of history and decision, he is therefore—let us accept the term—"personal," and in all these things he is thus able to be the partner of God.[129]

In this final theme of responsible freedom, we can see again the formal themes of man's existing in a relationship of unity, distinction and correspondence with God and the material themes of man's existing in correlation of his being and action with the election (calling and hearing), history of relationship, gratitude, and responsibility as knowledge, obedience, invocation and freedom. We can also see the themes underlying man's existing in a relationship of correlation as being covenantal, dynamic and eschatological, and extensive and so inclusive in the life of God. As the most comprehensive term of all we see Barth designating the being-in-relationship of God and man as a covenant partnership of personal existence. And all this has been founded upon a Christological perspective which reveals the ontological and noetic source and the ultimate determination of the life of humankind in such a personal existence of covenant partnership to be the inner triune life of God in himself.

Summary: The Grammar of Karl Barth's Theological Anthropology

Barth has claimed that in faith the knowledge of God is correlated with our knowledge of man because both are revealed in Jesus Christ. Furthermore, the knowledge of man is then related to the knowledge of God Himself in His intra-trinitarian life. In Jesus we meet God as Father, Son and Spirit and as Creator, Reconciler and Redeemer. Inasmuch as these actions of God cannot be essentially apportioned to only one person but are related to the one being of God, when we consider man as the creature of God the Creator we should expect that the entire triune being of God will be inferred as well as the other primary actions of God as Reconciler and Redeemer, although they will play only a supportive role.

What we discover in Jesus is that relationship to God the Creator is essential to human existence. But we do not just see this relationship abstractly. The form of this relationship has content, that is, it has activity. In fact it is God's activity which establishes the form. Thus, we see in the interaction of Jesus with God the content of man's relationship to God. But since Jesus reveals to us the nature of God, the content of Jesus' relationship to God reveals the intra-trinitarian relations in God. This means that our knowledge of man is rooted in Christology and so in the trinitarian knowledge of God. Our anthropology, as regards man's relationship to God, is both Christological and trinitarian, that is, it is founded upon the relationships of God and man in Jesus and in the relationships of Father, Son and Spirit present with and revealed in Jesus. This also means that because the relationships are ordered according to

---

[129] *Ibid.*, p. 202.

God himself, they will have similarities for all their dissimilarity. Barth has been tracing out the structure of these relationships.

What our foregoing explication of Barth's theological anthropology has indicated are the very contours of these relationships. We may now try to gather together the various strands that we have uncovered so far in an attempt to summarize them in a kind of formula (remembering all the provisos we have made regarding such categorizations).

What we propose are six characterizations of humankind under two primary categories, A and B. We will begin with these and then delineate the three characterizations under each of them, 1–3 and 4–6, respectively.

THE SIX DETERMINATIONS OF HUMANKIND AS BEING-IN-RELATIONSHIP WITH GOD

A) Humanity's being has the FORM OF RELATIONSHIP to God which indicates that humanity is **to, from** and **with** God as Jesus himself had this form of relationship with God and so *constitutes* the form of relationship with God through Him in which humankind participates.

1) Humanity's being has the form of a being FROM God and so a being UNITED to God, but he is not a being without God nor to be confused with God. Because Jesus is both like humankind and yet unlike humankind, persons in general are united with Him but not identical with him. There is a unity with Jesus as well as an independence of humankind.

2) Humanity's being is in the form of being DIFFERENTIATED YET DETERMINED FOR COMMUNION with God. Because Jesus has come from the Father and returns to the Father in the Spirit He exists in a fellowship and communion with God. Humankind too is determined for participation in the intra-trinitarian life of communion with the Father through the Son in the Spirit.

3) Humanity's being-in-relationship is a being of ORDERED CORRESPONDENCE of humanity with God and so his being is an IMAGE and WITNESS TO God. Jesus corresponds in his being to God in that He is God's presence with humanity, He embodies God's relationship with humanity for all. He is the enactment of the will and kingdom of God among humanity. Thus, we are to act in a way which corresponds to who we actually graciously are in relationship to God, the image of the Image, the sons and daughters of the Son of God, the children of the Father of Jesus.

B) Humanity's being in relation with God has also been given its COVENANTAL CONTENT (action) and is so constituted in both form and content as a being FOR God. Thus, Jesus' existence was not merely the revelation of who God and mankind are, but He existed only by virtue of the relationship of God and humanity with each other. He is the ontological reality of this relationship. He was Who He revealed. Humanity has being only as we engage in the action of relation just as

Jesus' person exists only in His action as God's image of his Creator and Reconciler.

4) Humanity's relationship with God is a COVENANTAL and so PERSONAL relationship of being FOR God. So Jesus is the one elected by God's initiative and who freely responds to God's calling in and through the history of his relationship with God which was a life of thanksgiving, obedience, invocation, and freedom for God. In this relationship we can indicate that in Jesus we find true human personhood, that God is personal, and that humankind, too, by the relationship (form and content) established with him in Jesus, is personal as well, corresponding to the image of God in Jesus.

5) Humanity's being in relationship to God is a DYNAMIC and ESCHATOLOGICAL history in which humankind BECOMES what he is graciously determined to be—FOR God. His covenantal relationship to God is not intrinsic to man *qua* man himself, but is the gift of the grace of God which became actual in Jesus Christ. In Jesus Christ humanity comes to exist and to exist in relation to God. We are maintained in relation to God and have a future in relation to God. Mankind's being is in becoming in relation to God.

6) Humanity's being in relationship means his being FOR God, transcending himself and GOING OUT of himself and GIVING of himself for others to be INCLUDED IN relationship with God as a response to God's own doing so toward him. So Jesus is God's own self-giving and outgoing to mankind that man might be included in the inner life of the Triune God. The relations of God and humanity as revealed in Jesus are not external but internal relationships in which each participates in the life of the other. God's action in Christ takes place so that humankind might participate in the life of God Himself. Humanity is not alien to God's divine existence. God in Jesus now exists in relation to humankind eternally and internally.

If we have understood Barth correctly, so far, what we should expect to see is how this primary vertical relationship with God is reflected for Barth in humankind's relationships with other human persons and how these horizontal relationships reflect and gain their proper order out of their Christological and trinitarian grounding.

Thus, we will proceed from here to survey in the next chapter Barth's theological anthropology for each one of these six determinations, delineated above, as it concerns inter-human relationships. We will follow along in the *Church Dogmatics* III/2, §45, "Man in His Determination as the Covenant-partner of God" for Barth's development of this.

The Relations of Relations are also Analogous

One last thing should be covered before we conclude this chapter. There is for Barth another level of complexity to the relations. The relations themselves can also be compared and characterized.

In discerning the humanity of Jesus, which occurs essentially as the history of His relationship originally with His Father and correspondingly with other persons, Barth will come to affirm a correspondence of *form* within all seven relationships: that is, between Father and Son, Jesus and God, Jesus and humankind, humans and God, human persons, the body and soul, time and eternity. Each relationship has its being as a unity establishing and maintaining a distinction with an ordering of one entity by the other.

Also, each relationship itself is related to the other relations in the same corresponding way: as a similarity yet a distinction with an ordering of one by the other. That is, the relationship of one set of relations to another set corresponds (that is, is in some respects different and in some respects similar) to all the relationships between any other two sets of relationships. How the relationships themselves are related is both the same (but the same in different ways in each case) and different (but different in different ways) in each case. For the five relations we are considering:

A. Father to Son (in the Spirit)
B. The man Jesus to the Father (in the Spirit)
C. The Disciples to God through Jesus
D. Jesus to His disciples
E. The Disciples to others.

The relations themselves are also comparable or analogous: e.g. A:E or C:D or A:C.

Each relation has itself the form of unity with distinctions; the distinctions are different with unique kinds of dissimilarity with similarity, an ordering and orientation of one by the other. Thus, the Father is not the Son ("not," in a unique way) yet is one with the Son ("one" in a unique way). Jesus is not one of his disciples yet is one with them (but Jesus is "not" one of the disciples in a different way than how he is "not" the Father and yet there is some similarity also) and is one with them in a way different yet similar to the way He is one with His Father. This we have already set out.

Concerning the correspondence of relations themselves: the way the Father and Son in the triune life, and Jesus and the Father are identical, the only distinction being that in Jesus the relation is made external. The Father's love for the Son and the Son's love for the Father have the same unity and distinction as Jesus' love for the Father and the Father's love for Jesus.

However, while Jesus' relationship to his disciples is all but incomparable to His relationship to his Father, yet there is a similarity and so it can be identified as being comparable: e.g., Jesus prays "that the love with which thou has loved me may be in them, and I in them" (Jn. 17:26) and says both that the Father will glorify him (Jn. 17:5) and that he will be glorified in his disciples (Jn. 17: 10).

Although there is great dissimilarity between Jesus' love for humankind and ours (His is a saving love) Jesus, nevertheless, because he enables there to be a correspondence, says "Love one another as I have loved you." "Forgive one another as you have been forgiven." When He prays that we will be one as He and the Father are one, including even those not yet identified as disciples of His, He compares the Father's love for the Son and the Son's love for the Father to our love for one another (Jn. 17:11, 22).

So while there are similarities and differences (i.e., a unity and distinction) between each relation, *how* they are similar and different, united yet distinct from each other, is also similar yet different in each case. In our characterizations of the grammar of being-in-relation, we are pointing out the similarities for the most part, but will have to note dissimilarities as well along the way as this is included in the grammar itself.

In terms of the ordering of the relations, the original orders the copy so that A (the intra-triune relations) is the original and so orders the copy B, while that relation orders its image C, which orders its image D. Note also that how each orders its copy is both similar and dissimilar in different ways for each ordering. The way one person provides an original for another person is much different from the way that Jesus is the Image of the Trinity. And yet there is a similarity so that in the New Testament we are directed to be imitators of Christ to each other. We are to be images of the Image. Jesus Christ is the externalization of the Son's imaging of the Father in the intra-trinitarian life. So the direction of comparison between the relations is unidirectional: from the original to its externalization or manifestation.

Finally, we should indicate that for Barth the way one is ordered by the other occurs in the interaction of the relationship itself. The copy participates in the original. The copy does not have or possess or control its own being a copy. It is only as the relationship continues by way of ordered covenant action that any participation of the copy in the original may occur. Were the relationship to dissipate there would be no correspondence, no participation, no ordering of one by the other.[130]

---

[130]This entire discussion anticipates Barth's unfolding of what he comes to call the *analogia relationis*. This anticipation without reference to the term is possible because Barth's own exposition of this concept is not introduced as a kind of datum or axiom, but emerges as he unfolds the Christological and Trinitarian approach to anthropology. The concept is a conclusion, a comprehensive term used to encapsulate what he has heretofore explicated. We anticipate it here so that we will better be able to follow along with Barth to see how it finally culminates in the *analogia relationis*.

Part Two

Humanity as Co-Humanity: Being in Covenantal Relations One With Another

Chapter 4

The Christological Determination of Our Co-Humanity

Here at the outset we should point out that Barth uses the term "humanity" (*Menschlichkeit*) to designate a person's existence in relationship to their world, or universe or cosmos. It designates the human creature as it relates on the horizontal plane "below" in contrast to man in his relationship with God "from above." Of course it is one of his major tasks to show how "real man" is related to "humanity." The key, and so the point of departure to investigate our humanity, is Jesus Christ. Barth's treatment of this Christological point of departure for understanding humanity in terms of its inter-relations is found in §45, "Man in His Determination as the Covenant-Partner of God," under the first part, "Jesus Christ: the Man for Others."

Jesus Christ: the "Man for Others"

In Jesus we discover "real man" as the one who is in relationship with God in a way that determines his existence. "He is determined by God for life with God."[1] As such real man is the covenant-partner (*Bundesgennosen*) of God as he lives in the history of this covenant of his election and responds to God's calling for him to enter fully into the relationship determined for him in Jesus Christ, and so live responsibly with, for and to God.

Yet humankind lives in the cosmos, in the creation. How is it that his being in the cosmos is related to his being in relation to God? The creature is not God nor God the creature. Mankind is distinct from God in his creaturely existence. Yet it is as a creature in creation that man is to be the covenant-partner of God, in his creatureliness, not apart from it. As Barth has explicated earlier he recalls how the creation is a reality distinct from God and is the external basis of the covenant. The covenant is the internal basis and possibility of creation as a reality distinct from God.[2] How does man live out, on the creaturely plane, his determination as the covenant-partner of God when they cannot be identical yet must both be pursued by one and the same person?

Thus, while there is a distinction between humankind's being with God and in the cosmos these are seemingly not in antithesis or contradiction. If there is a distinction yet harmony then there is some similarity of mankind's determination as the covenant-partner and his existence in the cosmos. Where, asks Barth, can this form of his humanity be discerned?

---

[1] *CD*, III/2, p. 203.
[2] *Ibid.*, p. 204. See *CD*, III/1, p. 41.

Sin Obscures but Cannot Obliterate God's Purposes

Again Barth must also consider the nature of man's involvement in sin. It is not only the fact that humanity and God are distinct but that sin has qualified humanity's existence. Thus, sin as well obscures the true nature of inter-human relationships. We may summarize Barth's point and say that certainly man breaks the covenant by sin and can deny and obscure the reality of his determination. This may lead one to think that his creaturely existence is in contradiction to some divine determination or that it obliterates whatever determination there was. The correspondence of his divine determination and creaturely form is indeed "covered over and made unrecognizable."[3] However, Barth finds no grounds in the witness of revelation to allow man's sinfulness to determine our starting point for considering the real détermination of man or to allow man's sin to annihilate God's good intentions for his creature. "The good creation of God which now concerns us knows nothing of a radical or absolute dualism in this respect."[4] Sin is not creative and so cannot replace the creature of God with another nor can it annul God's covenant with him.

The Mystery of Jesus Christ: "Man for God" and So Uniquely "Man for Humanity"

In order to discern the true form of our humanity (that is in its horizontal relations) and its interplay with our determination as God's covenant-partner "we must continue to base our anthropology on Christology."[5] In the person of Jesus we see a unity of Father and Son which "does not destroy the difference between the divinity and humanity even in Him." And neither detracts from the other. "That He is one with God, Himself God, does not mean that Godhead has taken the place of His manhood, that His manhood is as it were swallowed up or extinguished by Godhead, that His human form is a mere appearance...That he is true God and also in full differentiation true man is the mystery of Jesus Christ."[6]

Barth encapsulates his investigation into the person of Jesus by saying that Jesus' humanity is revealed in his relationships to others in distinction from his divinity which is revealed in his relationship with his Father.[7]

1. Jesus' Mission: "Man For God" and So Uniquely "Man For Humanity"

Jesus is the man who in His totality is both man for God and Man for man. And the way Jesus is for others is unique to him for, according to the will of God, it now shapes his entire incarnate existence. He, only and exclusively, has

---

[3] *Ibid.*, pp. 205, 206.
[4] *Ibid.*, p. 205.
[5] *Ibid.*, p. 207.
[6] *Ibid.*, p. 208.
[7] "If the divinity of the man Jesus is to be described comprehensively in the statement that He is man for God, His humanity can and must be described no less succinctly in the proposition that He is man for man, for other men, His fellows" (p. 208).

his being for others. He is his mission as Savior of humankind. His being now necessarily includes his humanity if he is to actually deliver them in their creaturely sphere. Jesus is human in order to accomplish the divine will, and this is the only reason for His incarnate humanity. He is completely with man in his humanity to be their Deliverer, for no other reason.

2. In His Being

Barth wants to "dig more deeply and say that in the being of the man Jesus for His fellows we have to do with something ontological."[8] That is, who Jesus is as mankind's Savior and Neighbor is not exhausted by a description of what he did, said or accomplished. For who Jesus is is not arbitrary or accidental. It is not the case that he might have been something different than he was. His person is identified with His mission. He is what he does. His humanity is determined by his divinity.[9]

3. Internally Related to Humankind

Barth goes on to note that Jesus is "immediately and directly affected" by humanity. There is no separation such that he is uninvolved with them in any way.[10] Thus, the help that Jesus brings is the Help for humanity that He is. He is uniquely and radically with and for other men in a most comprehensive way. The help is his total self-giving on behalf of humanity. His help is the establishment of a person to person history of exchange for their benefit at the core of their being. Such a relationship is internal to both Him and humanity.[11]

---

[8] *CD*, III/2, p. 210.

[9] *Ibid.*

[10] *CD*, III/2, p. 211. The Biblical passages Barth refers to here are instructive. He sees in Col. 1:15-18, "the first born of all creation...all things were created through him and for him....the Head of the body, the Church," Eph. 1:4: "he chose us in him before the foundation of the world...to be his sons," Rom. 8:29, "those whom [God] foreknew he also predestined to be conformed to the image of his Son, in order that he might be the first-born among many brethren," and Heb. 1:6: "when he brings the first-born [the Son] into the world" and passages in John (17:6,8,10,24; 20:17; 14:2) that humanity is eternally with God in the Son and so involves the relationship of the Father and the Son in their own eternal relationship in the incarnation of the Son on behalf of humankind. His exegesis of the compassion unique to Jesus in its depth and identification with the object of his compassion (σπλαγνίζεσθαι) is significant for the intrinsic source of his work of salvation.

[11] "He does not merely help His fellows from without, standing alongside, making a contribution and then withdrawing again and leaving them to themselves until further help is perhaps required....And so the being of Jesus for His fellows really means much more. It means that He interposes Himself for them, that He gives Himself to them, that He puts Himself in their place, that He makes their state and fate His own cause, so that it is no longer theirs but His, conducted by Him in His own name and on His own responsibility....It was not merely a matter of His turning to them with some great gift, but of His giving Himself, His life, for them....not merely to improve and alleviate their old life but to help them to a basically new one" (*CD*, III/2, p. 212). Barth here is reiterating the Cappadocian understanding of Christ's assumption of our humanity: ἀπροσληπτον θεραπευτον.

Six Implications of the Humanity of Jesus Christ

Barth draws together his discussion in six "implications" of Jesus' humanity (His relations with other humans) that are parallel to the six implications of His divinity (His relationship with His Father in the Spirit) which we have already covered. We will attempt to summarize them as they have import for the humanity of humankind in general.

THE HUMANITY OF JESUS CHRIST

1) His humanity is **from** humankind. It is determined by the nature of the humanity of his creatures. This is a fallen, guilt-ridden, imperilled humanity under judgment, not an ideal or "original" humanity untouched by sin.

2) His humanity is **to** humankind. It is exclusively for their benefit, deliverance, salvation. He is entirely with them and gives Himself entirely for them. He serves them utterly.

3) In these two ways Jesus is **with** all humanity and so is sovereignly their Master, Messiah, King and Lord. He is nothing in abstraction from those by whom He in his humanity is determined and for whom He has come.

4) Taken altogether, his being *from*, *to* and *with* means He is **for** man. He is towards others in a positive correspondence with his being *from*, *to*, *with*, and *for* God.[12] Thus, his being from, for and with man in his humanity is an obedience, that is, it is a correspondence of Jesus' action with God's will.

5) By fully serving, in His humanity, the will of God, He truly **serves** mankind because the saving work that He does is a task given Him by God. Jesus must be for man because he is first of all for God who is for man.[13] God in His eternal decree determined himself as Father, Son and Spirit to be the Salvation of man. Thus, He is eternally the Covenant Partner of man who appears in our time in Jesus Christ.

---

[12] "His humanity is in closest correspondence with His divinity. It mirrors and reflects it. Conversely, His divinity has its correspondence and image in the humanity in which it is mirrored. At this point, therefore, there is similarity. Each is to be recognised in the other. Thus even the life of the man Jesus stands under a twofold determination. But there is a harmony between the two. As he is for God, so He is for man; and as He is for man, so He is for God" (*CD*, III/2, p. 216).

[13] "God Himself is for man and is his Covenant-partner...God Himself is his Deliverer....The God who willed and resolved this, and acted in this way in His incarnate Son, is the basis of the saving work of the man Jesus which has man—His fellow-men exactly as they are—as its object. It is not by accident, then, that Jesus is for man as He is for God. Between His divinity and His humanity there is an inner material connexion as well as a formal parallelism. He could not be for God if He were not on that account for man. The correspondence and similarity between His divinity and humanity is not merely a fact, therefore, but has a material basis. The man Jesus is necessarily for His fellows as He is for God. For God first, as the One who gives Him His commission, as the Father of this Son, is for man. This excludes any possibility of the man Jesus not being for man as He is for God" (*CD*, III/2, p. 217).

6) In Jesus' humanity, i.e. in his being for humankind, God is **free** because in this He corresponds and is true to Himself in his inner-most Triune life.

In his interpretation of this last point, Barth gives the most profound and succinct paragraphs of his anthropology in which he brings together all his Christological criteria of human existence with its trinitarian grounding. We will quote it in full.

> If "God for man" is the eternal covenant, revealed and effective in time in the humanity of Jesus, in this decision of the Creator for the creature there arises a relationship which is not alien to the Creator, to God as God, but we might almost say appropriate and natural to Him. God repeats in their relationship *ad extra,* a relationship proper to Himself in His inner divine essence. Entering into this relationship, he makes a copy of Himself...Even in His inner divine being there is relationship. To be sure, God is One in Himself. But He is not alone. There is in Him a co-existence, a co-inherence and reciprocity. God in Himself is not just simple, but in the simplicity of His essence He is threefold—the Father, the Son and the Holy Ghost. He posits Himself, is posited by Himself, and confirms Himself in both respects, as His own origin and also as His own goal. He is in Himself the One who loves eternally, the One who is eternally loved, and eternal love, and in this triunity He is the origin and source of every I and Thou, of the I which is eternally from and to the Thou and therefore supremely I. And it is this relationship in the inner divine being which is repeated and reflected in God's eternal covenant with man as revealed and operative in time in the humanity of Jesus.
>
> Now we stand before the true and original correspondence and similarity of which we have to take note in this respect. We have to see that there is a factual, a materially necessary, and supremely, as the origin of the factual and materially necessary, an inner divine correspondence and similarity between the being of the man Jesus for God and His being for His fellows. The correspondence and similarity consists in the fact that the man Jesus in His being for man repeats and reflects the inner being or essence of God and this confirms His being for God. We obviously have to do here with the final and decisive basis indicated when we spoke of the ontological character, the reality and the radical nature of the being of Jesus for His fellow-men. It is from this context that these derive their truth and power. The humanity of Jesus is not merely the repetition and reflection of His divinity, or of God's controlling will; it is the repetition and reflection of God Himself no more and no less. It is the image of God, the *imago Dei.* [14]

---

[14] *CD*, III/2, pp. 218–219.

The Christological Determination of our Co-Humanity

We quote at great length here because this is the basis and crux of our entire exposition brought together at one point. Here we see Barth struggling to explicate the ontological and so theological foundation of the person of Jesus in his relationship with humanity and his imaging externally the divine Triune relationships in which He internally participates. All six of our basic characteristics under the two primary headings are brought together in this one succinct yet very complex exposition. Now we are at the most profound depths of the revelation. The being of Jesus for God and so for man arises out of the inner structure of the Triune life. God in Himself is with and for man, *ad intra*. The inner life of God has taken humanity into itself ontologically in the Son, reflected in the being of Jesus, *ad extra*. Jesus as divine and human is the image of God. He does not merely image the divine, for there is no merely divine or exclusively divine reality without humanity. This is the momentousness of the ontological character of the Election of humanity in the Word.

Barth's Grammar of the Triune Relations: *ad intra* and *ad extra*

We can now explicitly update our original characterizations of the intra-triune relations by correlating them with our summaries of the two Christological characterizations of Jesus' relationship with the Father (his divinity) and Jesus' relations with others (his humanity).

THE INTRA-TRIUNE RELATIONS

A) The Being of God has the FORM OF RELATIONSHIP.

1) The Being of God in Relationship has the form of the Father's and Son's being WITH one another in the Spirit, being united to each other, yet not being confused with or losing their distinctions as Father, Son, and Holy Spirit.

2) The Being of God in its relationships has the form of Father and Son being differentiated from one another in the Spirit and yet having their unity in that same Spirit.

3) The Being of God in Relationship takes the form of the Father and Son in the Spirit having an ordered correspondence to one another, working together, and so being images of one another, but each in a different way.

B) The Being of God in Relationship is CONSTITUTED BY ITS INTER-ACTIONS between Father, Son and Spirit.

4) The Being of God in Relationship between Father, Son, and Spirit is constituted by relationships which may be characterized as being covenantal and so personal relations of free life-giving initiative and reception of Father, Son and Spirit.

5) The Being of God in Relationship between Father, Son and Spirit is constituted as a dynamic history of relationship among them whereby God continually affirms and establishes Himself as the Living Triune God.

6) The Being of God in Relationship means that the relationships of Father, Son and Spirit are constituted by a going out and self-giving thereby becoming united with the others, each in a different way.

The Correspondence of Relations: The *Analogia Relationis*

This discussion leads us to the point of considering again the correspondence of the relations. How can we correlate the intra-trinitarian relations with Jesus' relations with God and others and our relations with God and others? Barth begins to make his most explicit answer at this point. He introduces us to his section on the *analogia relationis*.

It should be clear from the start, then, that Barth does not come to his conclusion that there is an analogy of relationship on the basis of some abstract philosophical or quasi-theological grounds.[15] The *analogia relationis* does not serve as a methodology by which to derive theological truths. For him it is the best way to sum up all that he has been driving at in this entire volume (and of of course, before that). "Analogy" is for him an ontological term. It is an explication of the person and work of Jesus Christ as the Elect of God revealing God Himself, as a saving of humanity that is *not external to humanity or God*. It designates the reality of "Immanuel" and keeps this Name from disintegrating into a metaphor. It guards the way to real relationship now and in eternity which involves the being of God and of man, which involves their very existence. It means that God Himself is what He does and so is freely sovereign and sovereignly free in his electing love. It means that God remains God even while being in actual communion with humanity. It means that humanity remains humanity even in actual communion with God Himself. It connotes that God is not arbitrary in His election but free in Himself for mankind. It denotes that God Himself is the one who saves and is none other than man's Salvation. The Redeemer is the redemption. Man is actually created according to His image, Jesus. And all this without God or humanity ceasing to be what they are or changing into something alien which they are not. This is, of course, why Barth must insist on no *analogia entis* in which case one could mistakenly deduce the interchangeability of humanity and divinity.[16] The being of God in Himself, in

---

[15] Barth indicates (*CD*, III/1, pp. 194ff.) that he was familiar with the term *analogia relationis* first used by Dietrich Bonhoeffer in his *Creation and Fall* (New York: The Macmillan Co., 1971, ET reprint. Original Germ. edit., 1937) pp. 38–39. It was Bonhoeffer who also suggested the contrast between it and *analogia entis*. Barth's usage seems largely to be in agreement with Bonhoeffer's as an interpretation of the *imago Dei* being a purposive relation given by God and not a capacity, possibility or a structure of humankind's being.

[16] Ultimately, Barth avoided speaking of being/ontology in the abstract because he believed this would misrepresent the relational nature of God's and our existence. Relations constitute being. So there is no being without being in relation in the triune life and in human life. Barth consequently focused on the relations. Alan Torrance points out, however, that this does not resolve all the issues. There are still individuated beings being in relationship. And if the relations are properly regarded as analogous (*analogia*

its internal, dynamic, covenantal relations of Father Son and Spirit, is externalized in Jesus Christ so that humanity might be brought into the sphere of and participate in those same relationships which are characterized by unity without confusion, differentiation without separation, and an ordering of the relationship to exhibit a correspondence of one to the other, of imaging and bearing witness of one to the other.

With this Barth bursts the bounds of the usual categories of much "rationalistic" discourse. He is offering an alternative "rationality" of being-in-living-relationship on the basis of his Christo-logic and trinitarian theo-logic and allows this to define the parameters of the "rationality" of personal relations. Barth has not given an alternative vocabulary for speaking of God and humankind, but has provided a new grammar. His grammar has a logic. It is a Christo-logic and so a trinitarian theo-logic. It allows for the ontological communion of beings which ontologically can never become their opposite because they are not of the same genus of being but exist in two distinct ways of being. However, his grammar disallows any ontological separation of God and man. Their unity and communion is one of ontological solidarity in the person of Jesus Christ. Yet there is no confusion or fusion of human persons with God.

In the end, what Barth offers re-frames what we mean by divinity and humanity. They are distinct, yet not nearly so distinct as might be indicated in rationalistic or Newtonian, Kantian or Cartesian frameworks. They do not denote mutually exclusive categories or realities. They are related in unique ways, and all at the ontological level, but are uniquely related such that their unity disallows any unity of a pantheistic, monistic, or a panentheistic kind. It is neither a dualism nor a monism, nor a platonism. It is an onto-logic embodied in the being of Jesus Christ: an onto-Christo-logic of relations between God and humanity. We could also say that Jesus Christ is, in his being, the "ana-logic" of human and divine being-in-relationship, of Covenant love, which God Himself is in His intra-trinitarian life.

---

relationis) and these relations constitute being, then there has to be some sort of analogy of being, *analogia entis*. Barth himself allowed a qualified acceptance of the *analogia entis*, namely, by way of the *analogia fidei*, the analogy of faith, and in Jesus Christ. We may speak of an *analogia entis* not by way of cause according to creation, but by way of covenant by way of redemption (see *CD*, II/1, p. 82). The former seems to represent the Thomistic way of rendering the *analogia entis*, and this Barth rejects. Alan Torrance points out that when Barth objects to the *analogia entis*, an analogy of proportion, or of two compared by a third, is assumed. Thomas Aquinas himself, however, acknowledged that these construals of analogy were inadequate. Primary theological analogy calls for making the comparison from above downwards, that is, it must be an *analogia unius ad alterum per prius et posterius*, the analogy of one to another according to priority and posteriority. The comparison must be unidirectional from God to creation and cannot be reversed. This orientation seems to have been lost by the Cajetanists and Barth's interlocutor, Eric Pryzwara. See Alan Torrance, *Persons in Communion*, pp. 135–189.

Imago Dei: Original, First and Second

Barth's discussion on the *analogia relationis* gives way and culminates with his discussion of the *imago Dei*. Here we find the theological home for Barth's discussion of analogy. It becomes clear that what is distinctive about Barth's approach is that:

1) for him the analogy can only be made in one direction and
2) that his understanding of relationship so qualifies his understanding of analogy that the former interprets the latter term.

Given the humanity of Jesus as grounded in the inner-trinitarian life, we must go on to explore the inter-human humanity of God's creatures. Here, Barth is quite clear. Humanity, which is to say personhood, is essentially constituted by its being in relationship with other persons. These inter-human relations are not arbitrary or accidental but necessary for human existence as human. This is a secondary determination of humanity compared to its relationship with God, but just as essential. This secondary determination of humankind is parallel to Jesus' own secondary determination of his existence by our humanity. Our being is determined by our vertical relation with God. But, because it is so determined, it is on that basis to be conditioned by the horizontal relationships as Jesus was both from, to and with and so for God so He is from, to, with and for mankind. Barth brings together the similarities of all four relationships: intra-trinitarian, Jesus to God, Jesus to others, and person to person.

Barth summarizes this relation of the images most explicitly in a response to a question concerning how man is the image of God transcribed in his *Table Talk*.

> Image has a double meaning: God lives in togetherness within Himself [the Original], then God lives in togetherness with man [first image] then men live in togetherness with one another [a second image].[17]

This defines for us the relationship between the two relationships. There is an original intra-trinitarian relation of Father, Son and Spirit; the God-God relationship. There is a corresponding relationship of man to God and man to man in Jesus which is the first image of God, of God in triune relationship. We then in our humanity are enabled in our existence to become the image of that Image, that is, be a second image in our human to human relationships. Thus, Barth says that man is not created to be the image but "in correspondence with the image of God."[18] We are to be conformed to Jesus Christ, who is the Image.

In an image, for Barth, there is both a similarity and dissimilarity between and an ordering of the copy according to the original. It is in his discussion of humanity as an image that we come to see how Barth understands that

---

[17] Ed. John D. Godsey, *Karl Barth's Table Talk* (London & Edinburgh: Oliver and Boyd, 1962), p. 57 (Hereafter, *Table Talk*).
[18] *CD*, III/1, p. 197.

humankind's interpersonal relations (humanity) are to correspond to (by being both like and unlike) the original Triune relations and the first imaging of those relations in Jesus Christ.

Dissimilarity of the God-Man and Person-Person Relationships

Barth indicates that there is also a dissimilarity between the way Jesus' relationship with the Father and others images God's own intra-trinitarian relations and the way human inter-relationships mirror Jesus Christ. The reality is present as Jesus images God. The Son is identical with Jesus. Jesus is the externalization of what internally the Son is to the Father for the sake of his creatures. Internally the Son images the Father. Externally Jesus images for us the Father. Jesus is the image for us. This is who He is. Humankind is, in a secondary way, an image of the Image in that humankind may correspond to the Image but is not itself the Image. Humanity itself cannot be identified with God's presence in the way that Jesus can. We are not united to Jesus as the Father and Son are united. Thus, we may only image the Image in our human relationships with God and to each other.

The concept of image is itself helpful in this connection because it usually carries with it a sense of limitation. The image cannot be confused with what it images. It points up a distinction and differentiation which Barth finds appropriate to the relationship of Jesus' humanity (his relations to other humans, in Barth's terms) and his divinity (his relationship to His Father which is identical with the Triune relationship). There is a distinction between the hypostatic union (our union with God in Christ) and the Son's relationship with the Father.[19]

Intra-Trinitarian Relations and Our Humanity: Two Dissimilarities

Yet even this distinction and dissimilarity between the relationship of God and God and God and man in Jesus reflects an intra-trinitarian dissimilarity, but of course a different dissimilarity. The Father is not the Son although united in

---

[19]"The 'image'—we must not forget the limitation implicit in this term. If the humanity of Jesus is the image of God, this means that it is only indirectly and not directly identical with God. It belongs intrinsically to the creaturely world, to the cosmos. Hence it does not belong to the inner sphere of the essence, but to the outer sphere of the work of God. In does not present God in Himself and in His relation to Himself, but in His relation to the reality distinct from Himself. In it we have to do with God and man rather than God and God. There is a real difference in this respect. We cannot, therefore, expect more than correspondence and similarity. We cannot maintain identity. Between God and God, the Father and the Son and the Son and the Father, there is unity of essence, the perfect satisfaction of self-grounded reality, and a blessedness eternally self-originated and self-renewed. But there can be no question of this between God and man, and it cannot therefore find expression in the humanity of Jesus, in His fellow-humanity as the image of God....Hence there is disparity between the relationship of God and man and the prior relationship of the Father to the Son and the Son to the Father, of God to Himself" (*CD*, III/2, pp. 219–220).

essence, neither is the Son the Father. Their union does not dissolve their distinctions. There is a distinguishing of one from another in God, so there is a distinguishing of God from His creation (similar in that it is a distinction, different in that it is a distinction that is created and external to God). So Barth comments:

> But God Himself is the Son who is the basic truth of that which is other than God. As the Son of God this Other is God Himself. But God Himself becomes Another in the person of His Son. The existence of the world is not needed in order that there should be otherness for Him. Before all worlds in His Son, He has otherness in Himself from eternity to eternity. But because this is so, the creation and preservation of the world, and relationship and fellowship with it, realised as they are in perfect freedom, without compulsion or necessity, do not signify an alien or contradictory expression of God's being, but a natural, *the natural expression of it ad extra.*[20]

Thus, Jesus the Son of the Father is, as the Son, the original internal image of God and, in the humanity of Jesus, is the external image of God (Father and Son in the Holy Spirit). Our humanity in our relations with each other is then the image of this Image. They are relationships which are similar but dissimilar to the Image of Jesus. We, in our relationships are not the origin of our being-in-relation. We are ordered by the original relation and its Image in Jesus Christ.

There is dissimilarity also in that we are the image of the Image only by God's grace. We are not created images but *become* images of the Image. Jesus is the Image (internally and externally) eternally in an uncreated way, in an original and unchanging way. We also exist as sinners in ourselves and so have denied our humanity as created for us. So we are images in a secondary way on two accounts: by creation and by reconciliation, the renewal of the imaging relationship with God.[21]

Thus, Barth must remind us that although we are for, with, from and to our fellow-man as Jesus is for, with, from and to us, Jesus is this in a way that is similar and dissimilar to the way we are "with" fellow humans. Jesus is the only one *totally for* others.[22]

---

[20] *CD*, II/1, p. 317.

[21] See *CD*, III/2, p. 255.

[22] "The difference between Jesus and ourselves is still indissoluble. It is quite fundamental. For of no other man can we say that from the very outset and in virtue of his existence he is for others. Of no other man can we say that he is the Word of God to men, and therefore that he is directly and inwardly affected by them, or sent, commissioned and empowered to be and act in their place and as their representative, interposing and giving himself for all others, making their life possible and actual in and with his own, and thus being for them, their guarantor, in this radical and universal sense. There can be no repetition of this in anthropology" (*CD*, III/2, p. 222).

The Similarity of Relations: A Co-Humanity

With this in place we can follow along with Barth and discover how we in our humanity may indeed image this Image. For all the dissimilarity between Jesus and our humanity there is a similarity nevertheless. Christology provides the key again.[23]

The basic form of humanity as revealed in the humanity of Jesus Christ is that on the horizontal plane of creation humanity is essentially a co-humanity (*Mitmenschlichkeit*), a co-existence (*Mitexistenz*) with and for others. We necessarily exist in relationships with others. We are to be who we are *in relationship with others*.[24]

As God in Jesus Christ is our covenant-partner so we in our humanity are to be covenant-partners with others. We must be so in a further sense because all other persons are also partners with God. Because God in His relations with others gives them personal being in correspondence with his own personal being, that is God addresses all human beings as Thou, then I too must acknowledge the other as a Thou, as one in covenant relation with God. To deny their "thou-ness," their personhood, is to deny their relation with God. Furthermore, this is to deny the reality of my own covenant relation with God. In perhaps his best single essay on theological anthropology, "The New Humanism and the Humanism of God" Barth summarizes:

> Man exists in free encounter of man with man, in the relation between the individual and his neighbour, in the relation between the "I" and the "You," in the relation between man and woman. An isolated man living for himself is not man...Humanity is the fellowship of men. Where there is no fellowship there is inhumanity.[25]

Humanity: a Being-With-Others as an Image of Jesus Christ

On this basis we can see how Barth goes on to indicate that the recognition of our humanity is dependent upon our recognition of the humanity of the other.

---

[23] "If the humanity of Jesus consists in the fact that He is for other men, this means that for all the disparity between Him and us He affirms these others as beings which are not merely unlike Him in His creaturely existence and therefore His humanity, but also like Him in some basic form. Where one being is for others, there is necessarily a common sphere or form of existence in which the 'for' can be possible and effective" (*CD*, III/2, p. 223).

[24] "The humanity of Jesus consists in his being for man. From the fact that this example is binding in humanity generally there follows the broad definition that humanity absolutely, the humanity of each and every man consists in the determination of man's being as a being with others, or rather with the other man....It is not as he is for himself but with others, not in loneliness but in fellowship that he is genuinely human, that he achieves true humanity, that he corresponds to his determination to be God's covenant partner" (*CD*, III/2, p. 243).

[25] Barth, *The New Humanism*, p. 162.

Barth traces out in progressively deeper spheres what it means for persons to be I, subjects, self. He does this in a notable passage where he discusses three aspects of being in relation as I and Thou, the form of the relation, and in four elements in the history of encounter of I and Thou, the content.

I and Thou: the Form of Humanity

1. "I am and Thou art:" Identification Yet Differentiation

Beginning with Jesus' own confession in His "I am" statements, we too may, in a similar way because of Him, say "I am." The essential action which corresponds to and confirms one's own being a personal subject in relationship to God is to affirm other persons as being true personal subjects in relationship to God by regarding them as ones who can recognize my being a personal subject in relationship to God. In doing so we recognize an essential likeness of one with another and the fact that each person is distinct from the other at the same time. We may do this when we regard each other as "I" and "Thou" in their deepest sense.[26]

What this shows, says Barth, is that "a pure, absolute and self-sufficient I is an illusion, for as an I, even as I think and express this I, I am not alone or self-sufficient, but am distinguished from and connected with a Thou in which I find

---

[26]"What is meant by 'I?' I pronounce the word, and in so doing, even if I only do so mentally or to myself, I make a distinction, but also a connexion. In thinking and speaking this word, I do not remain in isolation. I distinguish myself from another who is not I and yet also not It, not an object, but one who can receive and estimate and understand my declaration 'I' because he can make a similar declaration to me. In making this distinction, I presuppose, accept and make, as far as I am able, a connexion with him as one who is like me. Addressing this object as I, I distinguish him not only from myself but from all other objects, from every It, placing myself on the same level or in the same sphere with him, acknowledging that I am not without him in my sphere, that this sphere is not just mine but also his. The mere fact that I say 'I' means that I describe and distinguish the object to which I say it as something like myself; in other words, that with my 'I' I also address him as 'Thou.'....[Furthermore] when I say 'I' and therefore 'Thou' to someone else, I empower and invite and summon him to say 'Thou' to me in return....And it can only be a matter of fulfillment that he for his part would admit his recognition of this fact by pronouncing the word 'Thou' and thus proclaim himself not merely something like an I but actually as an I....The word 'I' with which I think and declare my humanity implies as such humanity with and not without the fellow-man. I cannot say 'I,' even to myself, without also saying 'Thou,' without making that distinction and connexion in relation to another. And only as I think and say 'I' in this way, only as I make this specific distinction and connexion with this word, can I expect to be recognised and acknowledged by others as a "Thou," as something like an 'I' and more than that as a real 'I,' and therefore to be confirmed in the human determination of my being, and regarded, treated and addressed as a human being" (*CD*, III/2, pp. 244–245). See also John Macmurray *Persons in Relation* (London: Faber and Faber Limited, 1966) for an excellent exploration from a philosophical perspective of how persons come to acknowledge their own personhood only in and through relationship, especially as it develops in the relationship of a child with its mother.

a being like my own..."[27] This is the radical nature of humanity's being-in-relationship.

2. "I and Thou in Relation:" an Ordered Correspondence of One with the Other

The nature of this relationship Barth explores further. Persons are those who are "in relation." To be in relationship as persons has the form of an interaction, the character of responding to each other as I and Thou. It involves a recognition of the otherness, undetermined by me, of others, which is yet a likeness and reflection of me. There is a sense of confrontation, of the other standing over against me, such that to remain in relationship one has to come to re-orient oneself to the other as one comes to see how they are independent and unlike me. Such an encounter means resisting projecting myself on to the other but coming to adjust my picture of them according to who they are. I must order how I regard the other in correspondence to who they actually are.[28]

To be in relation is to recognize the mutual reflection of persons in one another although totally distinct from each other and the essential and mutual need for this reflecting.[29] So, in a parallel way, neither can the other retreat from me. So, he necessarily exists in relation as well. The refusal to be in relation is to retreat into inhumanity—it is to deny my own and the other's humanity, for humanity *is* a being-in-fellowship.

3. "I am as Thou art:" Being in a History of Encounter

Finally, this all means, at the deepest level, that humanity exists as each recognizes that "I am as Thou art." Humanity is the unfolding of a history of interaction between persons who reflect and yet confront one another. The differentiation calls for the coming into unity of each with the other. The

---

[27] *CD*, III/2, p. 245. We must be careful here and not misconstrue Barth's argument. He is not resting his case on the fact that this is how we think and act. The interaction he is describing illustrates the fact "proved" in the humanity of Jesus Christ that we are beings in relationship with Him and with other human beings. As such this exploration serves as a confirmation of the humanity known in Jesus Christ. It is a description of true humanity based prescriptively on the "I am" of Jesus Christ and how he regards others as "Thou's."

[28] "I am as I am in a relation. And this means that as I posit myself—I should not be myself if it were otherwise—I at once come up against the fact that there takes place a corresponding self-positing and being on the part of the one whom I must see and treat as Thou. As I think and declare myself as I with this self-positing and being of his he comes towards me, or rather the Thou comes (for that is what he is as I am I in relation to him), and comes in such a way that I cannot evade him, since he is like myself and therefore Thou as surely as I am I, and therefore my sphere is not mine alone but his as well....The being and positing of this Thou reaches and affects me, for it is not that of an It, but of the Thou without which I should not be I....My own being and positing takes place in and with the fact that I am claimed by that of the other and occupied with it. That of the other sets limits to my own. It indicates its problems. It poses questions which must be answered. And there are answers for which it asks. I am in encounter with the other who is in the same way I am. I am under the condition imposed by this encounter" (*CD*, III/2, p. 246).

[29] *CD*, III/2, p. 247.

essential nature of our humanity comes into view here, where Barth expounds this formula.

In his explication of "I and Thou" Barth unfolds all six of our determinations (under their two comprehensive categories) in terms of the reflection of humankind's being-in-relation to God in the human-to-human relationship of I and Thou.

> The basic formula to describe it must be as follows: "I am as Thou art." Naturally the word "as" does not imply that the "thou art" is the cause, even the instrumental cause, or the true substance of the "I am."...Man has been constructed wholly in the light of the fellow-man, and the "I am" has formally disappeared in the "Thou art." The word "as" does not tell us where human being is created—for this we can turn only to God the Creator—but how. It tells us that every "I am" is qualified, marked and determined by the "Thou art." Owing it to God the Creator that I am as thou art; as, created by the same God, Thou art with me. Neither the I am nor the Thou art loses its own meaning and force. I do not become Thou, nor Thou I, in this co-existence. On the contrary, as I and Thou are together, their being acquires the character, the human style, of always being I for the self and Thou for the other. As we are in this encounter we are thus distinguished. On both sides...the being has its own validity, dignity and self-certainty. Nor is this human being static, but dynamic and active. It is not an *esse* but an *existere*. To say man is to say history. On a false understanding no less than a true we are forced to put the statement "I am" in the form of a little history, describing it as that self-positing. Similarly, the statement "Thou art" denotes a history. Therefore in our formula: "I am as Thou art" we do not describe the relationship between two static complexes of being, but between two which are dynamic which move out from themselves, which exist, and which meet or encounter each other in their existence. The "I am" and the "Thou art" encounter each other as two histories. It is to be noted that they do not just do this subsequently, as though there were one history here and another there which at a certain point became a common history; as though there were an "I am" here and a "Thou art" there which in the continuation of their two-sided movement came together and became a partnership. But in and with their creation and therefore in and with the two-sided beginning of their movement and history, they are in encounter: I am as Thou art, and Thou art as I am....Thus the formula: "I am as Thou art," tells us that the encounter between I and Thou is not arbitrary or accidental, that it is not incidentally but essentially proper to the concept of man...It tells us ontologically that we have to do with real man only when his existence

takes place in this encounter, only in the form of man with his fellow-man.[30]

We quote at length because we can see at least glimpses of all six determinations and their two primary categories of humanity in its person-to-person relationship in this one description. The primary emphasis, however, is that the form of humankind is essentially a being in relationship of a personal kind, acknowledging others as persons as they themselves are. It also involves acknowledging the interdependent nature of any self-affirmation with its invitation and need for the confirmation of another. In fact we could say that the nature of one's own self-affirmation *is* the confirmation of the personhood of the other as created by God. Upon confirming the "Thou" of the other to be an "I" before God like myself, I confirm myself: one who can confirm humanity as God confirms humanity. This indicates that our humanity can only be recognized in the act of being human, that is as I am "in-relationship."

Barth's exposition of the form of humanity in these three concentric spheres corresponds to the first three characteristics of his description of the form of real man in Jesus' relationship to God and so also to the first three criteria of humankind's relationship to God. There is unity with differentiation, a correspondence despite the differentiation, and this occurs as a history of relationship of each becoming united despite the differentiation. And in all, there is a decided Christological source for Barth's explication of I and Thou.[31] Barth also makes explicit the parallel to the intra-trinitarian relations.

The Original Trinitarian Relations and Humanity

Barth points out that the final basis of mankind's determination by God to be co-humanity lies in his being created according to the image of Christ who is the Image of God in his innermost Triune life:

> Humanity, the characteristic and essential mode of man's being, is in its root fellow-humanity. Humanity which is not fellow-humanity is inhumanity. For it cannot reflect but only contradict the determination of man to be God's covenant-partner, nor can the God who is no *Deus solitarius* but *Deus triunus*, God in relationship, be mirrored in a *homo solitarius*. As God offers man humanity and therefore freedom in fellowship, God summons him to prove and express himself as the image of God—for as such He has created him.[32]

Thus, Barth notes the original relations in the Triune life as being the source for humanity's being in I-Thou relation.

---

[30] *CD*, III/2, pp. 248–249.

[31] A number of Barth's critics have failed to see this and have rather assumed that Barth's reflections were essentially conditioned by Ferdinand Ebner and Martin Buber's writings or on the phenomena of human existence apart from Christology.

[32] *CD*, III/4, p. 117.

Included within his exposition of the form were hints at the second three characteristics and criteria which entail the content and action within the form of relationship. Barth now continues to unfold this content as it relates to mankind's humanity.

The Four Elements of Humanity as Being-in-Encounter—Its Content/Action

In one of the most illuminating sections of his anthropology, Barth delves into the content of the form of this interpersonal relationship. While we cannot pursue this section in detail we will give a summary of the four dimensions of interpersonal relationship which render them to be truly human and so humanizing.

1. Seeing Eye to Eye

"Being in encounter (*Begegnung*) is (1) a being in which one man looks the other in the eye."[33] When we see eye to eye we are both concerned to see the other for who they are and to let the other see me. There is a reciprocity, a give and take in this relationship. There is a kind of objectivity, an "openness" to the other to know them and be known by them without deception, without idealization, or derogation. There is a moving out of ourselves to see others and to reveal ourselves to them. What ensues in such an eye-to-eye interchange is a sharing of life together.

2. Mutual Speech and Hearing

Being in encounter means "that there is mutual speech and hearing."[34] This is a complex action of both I and Thou, both speaking to and hearing one another. Whereas the seeing is essentially receptive on each side, in speaking one makes one's own contribution to the other's perception. He participates in the revelation of himself so as to assist the other in drawing up his image of him. In this way one gives oneself to the other actively and in greater depth than merely being seen can offer. This reciprocal speaking is to be for the benefit of the other. Not just for the sake of expressing one's self but in order to give of one's self to the other. There is to be mutual listening with the intention of receiving from the other not just words and facts, but to receive the impartation of their unique person. This is because what the other has for us is something we do not have at all, and so is indeed something of vital importance to us. It is in this dialogue where lives are exchanged and so mutually enlarged and enriched that we speak and hear humanly.

3. Giving Mutual Assistance

Being-in-encounter means giving assistance in the act of being.[35] This means that we are for the other, we support the other in its life as we can, within

---

[33] *CD*, III/2, pp. 250–252.
[34] *Ibid.*, pp. 252–260.
[35] *Ibid.*, pp. 260–264.

its limits. And it means that we call for assistance because we know our own limitations and need the help of others. Assistance is mutual when the response with help corresponds to the call for support. There is no living of another's life or taking another's responsibility or substituting for another. But as a support alongside, with and for each other we both give and receive help. Our assistance is human insofar as we do act to help but only as we know our own need for assistance and as we do indeed call for assistance, admitting our need, only as we recognize that the other needs assistance as well. This is human fellowship.

4. Freely and With Gladness

Being in encounter means all this is "done on both sides with gladness," that is, "freely and from the heart."[36] The depth of relationship here is that there is a discovery of being with the other in such a way that there is recognized an inward correspondence of the other to me despite all his otherness. This is not a collapse of one into another, but the recognition that the law of my own being is fulfilled in being so completely with the other. In this correspondence there is the sense of an unimpeachable appropriateness and freedom and so joy.

> The secret of his humanity, however, is that in his being in the encounter of I and Thou we do not have to do with a determination which is accidental and later imposed from without, but with a self-determination which is free and intrinsic to his essence.[37]

In this he is glad, not being reluctant or neutral in relation to others, because in this relationship he is actualizing his very own humanity.[38]

Summary: The Correlation of Relations

With this four-fold description Barth presents a most in-depth portrait of mankind's humanity/personhood. It is found in the quality of relationship, in its content and so in its action, enjoined upon him as the creature of his Creator and heavenly Father. It points up the thoroughly relational nature of human existence on both the vertical and so the horizontal planes. These four characterizations correspond primarily to what we have called the personal-covenantal aspect of our interpretation. But they also have within them reference to humankind's dynamic becoming in relationship and the extension of one's self to include the

---

[36] *Ibid.*, pp. 265–285.

[37] *Ibid.*, p. 267.

[38] "The externality of the different fellow-man who encounters me has this in common with the very different externality of the God distinct from me—that it is also inward to me; inward in the sense that this external thing, the other man, is inward and intrinsic to me even in his otherness....To be sure there is a law here—the law of the Creator imposed as such on the creature. And there is a situation in which man finds himself—created by the fact that he is not alone, but the fellow-man is present with him. But that law of God is given him as his own law, the law which he himself has set up, the law of his own freedom. Only as such is its validity genuine according to the intention of its Giver" (*CD*, III/2, pp. 268–269).

other in loving fellowship. These four characterizations may serve as a summary for all of what Barth means by personal action-in-relationship.

There are also obvious parallels here to Barth's last three Christological characteristics of Jesus' being for God by his gratefully recognizing God's Lordship, being obedient and responsible, and so speaking and listening to his Father in order to obey, and His being a servant of God gladly in freely serving others. This is the Christological ground behind the description of humanity as seeing, speaking and hearing, serving and doing it all freely and joyfully.[39]

The correspondence of this horizontal relationship with humankind's relation to God with gratitude, responsibility and freedom is also now fairly obvious. As persons are grateful for being in relation to God, so they are grateful for being in relation to others and so are willing and able to see others and to be seen, to recognize others as differentiated from themselves. As persons are obedient and responsible in interacting with God, to the end of corresponding in their lives to God's purpose for them, so there is a mutual coordination of one person to another in their speaking and listening to one another for the self-revelation and self-knowledge which only occurs in such mutual interchange, and as a preparation for mutual service. As persons find freedom for service of God, God directs them to freely and gladly assist one another for their mutual joy and completion. In this way we become who God intends us to be, his

---

[39] J. G. Gibbs in his "A Secondary Point of Reference in Barth's Anthropology," *SJT*, Vol. 16 (Jan. 1963), pp. 132–135, has perhaps overstated his case when he says that the four criteria of human encounter "while connected by the thinnest line to a christological source, seem to have been formulated tacitly from this second point of reference" (p. 133–134). Barth's thinking on the trinitarian relations and God as personal more than prepared the way. His understanding of the Father's and Son's relationship is crucial to his exposition. The line is not nearly so thin as he seems to indicate. Furthermore, the "secondary point of reference" which Gibbs locates in the phenomena of *human* interaction, Barth has submitted as a whole to his primary Christological and trinitarian point of reference. This criteria provides for Barth a hermeneutical function of selecting, evaluating and interpreting the phenomena of human seeing, speaking, hearing, assisting and freely rejoicing. Barth does not ignore the phenomena but does interpret them in the light of the humanity of Jesus Christ. The fact that others have spoken of nearly the same things, especially those who have spoken of I and Thou, does not mean that Barth has failed to ground his observation theologically. This kind of correlation should be expected, says Barth. He is merely, at this point, expounding our creaturely humanity which is common to all persons and so available for observation to all. Some inevitably will then develop, without reference to its norm, a picture of humanity close to that revealed in Christ. This still does not amount to knowledge of or participation by the Holy Spirit in our actual relationship to God as his creatures or to knowledge of and participation in our being reconciled and redeemed in Christ. This also means that ultimately there is a correlation, no more, no less between our being human (and so being in relationship with others as I and Thou: seeing, speaking, and assisting each other gladly), even outside of faith, and our being determined or designated to be in eternal communion in the Triune life in the Word. See Barth's important discussion in *CD*, III/2, pp. 274–283, especially, pp. 279ff.

covenant partners in covenant love and fellowship. We participate in the gift of our humanity.

We have now come to a point of having laid out Barth's entire structure of personal being-in-relationship for his theological anthropology. It is this structure that makes his ethics comprehensible. The horizontal unfolding of humankind's being in covenantal fellowship is a reflection of the being in covenantal fellowship enacted in Jesus Christ and originally present in the Trinitarian life which has overflowed to us.

We will now continue to explore in detail Barth's presentation of his anthropology on the horizontal plane as presented in III/2 and III/4, with some references to IV in the *Church Dogmatics*. For there we have the beginnings of his ethics which will lead us to his section on "Parents and Children." We will take up in turn each of the six subheadings of our determinations. We will note how Barth develops these in terms of the various interpersonal relations (person to person, man to woman, in the Church, and with the neighbor) and how he sees the Christological and trinitarian foundations beneath them. This, then, will provide us a comprehensive framework within which to interpret the parent-child relationship as presented in III/4.

Chapter 5

Humanity as Being-in-Communion with Others: the Six-fold Grammar of Relations

I. Being-in-Communion

The Shape of Our Essential Relational Reality

The essential relational reality of humanity is, for Barth, to be delineated in its form in that this relationship on the horizontal plane involves a fellowship, even a unity of persons, yet not a union or fusion of persons such that there is confusion or a diminishment of the distinction of each person.

1. Neither Isolation nor Autonomy

Humanity does not exist either in an isolation or autonomy of individuals. The form of humanity is neither a collectivism nor an individualism of persons. But rather, each person finds his/her own true being only in unity with others, and not apart from them. We are distinct human beings for the sake of living in communion with one another.

Regarding the unity yet distinction in relationship Barth says: "Humanity is the realization of this togetherness of man and man grounded in human freedom and necessary in this freedom."[1] "From the very outset, as man, he is not without but with his fellow-man."[2] Being together is the intrinsic quality of their existence.

This unity Barth has filled out in terms of the marks of humanity discussed in his section on I-Thou relations and its four-fold activity of seeing, speaking and hearing, assisting, with joy. It means that persons are to be for each other by being from, to and with them, as Barth has already explained. It means that persons are not alien to one another and need not be hostile to one another. Persons are not to use others for their own ends but work together under the Lordship of God and his purposes. The antithesis of this being with others is Nietzsche's "Overman" who aims at existing without others, "Alone!"[3]

However, this unity must not be misunderstood. The unity of relationship envisioned here is not one of identification, of unification so that the two merge or collapse into one. This relation of intimate fellowship, while allowing no separation, maintains the distinction between one and the other in relationship.[4]

---

[1] *CD*, III/2, p. 269.

[2] *Ibid.*, p. 268.

[3] See Barth's discussion of what he is ruling out which culminates in his discussion of Nietzsche in *CD*, III/2, pp. 229–242.

[4] "We have to safeguard this statement against two misunderstandings. The first is this. Humanity in the highest sense cannot consist in the fact that the one loses himself in the

2. No Surrender or Tyranny; Voluntary or Involuntary

There is another misunderstanding of being in relationship which must also be recognized. This relationship of fellowship is neither a surrender of the self to the other nor using the other for oneself. The relationship and therefore the other person is not a means to my own ends of being human.[5] I cannot enslave myself to the other or enslave the other to me. I cannot allow the other to enslave himself nor allow the other to enslave me to him. There is no slavery nor tyranny in right relationship.[6]

The right relation of unity and intimacy and encounter is not a compromise of tyrannies or enslavements. It is not partial or moderate forms of these at all. Genuine human encounter avoids these orientations altogether. There is a free involvement, a free giving of oneself to the other and a free receiving of the other as well.

3. No Individualism or Collectivism

This orientation is neither an individualism nor a collectivism of humanity. These viewpoints describe inhuman relationships. Both of these alternatives in the end dissolve all true relationship. The one resolves into autonomous self-sufficient individuals with no necessary relationship to others. The other denies in the end the reality of the individual, recognizing only one collective entity.[7]

Thus, the individual never disappears nor does the fact of each individual's vital relationship with others diminish. We are as we continue in relationships of being with and for others and not in our being without or against them. This signifies a vital and essential life-giving exchange of one with the other.

4. The Individual

While we have been emphasizing Barth's concern to see humanity in relationship, the notion of what is meant by the term "individual" must also be scrutinized. What do we mean when we refer to the individuals who are in

---

other, surrendering or forgetting or neglecting his own life and task and responsibility, making himself a mere copy of the other, and the life and task and responsibility of the other a framework for his own life. Man is bound to his fellow-man, but he cannot belong to him, i.e., he cannot be his property. This is impossible because if he did he would not see and recognize in him what he is to him, namely, the other....He would encroach too much upon him by changing the encounter with him into a union...We cannot subject ourselves to a fellow-man without doing him the deepest injury. For what he can expect of me as another cannot be that I should cease to be his Thou, and therefore to stand before him in my distinction from him....Humanity is thus the realization of this togetherness only when I do not lose but maintain myself in it, living my own life with the other, accepting my own task and responsibility, and thus keeping and not overrunning the proper distance between us" (*CD*, III/2, p. 270).

[5] *CD*, III/2, p. 270.

[6] *CD*, III/2, p. 271.

[7] *CD*, III/2, p. 243–244, See also Barth's essay, *CA*: "If we base our thinking on this passage we can have nothing to do with either collectivism on the one hand or individualism on the other. It understands the true man in neither of these ways" (p. 44).

relationship? Barth develops a unique understanding of the individual because he purposely resists the temptation to allow any assumptions about it to serve as the norm for what he may go on to say. Thus, he rejects as normative the definitions of individuals as contained in, say, idealistic, romantic, or certain political notions.

a. Affirmed Theologically by the Word

Barth attempts to ground his perspective on the individual theologically. He takes as normative the biblical witness as to how God regards persons. From this perspective he acknowledges that the individual may be regarded as being in a certain sense unique, independent, and separate from others. Persons are distinguishable even from God's perspective.[8]

Barth accepts that the way the Word addresses persons indicates that they are indeed individuals, have a certain kind of autonomy from each other. The notion of the individual is theologically grounded in God's own action towards us. God Himself is free to interact with one and not another, with one in one way and another in another way, yet also always being true to Himself. Yet He does address each one with regard for others, never with disregard. God's dealing with persons indicates the enduring reality of individuals, yet never of individuals alone, but in relationship, most especially in relationship to God.[9] It is from this perspective that we may speak of individuals.

This understanding of the individual must be distinguished from other forms grounded differently. His is not a humanistic individualism, especially as colored by Romanticism and Neo-Romanticism.[10] Humankind has its independence "with God, not without God."[11] Mankind cannot humanize itself apart from Jesus Christ. Rather, "Before God, and as the one whom God addresses, every man is *sui generis*, an original, and he must will to be this."[12] Individuals are given by God a particular life (a body, span of life, a place, a vitality which can will, decide and act and be held responsible) and the task of

---

[8] *CD*, III/4, p. 328. One biblical example of this is the dialogue between God and Adam after his transgression.

[9] We may perhaps consider Jesus' calling of the disciples as an example of dealing with persons individually but always with the aim of gathering them together and also to send them out to others for the sake of the Kingdom.

[10] Although each of these orientations can be appropriately interpreted in the light of the revelation, as they are un-submitted to this revelation Barth resists the idealism of the world Spirit of Hegel where the individual is absorbed into the State which is identified with the Absolute Spirit of God. He rejects the Romanticism which identifies the individual's spirit with a manifestation of the Spirit of God. He resists the neo-romantic emphasis on the self-formation of the individual personality. The error in these approaches is in the identity of the human and divine in either the so called transcendent sphere or in the natural sphere. Such identities could be either individualistic, with a general disregard for the essential quality of relationships between persons, or collective, with a disregard for the irreducible significance of the individual person.

[11] *CD*, III/4, pp. 385–386.

[12] *CD*, III/2, p. 140.

growing into a particular distinctive "character" in the history of his/her relationship with God.[13] Each has his/her own soul under the guidance of the Holy Spirit. These characteristics mark out persons as individuals.

b. Individuality Established by Obedience not Self-Assertion

Furthermore, this being oneself is not essentially a self-oriented assertion. It occurs rightly and effectively only as an act of obedience to God, that is to say in relationship to God. "Even the affirmation of the life as self-affirmation is thus at root an act of obedience. It cannot possibly be the assertion of a claim and right if it happens in freedom and not in bondage."[14] Only in this way is it not an "act of desire, or rebellion or a bid for power" but rather is "supreme responsibility" which "fulfilled in this way as an act of obedience, it establishes, fashions and confirms as it should the particular, individual and personal character of man."[15] Each remains each as they are called to be a part of the one Body of Jesus Christ, each with his own time, place and vocation.[16]

Thus, the way persons are individuals in relationship is also Christologically and so theologically grounded. Individuality is a result of obedience, right relationship to God. Individuality then cannot be taken as autonomy, lacking all relationship. Consequently, what Barth means by an individual has a unique content to it in virtue of its connection to the God of Jesus Christ. Individuality is the product of real continuing relationship of obedience and manifests itself as a greater capacity for interrelationship. Individuality occurs in the context of Christological fellowship. This is what sets Barth's understanding of individuality apart.[17]

Fellowship (yet Differentiation): Humankind as Male and Female

1. A Duality that is Essential to Humankind's Fellowship

For Barth there are three spheres of polarity or essential differentiation or otherness in human relationship. 1) There is the polarity between one individual and another (as neighbors and as parents and children), 2) between the two genders, and 3) in the special sphere of marriage and sexual union. For Barth the distinction and unity of all persons which underlies all fellowship is gender.[18]

---

[13]*CD*, III/4, p. 386.

[14]*Ibid.* p. 387.

[15]*Ibid.*

[16]*Ibid.* p. 604.

[17]Admittedly, there are many questions, especially metaphysical ones, about the nature of individual existence which Barth does not directly address. Barth's purpose, however, is to disuss the theologically relevant issues. He is loath to engage in theological speculation by attempting to answer questions for which there is little material in the biblical witness. He regards such questions as of secondary importance not essential to the basic theological enterprise but which others may faithfully take up and which may come to have some secondary import even for theological discussion.

[18]It is important to remember that for Barth the sphere of the relations of man and woman should not be interpreted apart from what was said about relations in other

Our gender is essential to who we are and thus manifests itself in every sphere of relationship. It is in this sphere that we have depicted what is essential in all inter-human relationships: the essential likeness and unlikeness of each human person, the essential differential of one from another, yet each having the fulfillment of their being only in intimate relationship with the other.

For Barth there are only three other relations so essential to our being who we are. The first, of course, is our relationship to God in Christ, the other two are being the child of parents and being neighbors to others. These other relations are indeed just as essential to us. All other kinds of relations are secondary to these for Barth.[19] Each of these essential relations involve significant differentiations. But none of these differences is opposed to unity, but contribute to a true unity.

However, as we have said, the element of being gendered is the most fundamental creaturely distinction concerning who we are. The deepest aspect of who we are as acting, willing, deciding, fellowshipping persons has within it gender. We *are* masculine or feminine. This is an irreducible polarity of our existence never to be eradicated. It is the creaturely correspondence to the polarity between God and humankind. Barth calls this unique polarity a "structural differentiation."[20] In this polarity of humankind as male and female we see the duality yet the necessary unity and fellowship in its simplest and most poignant dimension. Humankind would not exist were it not both male and female and were there no communion between these two sexes. This duality and relationship of gender underlie all human interactions. Human life seeks its completion in the relationship of these two distinct forms of personhood. As such the true counterpart of man is woman and of woman is man.[21] Unity

---

spheres, including the trinitarian and Christological as well as other human spheres. The relations *are* analogous and should be taken as such. The interpretation of Barth has suffered because his section on "Man and Woman" has been discussed largely independently of what he says about other spheres of relationship, especially the other spheres of parent and child and the near and distant neighbor which follow this section in CD, III/4. It would be advisable, if we are to avoid misinterpreting and reacting to Barth, that the more controversial section on "Man and Woman" be interpreted in the light of the less controversial sections on relationships. This is what we are attempting to do here.

[19] CD, III/2, pp. 286–287, my emphasis.

[20] CD, III/2, p. 286. By structural differentiation (*structurellen Verscheidenheit*) Barth seems to be referring to a most basic and essential differentiation which is universal throughout all humanity, is not optional for human existence, is invariable and which is more comprehensive than other differences in that it colors, to one degree or another, all other differences rather than *vice versa*. Thus the differences between races are not of this order, they are variations of one and the same structure. Racial identity changes over time and is oriented around gender rather than gender being altered by racial concerns.

[21] Barth's consideration reflects the biblical observation that "Nevertheless, in the Lord woman is not independent of man nor man of woman; for as woman was made from

involves the dynamic relations of counterparts at the depths of such personal polarity.

Marriage, for Barth, is the sphere in which the meaning of our being gendered persons can be most completely expressed, is most obviously and simply manifested. Marriage is the paradigmatic expression of who we all are as we exist in the unity of love yet differentiation. This does not mean that all persons must be married to be completely human.[22] Marriage may serve as a particular *witness* and *reminder* of the true orientation of who we *all* are in *every* form of fellowship. Marriage arises out of and so points back to our fulfillment in being in a covenanted communion of even greater and more intrinsic polarity and so having a greater unity and intimacy with God. Marriage may be one form, albeit the simplest and strongest form, of witness to our essential being-in-relationship with God.[23]

2. Duality: not Essentially Psychological, Physiological or Sociological

The distinction Barth is making between men and women is, at its root, neither psychological nor physiological in nature.[24] Barth here is speaking of the unique dynamics of otherness, of polarity, in the relations between the genders which pose great dangers and tensions but also interest and energy. Men and women are for each other "supremely the other."[25]

Barth's deepest concern is gender not sexuality *per se*. His main concern is not even marriage *per se*. Gender may and must be distinguished from the physiological aspect of sexuality and sexual relations as that which ontologically grounds it.[26] His concern is the dynamic of relationship which occurs *wherever*

---

man, so man is now born of woman." (I Cor. 11:11–12). See Barth's comment on these verses in *CD*, III/4, p. 163.

[22] *CD*, III/2, p. 293.

[23] *Ibid.*, p. 288.

[24] *Ibid.*, p. 287.

[25] *Ibid.*, p. 288.

[26] The failure to distinguish and see gender as more foundational than sexuality is the mistake that many of Barth's critics make. This can be seen in Philip Hughes' book, *The True Image* (Leicester: Inter-Varsity Press, Grand Rapids: William B. Eerdmans, 1989). Ultimately for both Barth and Hughes, Jesus Christ alone is the Image. We are called to image the Image. Unfortunately Hughes does not point out this most crucial similarity between him and Barth. Rather he critiques Barth in the Genesis 1 passage as if Barth means that marriage and physiological sexuality is the ultimate image. Thus he argues that "relationship within the Godhead is in no sense a sexual relationship" and that "the interpersonal relationship in human society...is not dependent on sexuality; it is experienced in the bond of friendship...family...and in the multiplicity of daily associations of human society in which sexual identity is of little, if any, importance" (p. 19). Hughes interprets human differentiation in terms of animal differentiation and so identifies both with reproduction. For him gender is physiological and so involves sexual activity (p. 19). He fails to take into consideration that even reproduction is a much different affair for humans than for animals. This is seen in the Gen. 2 passage where Eve is called a helpmeet who answers man's aloneness and in whom Adam

persons are together because humanity occurs in two genders.[27] Gender is a personal category for Barth. Gender is personally and ontologically intrinsic to who we essentially are. Our physiology expresses outwardly this inward reality. It is the personal quality of relationship as it is affected by the polarity of the gender that grounds Barth's discussion. Marriage and sexual relations are heightened forms and concrete manifestations of this interplay of the deeper reality of our being gendered beings. Thus, physiological differentiation allows for physiological intercourse. Marriage is the context where the meaning of gender may properly be allowed its full scope and completion—manifesting itself physically, psychologically and sociologically. Our physiology and capacity for sexual relations are the external basis for the expression of the reality for all of the internal meaning of our being gendered. We are created distinct for the sake of being in communion. Marriage is the "simplest and yet its strongest form" of human unity yet polarity. It is the "primary form of all that has occupied us as humanity."[28] But marriage is not a necessary form for our living human lives.

3. Duality: the Dynamic in all Fellowship

Thus, this "structural" differentiation and likeness is not limited to the sexual sphere at all. It is "the subterranean motive" in all forms of fellowship involving males and females and related to all intra-gender relationships as well. It happens that "it is always in relation to their opposite that a man and woman are what they are in themselves."[29] This is not a matter of social determination or stereotyping, but can only be *discovered* in actual relationship. As such it can

---

rejoices saying "at last, bone of my bone and flesh of my flesh." The creation of Eve, in contrast to the animals, opens the way to a personal, volitional act of leaving and cleaving to her as a wife. For Barth the Gen. 2 passage is more crucial than Gen. 1 for understanding humanity as male and female. The "sexual" difference for humankind is different than for animals. It is personal, relational, volitional. Barth brings this out. Apparently for Hughes, the biblical witness gives gender no personal theological meaning. In Hughes' frame this aspect of man's creatureliness is cut off from his being human, it remains animal and merely a physiological fact. Furthermore, Hughes notes that Barth is only suggesting an analogy but fails to grasp the necessary direction of the analogy as Barth uses it. Claiming that he is contradicting Barth, he actually says, regarding the one Image, nearly what Barth does. "Man's person-to-Person relationship with his Maker, itself undoubtedly an indicator of that "image" is not determined by the fact of human sexuality. It exists independently of sexuality. Of this the perfect paradigm is the unclouded interpersonal harmony that informed the relationship between the incarnate Son and the heavenly Father, for in his incarnation the Son, who is himself the Image of God, expressed the fulness of life in that image, that is to say, as our fellow man, in a manner that was not in any way dictated by the issue of sexuality" (p. 20). Barth would agree entirely. Our being gendered is determined by the Image, not *vice versa*.

[27] *CD*, III/2, p. 288.
[28] *Ibid.*, p. 289.
[29] *CD*, III/4, p. 163.

never be defined *a priori* but "is to be constantly experienced in their mutual exchanges and co-existence."[30] In fact Barth specifically rules out the making of any psychological or sociological generalizations, any stereotyping.[31]

So what then is Barth driving at? He is pointing to the fact that there is a theological meaning, an ontological significance for our being male and female. He is saying that the fact that we as humans exist in a gendered way is not accidental or insignificant. In fact, it plays an essential part in our being and becoming who we are as we engage in relationship with persons of the opposite gender. *We exist in this essential polarity for the sake of human communion.*

Barth's discussion serves as a warning that we must seek and have positive ("for," "with," "to") relations with persons of the opposite gender if we are to not jeopardize our humanity. Barth is describing not the physiology, the psychology, or the sociology of gender distinctions but *is setting out its personal meaning*. What the particular content, meaning, or particular form of the fellowship in polarity will be can only be discovered in each case in the history of relationship with the person(s) of the opposite gender. But who I am, as male or female, will be essentially conditioned and confirmed in those relationships.[32]

4. The Intrinsic Necessity of the Duality for Fellowship

Thus, male and female need not threaten one another. This differentiation is a blessing as Adam recognized as he stood before Eve. It is the differentiation in relation that allows for each to become what they are. There is no such thing as the autonomous male or female. Masculinity can only come into existence in relation of fellowship with its polar "opposite." So too femininity. Each is co-determined in the fulfillment of relation with the other. Social roles have no absolute normative determination for what constitutes masculine and feminine. Nor can the dominance of one gender or the other independently legislate the contours of gender. Masculinity and femininity are to be discovered in the mutual dialogue between members of both genders as they recognize an interdependence in their becoming fully what they are as male or female. In the male-female relationship we see our humanity as two distinct individuals which cannot be interchanged. They cannot be dissolved or interchanged because each needs the distinctiveness of the other to fully realize itself and enable the other to be fully realized as well.

The Theological Grounding of Fellowship (yet Distinction)

1. The Created Relationship Based on the Gracious Relationship

This form of man's being in fellowship is given; it is mankind's natural determination. It has its root of course in humanity's relationship with God. This latter relationship is not given, it is not established on the basis of the nature of

---

[30]*CD*, III/2, p. 287.
[31]*CD*, III/4, p. 287.
[32]*Ibid.*, p. 158.

things. Therefore Barth can only speak of the male-female relationship as a copy, an analogy, a likeness to the original God-man relationship established by God's free electing grace, an overflow of His internal goodness.[33]

So, for example, the relationship of man and woman is given a crucial place in both Old and New Testaments because it has in mind its "prototype" "which in the plan and election of God is primarily the relationship between Jesus Christ and His Church, secondarily the relationship between Yahweh and Israel, and only finally—although very directly in view of its origin—the relationship between the sexes."[34]

The fact of human gender is founded on the fact of the being of God and His determination that humanity should be like Him, in His image. "God created them male and female corresponding to the fact that God Himself exists in relationship and not in isolation."[35] It is only as both men and women exist in their proper relationship that humankind will image its Creator, will be fully and truly human. Gender exists for the sake of engaging in covenantal relationships of differentiation and unity which bear witness to the unity and polarity of God's relation with humankind in Jesus Christ.[36]

---

[33] *CD*, III/1, p. 319.

[34] *Ibid.*, p. 322. The importance of gender and its special and particular form of fellowship in marriage does not arise alone, for Barth, from the Genesis 1 and 2 passages. It is a mistake to think so. Many have questioned Barth's exegesis of the Genesis passages. Much of the discussion has been limited to his interpretation of the few verses in Gen. 1:26–28. Interpreted on its own, within the frameworks of various hermeneutics, it seems the question must remain open about the relation of the image and humankind being male and female. However what Barth says about man and woman is grounded on the whole witness not just a few verses. He interprets Gen. 1:26, 27 *in terms of* Gen. 2:18–24. Furthermore, he interprets it in the light of the repeated usage of marriage as imaging God's own relation with his people found in the covenant and betrothing language of Genesis, the book of Hosea and the prophetical likening of idolatry with marital unfaithfulness, the Song of Songs, and finally putting this all in the light of Christ being the bride of the Church, e.g. in Jesus' parable of the bride and groom in Mk. 2:19f.; Lk. 5:34; Jn. 3:29 and the marriage feast of Mt. 22:2, the comparison in 2 Cor. 11:2 and in Rev. 21 and in the direct correlation of Christ and the Church with husband and wife in Eph. 5:23. Also important in this connection the parallel of the unique relationship between sexual union and our relationship with God by the Spirit in I Cor. 6:12–20 which refers itself to the Gen. 2 passage of becoming one flesh. If Barth's argument for the unique witness of gender in general and marriage in particular is to fail it must be challenged by taking into consideration the whole of the biblical witness. Given his hermeneutic of interpreting the whole of the biblical witness in terms of its fulfillment in Christ it would seem his position has not yet been invalidated. We will return to this discussion again.

[35] *CD*, III/4, p. 117. We must remember the order here. The differentiation and unity within God, and the Christological differentiation and unity gives rise to humankind's being created in a gendered way. We have no warrant here to argue that on this basis there must be sexual differentiation in God. This is to reverse the order of analogy.

[36] *CD*, III/2, p. 320.

Thus, the covenant-partnership of man and woman is created after the likeness of the covenant-relationship of God with man. In both there is a distinction of partners, never to be dissolved, but a union and communion of life in fellowship, where one is never without the other. All this is said, of course, noting the dissimilarity between the otherness of God and the otherness of the genders and the kind of union between God and man in Jesus and the one flesh union of husband and wife. The original relationship is one of grace; the copy is given in and with creation. The latter is the external basis, the former the internal basis. The latter we are, the former we must become on the basis of the promise given us in Christ.

2. The God-Man Prototype of Fellowship (yet Distinction)

Nevertheless there is a likeness. The creature of God is indeed to be differentiated from God even though derived from and dependent upon God. Humankind is in a way independent, not a mere extension of God and His will. And this is so by God's own determination and as such is a reflection of God's own independence.

In Jesus we are persons confronted by a "divine Other" who is distinct and so independent. This means that humankind too is, in a similar but not identical sense, independent. Thus, Jesus stands as the true Counterpart (*Gegenüber*) of every person.[37]

In the God-man relationship persons do have their own space, time and actuality. There is an actual co-existence of mankind with God. God Himself respects man's creaturely independence, actuality and activity. In this sense, God may be said to cooperate with the creature. God acts towards and with the creature. Yet in all this man is never alone, never without God nor God alone without man.[38]

God never ceases to be God by changing into man, man never becomes God. Yet humanity has a place in the divine Triune life itself in Jesus Christ. There is a unity of co-existence unparalleled in the horizontal plane. "God in absoluteness has freedom to be present with that which is not God, to communicate Himself and unite Himself with the other and the other with Himself that surpasses all other human reciprocal fellowship."[39]

This unique communion with mankind, although far surpassing any human relationship in unity and fellowship, is nevertheless one which does not violate man's being. In fact, the communion forms the basis for God's upholding the person as distinct from Himself.[40]

This, of course, has occurred in Jesus Christ. As the Son of God assumed our fallen humanity and realized it in the creaturely sphere, i.e. our humanity, so

---

[37] *CD*, III/2, p. 135.
[38] *CD*, III/3, pp. 91–93. Cf. III/2, p. 140.
[39] *CD*, II/1, p. 313.
[40] *Ibid.*, p. 314.

in Him we are given the gift of participating in the inner life of God Himself.[41] This is the deepest significance of the Incarnation, Crucifixion and Resurrection of Jesus Christ for us. It establishes by grace an all-surpassing fellowship not resulting in our obliteration but rather our full establishment as human persons. By the Spirit we may participate in his relationship to the Father.[42]

This is the eternal distinction and union of God and man in covenant partnership that is reflected in the creaturely sphere of the relationship of man and woman, and all human relationships. In this way Barth can designate, along with the Genesis text, that the man-woman relationship is the "*imago Dei*" because it is "an I-Thou relation similar to the I-Thou relation in God Himself."[43]

3. The Trinitarian Relations: Fellowship (yet Differentiation)

We come to see then, at bottom, that the human sphere of relationship reflects the very depths of the intra-trinitarian life in which we have revealed to us the distinction of the persons of the Trinity and yet their indissoluble unity. We will quote at length perhaps Barth's best explication of these intra- and inter-relationships.

> What God does in all this He is...But what is it that he does in virtue of His triune name...we must say that He wills to be ours, and He wills that we should belong to Him. He does not will to be without us, and He does not will that we should be without Him. He wills certainly to be God and He does not will that we should be God. But He does not will to be God for Himself nor as God to be alone with Himself. He wills as God to be for us and with us who are not God. In as much as He is Himself and affirms Himself, in distinction and opposition to everything that He is not, He places Himself in this relation to us. He does not will to be Himself in any other way than He is in this relationship. His life, that is His life in Himself, which is originally and properly the one and only life, leans towards this unity with our life.[44]

Once again Barth has led us within the sphere of human relationship to discover the trinitarian grounding of our being in communion and yet differentiated from one another in that very fellowship.

---

[41] *CD*, II/2, p. 780.
[42] *CD*, III/2, p. 65.
[43] Barth, *Table Talk*, p. 41.
[44] *CD*, II/1, p. 274.

II. Being-in-Relation in a Differentiated Order

The Shape of our Differentiated Relations

Humanity is essentially humankind's being in relationship on the horizontal plane as well as on the vertical plane. The form of this relationship has been further delineated as a duality or polarity of two persons unified in a fellowship. We must now follow Barth further concerning the differentiation of persons one from another. Differentiation is the structural correlate of the fact that humanity must be a co-humanity, a being in relationship. This differentiation, however, calls for an ordering of one by the other, a reorientation of the one to the other. These distinctions which call for mutual adjustment of one to the other are not inimical to fellowship. Their differentiation is essentially ordered to their true communion.

Because the human to human relationships are theologically and so ontologically grounded, the differentiation of human life in the God-to-man relationship will have a corresponding differentiation on the horizontal plane as well. We must remember that, again, there will be similarities and distinctions between the divine-human distinction and the human-human distinction in relationship. The originality and primacy of the divine-human differentiation will still take precedence in this sphere of human to human relationship.

Ordered Differentiation in Male-Female Fellowship

The differentiation of humanity in relationship is most clearly present in the male and female relationship, but this differentiation is operative in all other relationships as well. All persons, Barth points out, are male and female, male or female. This is the only differentiation among creatures that is structural (*structurellen Verscheidenheit*)[45] unlike race, physiological features, social roles, biological roles (being fathers or mothers), or kinship relations, which are variations within this dual structure. In all other essential or non-essential differentiations, persons are either male or female in their "being, feeling, willing, thinking, speaking, conduct and action...co-existence and co-operation in all these things."[46] This structural differentiation is a confirmation of the Christological truth that humankind is essentially a being in relation. Men are to women and women to men distinctly and uniquely others.[47]

---

[45]See our previous discussion of this in the section on "Fellowship (yet Distinction)" for Barth's arguments. See *CD*, III/2, p. 286.

[46]*CD*, III/2, p. 286

[47]Men are to women and women are to men "supremely the other, the fellow man, to see and to be seen by whom, to speak with and to listen to whom, to receive from and to render assistance to whom is necessarily a supreme human need and problem and fulfillment, so that whatever may take place between man and man and woman and woman is only as it were a preliminary and accompaniment for this true encounter between man and fellow-man, for this true being in fellow-humanity" (*Ibid.*, p. 288).

Thus, "the human is the male and female in its differentiation and connexion."[48] Each can be what it is only by virtue of its actual relationship with the other. One cannot be without the other. Marriage, then, is the "simplest and strongest form" of this differentiation essential for humanity.[49]

Right relationship, humanizing relationship, requires a differentiation so that one may become for the other a mirror of the other thereby assisting each other in self-recognition through encounter with the other. In this way there is mutual completion of one with the other, a true being-in-communion.

For Barth, the essential exegetical source for his perspective is the Genesis 2 creation narrative of man and woman.[50] Woman's being is from man but man discovers for himself that she is distinct and yet a counterpart, "bone of my bone, and flesh of my flesh." This is the confirmation that it was not good for man to be alone, and that it was only by communion with his counterpart that humanity could be completely good.[51] The other greatest single source of confirmation comes, for Barth, in the Song of Songs where we find man and woman in their differentiation and communion.[52]

The ultimate theological grounding for this essential differentiation is the differentiated communion and imaging of Father and Son, Yahweh and Israel, and Jesus Christ to the Church.[53] The human differentiation follows the contours of the theological grammar of these relationships. Thus, human relationships will have a form that is indeed related to but also distinct from the divine order. It, nevertheless, will be able to correlate to it so as to be an indirect and human image and witness.

Barth is willing to use the terms "super-" and "subordination" to describe the ordered differentiation of relationship.[54] Barth finds no reason to dismiss the biblical testimony at this point but rather finds reason to retain it. This, of course, puts Barth at odds with much contemporary discussion which finds these terms altogether unacceptable.[55] We will attempt to fill out some of what he

---

[48] *CD*, III/2, p. 292.

[49] *Ibid.*, p. 289.

[50] Not Genesis 1. As we pointed out earlier, for Barth, Gen. 1 is to be interpreted in light of Gen. 2.

[51] *CD*, III/2, pp. 291–293.

[52] *Ibid.*, p. 294.

[53] *Ibid.*, pp. 297–316.

[54] We have been following Barth's shorter discussion in III/2, pp. 309–321. However to fill out his argument we will now follow his lengthier discussion in III/4, pp. 149–181.

[55] To follow Barth at this point will be difficult if we do not pay attention to why he maintains this terminology and also to how he qualifies its usage. We may cite a number of those who do not seem to see the point Barth is making, even though once they have seen it they may still reject his position. See for example: Rosemary Ruether's *Religion and Sexism* (New York: Simon & Schuster, 1974) who in turn cites Eleanor Commo McLaughlin who claims that Barth engages in a "platonizing" of relationships into fixed hierarchical structures (p. 259) and also Jane Arnold Romero who charges that Barth rejects "any view that would make man and woman equal" (p. 324). Mary Daly comes

means by this ordered distinction but emphasize the theological grounding and context by which he interprets what is meant by this ordered differentiation. His

---

out quite strongly in condemning Barth's theology with being "sadomasochistic" in her *Pure Lust* (Boston: Beacon Press, 1984) p. 2. Letty Russell cautions that Barth is "closer to the way it is after the fall than descriptive of God's intention for partnership" in her *Becoming Human* (Philadelphia: The Westminster Press, 1982) p. 68. Paul K. Jewett in his *Man as Male and Female: A Study in Sexual Relationship from a Theological Point of View* (Grand Rapids: Wm. B. Eerdmans Publishing Co., 1975) levels criticisms that Barth's argument "dies of a thousand qualifications" (p. 82), is equivocal (p. 82), "does not seem to advance anywhere, it does not move toward any resolution of the issue" (p. 83), is designated *sui generis* to the extent that it cannot be related to anything we know (p. 85), and finally that the more basic thrust of Barth's own theology is not of subordination and hierarchy but of "a fellowship of equals under God" (p. 85). See also Cynthia Campbell's Ph.D. dissertation, "Imago Trinitatis: An Appraisal of Karl Barth's Doctrine of the *Imago Dei* in the Light of His Doctrine of the Trinity" (Southern Methodist University, 1981) where she asserts that Barth uses these terms, by way of his qualifications, in "non–ordinary ways" citing the *Oxford Dictionary* as the criterion for ordinary. "The problem is that this is an idiosyncratic use of language differing from ordinary experience so much as to create significant doubt as to what is in fact meant...we would argue that the term 'subordination' has no place in describing a relation which is also to be described as 'equal' or 'mutual.' " pp. 169–170. While she acknowledges that Barth's theological design is to reclaim language to its "proper meaning" the reason she dismisses this aim is not clear. Presumably because she regards it as irrelevant, impossible or confusing. It is not convincing that this is sufficient grounds on which to dismiss Barth's program, because, for Barth, this is the essence of the theological enterprise itself at all points, not just in this issue.

While it is not our task to resolve these issues, our presentation suggests that Barth is compelled to retain the concept of differentiated order because of the ordering of relationship of Jesus to His Father and so revealing the ordering of the Son's relation to the Father, the imaging of this relation in the male and female relationship. What his critics also generally miss is the contextualization of any order within mutuality (thus Barth's acknowledgement of his Christological and trinitarian orientation, not the overlooking of it) and the fact that Barth is not attempting to give a phenomenological description of roles although some insist that this is what he has done or insist that he has said nothing helpful if he hasn't done so. Barth has perhaps left himself somewhat open to such misunderstanding by using the two particular terms of "leadership" and "initiative" even if these occur in the context of an essential ordering rather than phenomenological description. A. J. McKelway seems to have a much better grasp of Barth's theological context and interpretation of the ordering in his article "The Concept of Subordination in Barth's Special Ethics" *SJT*, Vol. 32, 1979, pp. 345–357, where he indicates that "In the ordering of the sexes which requires subordination without inferiority, we are confronted, it seems to me, with a reference to precisely that order within the Trinity which *perichoresis* describes" (p. 352). Here he seems to acknowledge that *analogia relationis* and *perichoresis* allow for mutuality *and* subordination. However, see his other article "Perichoretic Possibilities in Barth's Doctrine of Male and Female" *The Princeton Seminary Bulletin* (Vol. 1, 1986) pp. 231–243, which seems to retract the possibility of subordination, at least as understood in terms of authority or leadership, being an aspect of perichoretic mutuality and argues that Barth's own view of the intra-trinitarian relations really disallows this. See below.

own grasp of these terms in that context addresses most, if not all, objections to their usage.

1. Ordered Relationships Presuppose Mutuality

To summarize his lengthy presentation we may say at the outset that the entire context of any discussion regarding the ordering of the relationship *presupposes* the mutuality and equality of that relationship. Mutuality is the more comprehensive category and super- and subordination must be interpreted in terms of it, not *vice versa*. The order does not create the relationship.[56] Rather the mutual relationship includes within it an order subordinate to it. If one is to mirror or image the other there must be a submission of the "copy" to the "original." However, there must be a mutuality, an equality and similarity presupposed if there is to be a significant imaging of and fellowship with each other.[57]

The significance of this more comprehensive context for any discussion of Barth's view of order should not be overlooked.[58] Each, in two ways, is equal.

---

[56] *CD*, III/2, pp. 291–292, 312.

[57] *CD*, III/4, p. 164 and III/2, p. 309, where he notes that it is the equality announced in the Gospel in the first place that gives rise to the issue of the proper new ordering of the sexes.

[58] Most often critics have offered only mutually exclusive alternatives: mutuality or static hierarchy. However, as we have seen, Barth's grammar allows for unity, distinction, ordering and correlation of relationship as well as dynamic interaction and becoming. Thus the grammar of Christology and Trinity calls for both mutuality and order but not order of a static or hierarchical kind.

Barth's critics at the outset often reject such a logic, demanding that Barth utilize some other (and non-theological) grammar. So for example, A. J. McKelway, who in his article, "Perichoretic Possibilities," overlooks the grammar intrinsic to Barth's understanding of relationship and concludes that *analogia relationis* (p. 240) and "co-humanity" (p. 241) and perichoresis (p. 232) must necessarily eliminate any 'thought of authority and leadership which is not shared' (p. 241) and that 'shared authority implies an exchange of roles of leadership and following' (p. 241) so that there must be equal exchange, reciprocity and mutuality rather than 'the static hierarchical structure' (p. 232) of Barth. He assumes that these concepts exclude the ordering whereas Barth has shown how it is included in these relationships especially in the Christological and trinitarian spheres. Perichoresis does not eliminate an ordered differentiation. It in no way calls for an interchangeability of divine roles. There is reciprocity but not interchangeability or a mutuality taken in this way. McKelway emphasizes the issue of roles, and an antithesis between mutuality and ordering. Barth is not essentially speaking about roles and for Barth, mutuality is indeed the more comprehensive category, but this does not exclude an order, especially one he insists is not hierarchical. (See his other article, "The Concept of Subordination in Barth's Special Ethics," for a slightly more adequate understanding of Barth.)

Given the inability to accept what Barth explicitly says (e.g. that he is not presenting a hierarchy and that the content of any super- and subordination cannot be pre-determined but only discovered in the history and dynamic of the actual relationship), the inability (unwillingness?) to recognize the grammar he uses, and often arguing that they themselves are able to be more theologically consistent than Barth, it seems that many of his critics are using an alien grammar to evaluate Barth's language and are

First, each is called by the command of God to be faithful to the distinction of their gender.[59] Second, each cannot be faithful to their own gender except by being in mutual relationship with the opposite sex.[60] The ways of this relationship, Barth reiterates, are *identical* to the ones he used to describe the essence of humanity in fellowship: mutual seeing, hearing, speaking, assisting, and glad freedom in responsibility.[61] Thus, their mutuality before the grace of the electing and determining and ordering God stands as their mutual orientation. And so they are equally dependent upon the necessity of their mutual relationship and orientation.[62] What Barth means by super- and sub-ordination cannot be interpreted to be in contradiction to the content of the grammar of personal relations. Rather these terms are to be interpreted in terms of what he says of relations elsewhere.

The issue of mutuality is not merely one of ontological status, but also of reciprocity. Barth is clear that the ordering of the differentiation is to be understood within a "reciprocal sub-ordination in which each gives to the other that which is proper to him...It has nothing really to do with patriarchalism, or with a hierarchy of domestic and civil values and powers. It does not give one control over the other, or put any one under the dominion of the other."[63] There is no inferiority in subordination when it is appropriately understood.[64]

The unity and differentiation of *reciprocal* giving and receiving provide the context for any other dynamics of so-called ordering.[65] Consequently, if there is to be a "first and a second," a "succession," a "precedence" or "initiative," this means for Barth only the establishment of the unity with its differentiations.

---

insisting at the outset that their own grammar is normative. McKelway accuses Barth of having 'culturally conditioned elements' (p. 232) in his ethics. It remains to be seen whether or not the "logic" insisted upon by McKelway and others is not itself at least equally culturally conditioned. At any rate the charge of cultural conditioning cuts both ways and does not serve to advance the discussion.

[59] *CD*, III/4, p. 152.

[60] *Ibid.*, p. 163.

[61] *CD*, III/2, pp. 250–274

[62] *CD*, III/4, p. 169.

[63] *CD*, III/2, p. 313. There are some who overlook Barth's acknowledgment of this mutual subordination in Ephesians 5. The question is whether such mutuality entails an inter-changeability, whether it requires complete symmetry. Mutuality, as understood by many, necessarily involves such. It is usually subsumed under the term "equality." For Barth mutuality does not necessarily entail equality in the sense of symmetry, inter-changeability. The essential aspect of mutuality is, it seems, reciprocity.

[64] "Man speaks against himself if he assesses and treats woman as an inferior being..." *CD*, III/4, p. 287.

[65] See especially III/4, pp. 190–192. Bromiley translates the clause "*daß Mann und Frau in dieser liebenden Treue miteinander und and zueinander stehen*"—"the reciprocal co-existence and orientation of husband and wife in this faithfulness and love" (p. 192, *KD*, p. 215).

For in what way does he take precedence of her? Certainly not in order to be something more and greater and other than she! Certainly not to his own advantage and her disadvantage! But for her sake, that she might follow him! And where does this course lead her? Not into an unworthy and irksome dependence upon him, but into her own characteristic freedom in relation to him! Not into a great depth beneath him but upwards into fellowship with him! He is her head in the fact that he summons her to this goal, i.e., that he makes himself primarily responsible for their common advance towards it, to freedom in fellowship.[66]

2. *What Mutuality Rules out* a limine

It is this mutuality and reciprocity which controls the boundaries of what can be meant by any ordering. Barth is clear. There is no warrant here for control, domination, servility, manipulation, depersonalization, inferiority or hostility. Additionally, on the one hand, what this rules out, then, is any "jealousy, envy, imitation, or usurpation" of one sex by the other.[67] On the other, it rules out any denial of gender identity especially in some kind of androgeny or bi-sexuality.[68] It means to accept ones own gender as a benefit, neither fleeing it by attempting to be other than what one is, by seeking ones self in the other sex, nor escaping gender through some attempted transcendence of it.

Also, there can be no simple interchangeability or substitution of one sex for another.[69] The mutuality of the sexes does not eliminate a certain asymmetry which must be honored if we are to benefit from this distinction and fellowship. The most essential and reliable criterion for discerning the faithful ordering of the sexes, says Barth, is each being fully aware and honestly glad of their gender.[70] This is Barth's primary orientation and is the most important issue at stake. Only from this vantage point may we continue to comprehend accurately what Barth is saying.

3. *The Ordering of Relationships*

a. *Ordering within Unity and Differentiation*

The "ordering" of the relationship is for Barth the third aspect within the two-fold mutuality.[71] When describing marriage he precedes the section on order with one each on the unity and the differentiation.[72] This follows, of

---

[66] *Ibid.*, p. 194.
[67] *Ibid.*, p. 154.
[68] *Ibid.*
[69] *Ibid.*, p. 169.
[70] *Ibid.*, p. 159.
[71] *Ibid.*, p. 168.
[72] *Ibid.*, pp. 189–195.

course, the pattern we have seen, first in Christology and then, in terms of the trinitarian relations: unity, correspondence, ordered unifying differentiation.

b. Not a Phenomenological Prescription

Also, at the outset we must indicate that Barth is not attempting to develop a typology of gender roles, that is, a phenomenological description of sociologically and psychologically observed and measured patterns. Thus, Barth says, "we definitely reject every phenomenology or typology of the sexes." [73] and gives examples of two other theologians who mistakenly do so. This Barth takes to be an exercise of imposing cultural values into the theological explication of humanity. He is seeking the basis of gender beneath "psychology, pedagogy, hygiene, and the like."[74]

c. A Dynamic Discernment: Neither Pre-Determined nor Culturally Defined

Consequently, what at the behavioral level, such ordering of relationship will look like cannot be pre-determined, "it can never be known in advance"[75] for

> The summons to both man and woman to be true to themselves may take completely unforeseen forms right outside the systems in which we like to think. In no event is it bound to a scheme which we may presuppose. It is thus a mistake to attach oneself to any such scheme, however well considered and illuminating it might appear to be.[76]

Thus, at the level of behavior and roles the ordering can only be discovered in each relationship as it actually occurs, as it is lived out in encounter.

> What distinguishes man from woman and woman from man even in this relationship of super- and subordination is more easily discovered, perceived, respected and valued in the encounter between them than it is defined. It is to be constantly experienced in their *mutual* exchanges and co-existence.[77]

As such it becomes a *mutual* ordering, but an ordering nevertheless. Barth clearly acknowledges the biblical witness to a "mutual" or "reciprocal" subordination especially as found in Eph. 5:22ff.[78] However, there is still an ordering that will take place in this relationship which nevertheless cannot be stated in general terms at all.

---

[73] *Ibid.*, p. 152. Barth advocates making no "generalized pronouncements about the phenomenological differences" (III/2, p. 287).
[74] *CD*, III/4, p. 150.
[75] *Ibid.*, p.151
[76] *Ibid.*
[77] *CD*, III/2, p. 287, emphasis mine.
[78] *Ibid.*, pp. 312, 313.

d. A Succession, not a Hierarchy

Most simply, Barth describes this ordering as one of succession and of succession only, as B follows A.[79] This ordering is not a hierarchy and implies no inequality before God nor denies the equality of each needing to be in relationship with the other.[80] He further defines super- and sub-ordination as an "inspiring," "initiating," "leading" of the masculine and a "following," "responding," "being stimulated" by the female.[81] Barth recognizes the danger even of this attempted non-phenomenological characterizing of the order, but senses he has grounds to do so this far and yet, not further.[82]

e. Essentially a Subordination to Jesus Christ

This ordering itself is qualified in that it may faithfully be done only as an obedience to Jesus Christ.[83] Thus, the male, too, is ordered, is subordinate. Likewise, the female is not essentially subordinate to the male but to the Lordship of Jesus. Her following is just as much a free and voluntary act as the male's taking the first step in obedience towards the woman.[84] Thus, there is neither room for the tyranny of the male over the female[85] nor is there room for the female to exercise a false compliance and irresponsibility towards a man.[86] The distinction of gender has nothing to do with matters of the pride of one's own gender, or maintaining one's dignity. It is all a matter of responsibility, of masculine responsibility and of feminine responsibility.[87] Thus, Barth is not attempting to impose an external law upon these relationships but expose a contour which will arise in the interaction of men and women and to a certain extent all persons.

Summary

After all has been said in terms of the male female relationship, we should point out that much of what Barth indicates is in the negative: what super- and

---

[79] *"Ordnung heißt Folge"* says Barth, (*KD*, p. 189).

[80] *CD*, III/4, p. 169, 170 Cf. III/2, pp. 311, 312.

[81] *CD*, III/4, p. 170, 171. Barth uses the words *"Anreger," "Führer," "Erwecker," Initiative"* and their verbal forms.

[82] *Ibid.*, pp. 169–170: "Every word is dangerous and liable to be misunderstood (*mißverständlich und gefährlich*) when we try to characterize this order. But it exists....we utter the very dangerous words which are unavoidable if we are to describe what is at issue in the being and fellowship of man and woman." This is the point where Barth opens himself to the greatest challenge. With this step has Barth gone too far? Are these indeed the appropriate words to characterize the relationship? Given Barth's grounding it would seem that they both could be but do not have to be the only ones or even the correct ones. Alternatives would most likely not be entirely dissimilar however.

[83] *Ibid.*, p. 173, Cf. III/2, p. 311.

[84] *Ibid.*, p. 172.

[85] *Ibid.*, p. 177.

[86] *Ibid.*, pp. 178–179.

[87] *Ibid.*, p. 176.

subordination is not. This aspect, we think, is an important service rendered. Barth has ruled out much that passes for the ordering of relations. This we need to keep in mind. Most importantly he has ruled out domination, enslavement, and socially defined roles as norms for male-female relationships.

Positively he has said some important things. First, that being male and female, as such, is indeed a blessing from God which can provide a basis for fellowship. Secondly, that men and women should seek to be in positive self-giving relationships with each other. Third, we should not be disturbed about an asymmetry arising in such loving relationships. This may enhance the fellowship not threaten it. Fourth, that we should be glad about the gender which we are given, accept it and live it out in confidence that it will be a blessing. Fifth, that the true ordering of relationships according to their gendered differentiation can only be found through the living out of the relationship in a covenantal way.

Barth has also offered some timely warnings. First if we do not have positive relations between men and women we jeopardize our humanity. Second that jealousy, envy or animosity towards the other gender is damaging to our humanity. Third, that men and women are not interchangeable parts and to treat them as such will dehumanize us. And fourth, an implication which we bring out of Barth's understanding of this relationship being a subordination to Christ, is that the demand for personal equality between men and women cannot be made into an external law of our relating, the first priority of our relationships. As Jesus did not try to secure equality with his Father, our doing so, contrariwise, on the horizontal plane, will only dehumanize our relationships. Being in fellowship is *a gift* of one to another. The proper fellowship and whatever mutuality is accomplished between men and women will arise out of a free and joyful response of giving on the part of both men and women, not out of a determined and self-righteous defensiveness or a jealous self-righteous anger or demand.[88]

While what Barth has to say is significant, it is often overlooked. Some, to be sure, will still say he has not been specific enough about what the ordering should look like. Others will say he has said too much in designating it as a leading and following, initiating and responding. Certainly, many critics have reacted negatively to these terms. Understood in context they should not cause as much offense as is often the case. Perhaps they are not the most useful terms he could have chosen. Whatever terms are chosen it is doubtful that they will be any less offensive than the biblical texts from which they derive. From Barth's perspective they should be neither more nor less scandalous than the communion

---

[88]This statement does not overlook the fact that there is sin and injustice and violence in the relations between men and women. It is meant to point out that certain attempts to make these relationships right can be just as evil and damaging to our humanity. We must question what means we may use to pursue God's intentions. It does not question whether justice and reconciliation ought to be sought. It calls into question the justification of the use of any and every means. Means opposed to the ends will inevitably pollute the accomplishment of the ends, thereby preventing their realization.

and obedience of Jesus to the Father, his refusing to grasp on to equality with the Father as his right, and his call to die to ourselves for the sake of others.

Ordered Communion Grounded in the Humiliation and Exaltation of Jesus Christ

This responsibility of ordered differentiation in human communion, as carefully defined above, applies to all relationships because it is essentially a subordination to Jesus Christ who is far "superior" to men and far more "subordinate" than any woman might properly be. Thus, both the preceding and the following are done according to Jesus Christ. The equality and distinction they have is like the equality and the distinction of the divinity and humanity (exalted and humbled) of Jesus himself and in fact mirrors it.[89]

In the obedience of Jesus to the Father we find the original of this ordering among persons within the creaturely sphere. And here is where we see that the ordering of relationship is no tyranny, no lack of freedom, no disunity of one with the other. Rather we see true unity of relationship and freedom, honor and dignity in obedience.[90] The freedom of Jesus from all others is founded in his subordination to the Father.[91]

Grounded in Christ's Relationship with Israel and the Church

Barth also picks up another sphere of relationship in which he finds a correspondence of ordered relationship. The biblical witness throughout Old and New Testaments makes an analogy and comparison of the relationship of God with Israel and Christ with the Church with the relation of man and woman. Barth is clear, we have only an image, a reflection, a type which "may reflect, represent and attest" the reality of the community's relationship to God.[92] This

---

[89] *CD*, III/4, p. 173, cf. III/2, pp. 311–313. It is beyond the scope of this book to discuss Barth's exegesis which underlay this whole discussion of order. We can say that the extensive work that Barth did in this area demonstrates a commitment to the biblical witness which he found no legitimate way to dismiss, in whole or part, on some hermeneutical grounds. The passages he used are not unusual: Gen. 2:18ff.; Gal. 3:28; I Cor. 14:33; I Cor. 11, 14; Col. 3:18ff.; Eph. 5:22–24; I Tim. 2:11; Tit. 2:5; I Pet. 3:1; Rom. 13; but, as he notes, their translation is crucial (III/4 pp. 172–176 and III/2, pp. 309–316). What Barth offers is a comprehensive look at them all taken together and in terms of the whole grammar of relations in the seven spheres of relationship, the relation of Father and Son being the determinative sphere for interpreting the human sphere of relationships.

[90] "And this obedience of Jesus is the clear reflection of the unity of the Father and Son by the bond of the Holy Spirit in the being of the eternal God Himself who is the fullness of freedom Himself" (*CD*, II/2, p. 605).

[91] "Jesus is the man who is free from all other forces and lords because He is completely bound to God" (*CD*, II/2, p. 623).

[92] *CD*, III/2, pp. 314, 315. Biblical texts Barth discusses are Eph 5:22–33; Gen. 2; Gen. 24; the Song of Songs; Hosea; II Cor. 11:2f.; Rom. 7:1–6; I Cor. 6:12–20. See *CD*, III/2, pp. 291–318.

is another aspect of the Christological grounding of the ordering of relationships which is a freedom and responsibility with gladness.

Originally Grounded in the Triune Life of God

There is within the intra-trinitarian life a unity, a differentiation, and an order within the one essence of God. There is a first and a second, there is a leading and a following in the inner life of the Triune God according to Barth.

> As we look at Jesus Christ we cannot avoid the astounding conclusion of a divine obedience. Therefore we have to draw the no less astounding deduction that in equal Godhead the one God is, in fact, the One and also Another, that He is indeed a First and a Second, One who rules and commands in majesty and One who obeys in humility. The one God is both the one and the other. And, we continue, He is the one and the other without any cleft or differentiation but in perfect unity and equality because in the same perfect unity and equality He is also a Third, the One who affirms the one and equal Godhead through and by and in the two modes of being, the One who makes possible and maintains His fellowship with Himself as the one and the other...He is God only in these relationships and therefore not in a Godhead which does not take part in this history which takes place between them.[93]

We should also note some parallels between the succession of the triune Persons and that of succession among persons. Certainly, the succession in God presupposes equality of essence and presupposes mutuality. Yet within God we find a succession, a following of B after A. What Barth means by succession in human relationships is analogous to the intra-trinitarian successions of begetting, being begotten and procession. There is a direction of orientation, an asymmetry, a non-interchangeability of one "person" with another.

Thus, the order reflected in human relationships is originally an order in the intra-trinitarian life. Thus, order and obedience can hardly be necessarily regarded as injustice, inequity, inequality. Thus, we come to Barth's reminder that obedience itself is no dishonor, no disgrace, no inequity. The obedience of man to God is his proper honor and dignity and freedom. Thus, in human relationships the mere fact of one's obeying another need not be a dishonor, injustice, inequity as it orders itself along the lines of the commanding Lordship and the obeying humanity of Jesus Christ, revealing to us the very order within God Himself.

The Ordered Community of Believers

The place where Barth most explicitly expounds the general ordering of all human relationships is found in sections where he describes the life of the Church. The ordering occurs between individuals and also among all the

---

[93] *CD*, IV/1, p. 203.

members of the whole community under Christ. On a person-to-person basis Barth takes note of the task within the Church of spiritual oversight of the elders over the younger. In this, the elder precedes the younger as one who has known God and has engaged in a history of relationship with God. Given this wisdom, the elder is responsible to pass this on to those beginning to discern their true relationship with God. The "superiority" of the elder is only one of precedence, being before the younger in his history. But the elder stands under the same God and His grace as does the younger. His witness to God is in order to see that the younger does indeed place himself along with him under that gracious Lordship as brothers of Jesus Christ.[94]

More comprehensively, Barth considers the life of the community of faith to be an ordered relationship. A helpful description of this is found in his later Volume IV. The marks of the community are that it is 1) regulated by the law of service, 2) based on mutual trust, not compulsion, 3) where each assumes tasks of freedom and responsibility for the common good, 4) and so is a dynamic, living, growing, and reforming community.[95] It is where Christ's Lordship is acknowledged and where He is its norm for that which it is and is to become.[96]

Thus, Barth finds reflected in the sphere of humanity an ordered differentiation which presupposes a fellowship and correspondence of persons in a dynamic history of covenantal relationship grounded in Christ's own relationship to us and which is originally found within the inner Triune relationships. It also finds provisional representation in the life of the Church. We will now go on to show how Barth sees the unity and ordered differentiation of humanity culminating in humanity's corresponding with and so being a witness to its Creator.

III. Being-in-Relationship: Image, Analogy, Correspondence and Witness

We come now to the most comprehensive categorization of the form of humanity as being-in-relationship. It holds within it and coordinates the determination of humanity in its differentiation and communion so that there is an actual interchange of lives one to the other. This means that humanity exists as its inter-human relationships correspond, image, or bear witness to the divine-

---

[94] See *CD*, III/4, pp. 241–243.

[95] *CD*, IV/2, pp. 690–718.

[96] *Ibid.*, pp. 661–666. While we cannot develop this theme of humanity as it expresses itself in the community of believers and Barth does not fully develop this theme until Part IV, we should say that all that we say here in his anthropology points to and culminates in the Body of Christ. See Verne H. Fletcher, "Karl Barth's Conception of Co-Humanity and the Search for Human Community" *South East Asia Journal of Theology*, Vol. 9, No. 1 (July 1967), pp. 41–53, for an excellent survey of Barth's anthropology in Part IV of the *Church Dogmatics*.

human relationship in Jesus Christ and so to the intra-trinitarian relations in God Himself revealed in Jesus Christ.

Barth's Theological Interpretation of *Analogia*

1. A Constellation of Terms

What must be said at the outset is that what Barth has attempted to do is to adopt and adapt, where helpful, the language of analogy for theological purposes. He interprets it in a way such that it assists him in expounding the reality of the Word of God indicated by the more strictly biblical terms, such as image, likeness and witness, and the myriad biblical comparisons (and contrasts) between God and humankind. So while the concept of *analogia* is indeed crucial for Barth himself (as so many of his interpreters note),[97] and so must be also for our understanding of Barth, we must point out that he immediately interprets and qualifies it. He speaks of the *analogia relationis, gratiae* and *fidei*.

While Barth dialogues with many theologians who have utilized the concept of analogy, his most valuable contribution is how he transforms its usage. In his anthropology it is qualified by the term relation. We contend that Barth's qualification is so radical that analogy should be understood in terms of relation rather than *vice versa*. Ultimately, for Barth, the proper usage of terms is measured by its faithfulness to the object of faith, Jesus Christ. For Barth, there is only one analogy between God and humankind, Jesus Christ. His terminology of analogy must be measured against the reality revealed in Him.

The term "analogy" does indeed seem to provide a basic building block in Barth's method. However, how it functions, how it is grounded, and how it is related to the whole family of terms he uses is also crucial for understanding him, as he himself points out.[98] For Barth it is the personal relationships themselves which are analogous, that is, which are to be compared. Barth, in his usage of the concept of analogy, is not essentially concerned with *how* we can conceptualize truth or in working out an *a priori* valid theological methodology. Analogy, for him, is not essentially a matter of predication or attribution. What are analogous are the personal relationships in each of the five spheres of relationship Barth has been considering all along. In the person and work of Jesus Christ the life of God and the life of humankind have been coordinated and so exist in a reciprocal relationship in which the being and act of God finds its reflection in the response of the being and act of man. The concept of *analogia relationis* is not a methodological starting point, but Barth's attempt to sum up in one term what he has been unfolding all along. There is a likeness, despite all

---

[97] Hans Urs Von Balthasar was one of the first interpreters to suggest that there was a major shift in Barth's theological development from a dialectical to an analogical method. See his *The Theology of Karl Barth*, trans. John Drury (New York, Chicago, San Francisco: Holt, Rinehart, and Winston, 1971), orig. Germ. edit., 1951. The discussion of Barth's use of analogy is extensive. We will deal with some of this material.

[98] *CD*, II/1, pp. 237–243, in his comparison with Quenstedt's approach.

the differences, in the essential spheres of relationship in God, between God and humankind, and between persons. What we have summed up as Barth's grammar in six determinations is a formulation of the nature of these relationships.[99]

Barth uses this term as the most comprehensive one of those dealing with the *form* of human being-in-relationship. It encloses the concepts of unity, differentiation and ordering. But it also incorporates the additional dimensions of likeness and unlikeness, or similarity and dissimilarity. But ultimately the *analogia* must be interpreted also in the light of the *content* of the being-in-relationship of humankind. There can be no separation of form and content, being and action, the person and work of Jesus Christ. We can already see this in Barth's special qualification of *analogia* by *gratiae* and *fidei*.[100] All these relationships are gracious ones. Humanity may exist in these relationships because of the grace of God in Jesus Christ. Humanity may make active and faithful response to God because of the gracious relationship established in Jesus Christ. These qualifications point out the actional content of the relationship.[101] They signify the kind of unity, distinction, ordering and correspondence he has been expounding all along. They are gracious and faithful relationships.[102] In

---

[99] Barth's primary aim is to avoid making *a priori*, speculative and so abstract ontological claims. He does this because *a posteriori*, within the Christian frame, ontological consideration apart from relations could only contribute to an abstract description alien to the Christian faith. However, *a posteriori ontological* considerations within a relational framework should certainly not be ruled out. There must be ontological implications within such a relational frame. It seems that Barth did not explore this possibility and so did not entirely escape the issue of the *analogia entis*. See Alan Torrance's important discussion, *Persons in Communion*, pp. 140, 186f.

[100] John McIntyre in his article "Analogy" *SJT*, Vol. 12 (1959) says, "It is a pity that it is the phrase *analogia fidei* rather than *analogia gratiae* which has been popularised as the summary of Barth's position in this matter. The subjective nuances attaching to the word 'faith' open up the possibility that the analogia fidei is something created by our subjective act of faith; whereas it is because grace sets up the analogy that faith takes place" (p. 15). We concur with McIntyre in suggesting the primacy of grace as the foundation for the response of a corresponding faith.

[101] Henri Bouillard says that "Barth has rendered a service to Christian thought in introducing into the classic doctrine of analogy the point of view of event, of historical revelation." He goes on to note that Barth neglected the exploration of the structure and meaning of analogy. See *The Knowledge of God*, trans. Samuel D. Femiano (London: Burns & Oates/Herder and Herder, 1969) orig. *Connaissance De Dieu* (Paris: Aubier, 1967), p. 116. This seems to be an accurate critique. However, Barth has little interest in doing so because the concept and possibility of analogical predication play no decisive role in his method or theology. It is a term he adopts and adapts (for better or worse). It is interpreted theologically and this is what Barth develops. And in such a framework the crucial aspect for Barth is the personal event of correlating in our action with God's. The biblical witness assumes that such is an actuality in Christ and so a possibility for us. The event nature of the analogy is theologically its structure and meaning.

[102] This is the real difference between Barth and Thomas Aquinas according to Alan Torrance. Aquinas argued that the primary form of analogy was from the prior to

terms which we have been using they are of a covenantal kind: personal, free and responsible, dynamic and eschatological, and extensive to the end of being inclusive. The *analogia relationis* is the most comprehensive term Barth uses to represent the nature of the whole of Barth's basic grammar and theo-logic of relationships.

The constellation of terms occurring in the *Church Dogmatics* which bring out the same understanding of relationships include: correspondence, analogy, original (*Urbild*) and copy (*Abbild*), prototype (*Vorbild*) and type/imitation/copy (*Nachbild*), representation, witness, image (*imago*) and *analogia: relationis, fidei* and *gratiae*.

Barth explains, in a general way, what he means by correspondence: there is a relationship between God and ourselves which is neither one of parity nor disparity but rather of similarity, of partial correspondence and agreement. This could also be termed a relationship of analogy. Of course given the limitations of language to communicate the absolutely unique event of God's relating to humankind, there can be only a partial correspondence of the word "analogy" itself to the reality of the relationship it indicates since the reality of God is unique, it has no strict analogies, for there is no category of which both terms (God and man) are members, in whole or part, or in any kind of proportion whatsoever.[103] It is a relationship *sui generis*. God is not one of many gods. Our relationship to God is not repeated in relationship to others who are not God. It is essential to remember Barth's acknowledgement of this if he not to be misunderstood. The use of the term analogy will be inadequate to the reality to which he wants to point.[104] Nevertheless, the revelation of the reality revealed,

---

posterior. But this relation was understood by him to be a matter of causation, of being naturally intrinsic by virtue of creation. For Barth, considered theologically *a posteriori*, there could be no such intrinsic comparison. However, according to faith (*analogia gratiae, analogia fidei*) in the transforming, reconciling, action of God's grace in Christ's assumption of our humanity, we may speak of an *analogia entis*. Subsequent to the faithful acknowledgement of the gracious *analogia relationis* we may speak of an *analogia entis*. See CD, 2/1, p. 82 and A. Torrance, *Persons in Communion*, pp. 162–163.

[103] So Thomas Aquinas says: "*Deus non est in genera*" (God does not belong to a genus), *Summa*, 1A. 3, 5.

[104] Robert Jenson, in his book *God After God* (Indianapolis, New York: Bobbs-Merrill Company, 1969), levels a radical critique of Barth when he says that "the relation of what Barth says of our lives as they are in God to what we know and experience of our lives shifts and shimmers. One moment Barth's entire theology seems to be the first wholly existential theology the next moment the whole thing seems a dream having nothing to do with us....This ambiguity results from Barth's retention now within a Christological and trinitarian theology, of an analogy-principle which has its home in a quite different sort of theology. After all "analogous" is just another word for "ambiguous" and to say that we and God are united by "analogies" may only be to say that our relation is ambiguous that he both does and doesn't have to do with us" (p. 92).

It is difficult to see the reason why we should follow Jenson's interpretation of

Jesus Christ, seems to indicate that, of the concepts available, that of analogy may be the most useful one to refer to it.[105]

Barth. The fact, the existence, the reality of our relationship to God is no more ambiguous than the existence of Jesus Christ Himself. Barth does not say that we are united to God by analogies, but by Jesus Christ. What Barth does say is that the kind of relationship which this is, which is actual and real, may be compared analogously to other relationships which also actually exist. The quality of relationships is similar and dissimilar but not the fact of the relationships themselves. Jenson misrepresents Barth's usage of analogy. Barth cannot possibly be taken to mean that God's relation to us is ambiguous such that he may or may not have to do with us. Jenson's interpretation involves the misapplication of Barth's usage of analogy, and also the reduction of analogical predication to equivocal predication. Equivocal predication, in classical terms, is open to the charge of ambiguity, not analogical. To equate these two categories and critique Barth on this basis misrepresents Barth's position. Finally, Jenson clearly cannot decide whether we should interpret the reality of our relation to God on the basis of our own present experience or on the basis of the reality as depicted in the revelation, or at least Barth's representation of revelation. For Barth our actual union with Christ is a given reality and we are to interpret our experience in terms of this. Our experience is not self-interpreting but is obscure. Thus Barth's whole theological method is oriented to the proper ordering of the analogical understanding of our experience. We move from the revelation to our language and experience, not *vice versa*. Jenson has failed to see, or at least assent to, Barth's insistence on this ordering of analogy so that theologically we must first seek to speak of the Christ of our experience rather than our experience of Christ. For only the former will reveal the true status of the latter. (Cf. a recent article of Jenson's on Barth where his reservations about Barth are still detectable but are not discussed. There is no doubt that he has a secure grasp on the importance of Barth's seminal contributions for doing theology now in our [still!] post Enlightenment context. He highlights many of the points we will make in the course of our discussion on Barth's methodology. See, "Karl Barth," *The Modern Theologians*, Vol. I, ed. David F. Ford (Oxford: Basil Blackwell, 1989).

Barth's use of the concept of analogy stirred up considerable debate which remains largely unresolved. We have attempted to make clearer Barth's usage of the concept of analogy. However, given the fact of the continuing debate regarding the concept of analogy, even if there are better and worse ways to use it, we must ask whether the term has outlived its usefulness. It is not clear that it has. If properly qualified, as Alan Torrance has so helpfully done, it certainly can be of theological service. Barth seems to have overstated his case against the *analogia entis* in general. But he has also acknowledged the proper parameters within which even this comparison may be made. Given that accomplishment, the way seems to be clear for a proper usage of the *analogia relationis*.

[105] *CD*, II/1, pp. 237–243, see also p. 226 and p. 75. In his discussion of Quenstedt, Barth suggests that given this discrepancy between the language and the unique reality, a further refinement could be made. Barth thinks that the analogy of extrinsic attribution rather than intrinsic attribution is the most adequate. Others have suggested other modifications. Harold G. Wells, in his article "Karl Barth's Doctrine of Analogy" *Canadian Journal of Theology*, Vol. XV, 3 & 4 (1969), pp. 203–213 suggests "a combination of intrinsic attribution with proportionality in a very carefully defined analogia *entis*" (p. 212) and John McIntyre in his "Analogy" *SJT*, Vol. 12 (1959), pp. 1–20, thinks an analogy of proportionality with a more adequate definition than Barth was

Humanity as Being-in-Communion with Others 135

Since our main concern here is not primarily epistemological, but rather theological, ontological and anthropological, we will be concerned specifically with how Barth sees the relationship between *analogia relationis* and the *imago Dei*. In *Church Dogmatics* III/2 this is the central issue in his discussion.[106]

---

using would be more appropriate. Ultimately what is at stake for Barth is not finding a concept into which the reality of our relationship to God can fit, or the using of certain concepts appropriately, but rather it is letting the reality itself fill out its own definition to which we apply our terms as adequately as possible. Perhaps this is why Barth had to uniquely qualify the term *analogia* with *relationis*. In this move he virtually created another term which is analogous, both related to but also distinct from, the previous history of its usage. Rather than further critique his usage we will attempt to fill it out as completely as possible given Barth's Christological and anthropological explication of it.

[106] We cannot begin to discuss the issues that arise, but can only point out some of them. The literature on this aspect of Barth's theology is extensive. Most of it approaches the issue from the epistemological angle addressing the issue of the nature of theological language and the philosophical and theological history and usage of the related concepts. See for example: Battista Mondin, *The Principle of Analogy in Protestant and Catholic Thought* (The Hague: Martinus Nijhoff, 1963); Hans Urs von Balthasar, *The Theology of Karl Barth*; Jung Young Lee, "Karl Barth's Use of Analogy in His *Church Dogmatics*" *SJT*, Vol. 22 (1969) pp. 129–151; Sueo Oshima "Barth's *Analogia Relationis* and Heidegger's Ontological Difference" *The Journal of Religion*, Vol. 53 (1973), pp. 176–194; Harold G. Wells, "Karl Barth's Doctrine of Analogy" *Canadian Journal of Theology*, Vol. XV, 3 and 4 (1969), pp. 203–213; Christopher Morse "Raising God's Eyebrow's: Some Further Thoughts on the Concept of the *Analogia Fidei* Union Seminary Quarterly Review, Vol. XXXVII, Nos. 1 and 2 (Fall/ Winter, 1981–1982), pp. 39–49; John McIntyre "Analogy," *SJT*, Vol. 12 (1959), pp. 1–20; Horst Georg Pöhlmann *Analogia entis oder Analogia fidei?: Die Frage der analogie bei Karl Barth* (Göttingen: Vandenhoeck & Ruprecht, 1965). Pöhlmann's critique of Barth's total rejection of the Roman Catholic usage of *analogia entis* (See *CD*, I/1, p. x) has been sustained by most of Barth's critics, even sympathetic ones. Although some of Thomas's successors such as Cajetan and Suarez may have understood Being as a *genus* in which God and man participate, Thomas himself did not and specifically says so: "creatures are not related to God as to a thing of a different genus but as to something outside of and prior to all *genera*" (*Summa* 1A. 3, 5). Henri Bouillard in his *Knowledge of God* brings this out (p. 104ff.). In fact some, Lee for example, hold that Barth himself became less polemical and minimized the contrast between it and his *analogia relationis* (*op cit.* p. 132). Barth does acknowledge that there is an appropriate way to render the *analogia entis* as the Roman Catholic, Söhngen, had done (see *CD*, II/1, pp. 81–82).

What becomes clear through the discussion is that for Barth 1) the doctrine of our knowledge of God had to follow from the doctrine and reality of grace and justification (and so God's hiddenness and revealedness) and be analogous with it, and could not follow from some pre-theological ground such as a sharing, even in some secondary way, of being with God, even if there is in some sense something in common; 2) the static and substantival ontology which often accompanied the *analogia entis* is inadequate to the relational and dynamic nature of our knowledge of God. Without continuing relationship with God there would be no knowledge of God; 3) that the movement must be *from* God *to* humankind. God is the one who makes the analogy, who adapts man's being and language to himself and calls for persons to do the same in light of God's own activity and promise, and 4) that Jesus Christ Himself is the analogy

For Barth the conception of human relationships corresponding in some way to the divine-human relationship is a conclusion, rather than a presupposition. Barth, given the terminology and options at hand in the history of theology is "forced to avail [himself] of the concept of analogy..."[107] Barth is seeking a term adequate to the object of faith. This is why he can at times use interchangeably the terms *analogia fidei* or *analogia gratia* with it. A survey of the biblical and Christological grounding of *imago Dei* and *analogia relationis* will further illuminate for us Barth's understanding of faith and grace.

2. The Biblical and Christological Grounding of Humanity as Image

The biblical witness compares God's relationship to humankind with various human relationships: husband to wife, a father and mother to their children, as friend to friend, and as mother and father to a child, etc. In the light of the relationship of God and mankind in Jesus Christ, Barth sees no reason to regard such talk as mythological.[108] There is a real likeness, for all the dissimilarity, of the human relationships with the God-man relationship because they are founded on that original relation with God. The original relations in the Triune life are played out in the creaturely realm in multifaceted ways because creation, reconciliation and redemption are from, through and to the Word to which humanity is united.

There are also explicit references to the likeness of humanity to the man-God relationship. The Old Testament indentifies humankind as being created in the likeness and after the image of God. Furthermore, God commands humankind to exhibit in their relationships the same character as does He: justice, mercy, humility, faithfulness, love and even sanctity. The possibility of correspondence is assumed. In the New Testament there is even greater reason to accept as real the correspondence. There humankind is regarded as created in

---

in person, the essential point of contact in word and being, whatever else we say about our language or being. One of Barth's most significant contributions to the discussion, it seems, is point 3) above. Barth attempted to reverse the direction of making analogies which has characterized much of the history of theology. While Barth has integrated this insight into his theological methodology, he does not make use of Thomas Aquinas's conclusion that our primary use of analogical predication must not be one of proportion which allows bi-directional comparisons, but, rather, must be a unidirectional comparison, one made *unius ad alterum*, or *per prius et posterius*. Barth's arguments have force against Thomists who have lost Aquinas's insight rather than against Aquinas himself. See Alan Torrance, *Persons in Communion,* pp. 127ff., for a comprehensive discussion of the issues.

[107] *CD*, II/1, p. 236.

[108] F. W. Camfield notes the implications of Christology for our ability to speak of God as he has revealed himself and not remain trapped in self-projection, i.e. mythologizing. "In fact all mythologizing is unmasked as such in the conception of the God-man, and branded as idolatry. And it may very well be asked whether all human thinking which rejects the conception of the God-man can be anything more than mythology at last" in *Reformation Old and New (A Tribute to Karl Barth)* (London and Redhill: Lutterworth Press: 1947) p. 85.

the image of God, but even more, as recreated in that image. Human action is to follow after God's action so that men are to forgive as God forgives, are to be holy as God is holy. Specifically persons are directed to imitate God and on many occasions to bear witness in word and deed to the character of God.[109]

Of course, the culmination of this correspondence of relationship is embodied in Jesus Christ who is the Image, the presence of God in humanity. In Him we have complete correspondence of God and His Word with man in our sphere of life.[110] Thus, the one who has made the analogy and made it appropriate is not an autonomous human. God Himself in Jesus Christ has made our human realm adequate to the reality present and revealed in it. Strictly speaking, there is only one true case of analogy in time and space, one point of contact, it is Jesus Christ Himself.[111] This is Barth's most essential point.

Yet, it is He who calls us, and so our words, to correspond to Him and so to God.[112] Thus, we are to do the will of God, participate in his sufferings, share in his righteousness, his union and communion with the Father, His knowledge of and relationship with God, and announce the Gospel of His kingdom. For us to speak analogously is, then, an act of obedience grounded in a promise of God. It is an act of faith in God's grace embodied in Jesus Christ. Humankind arrogates nothing to itself in doing this. It is given this task.[113] In the process of announcing the Kingdom our categories are to be reinterpreted in terms of God's personal revelation. We have this possibility only by God Himself through the Son by the Spirit.

Barth finds no reason to regard the Biblical witness as mythological projections or anthropomorphisms. They are not regarded as such by the witnesses themselves. In fact, just the opposite is presupposed: a tremendous realism of correspondence despite all dissimilarity. Barth will not attempt to demythologize this correspondence of humanity with God. It is the center of the Gospel, it is Jesus Christ Himself, God with us. To dismiss this as mythological

---

[109] Biblical texts abound with comparisons indicating and anticipating a correspondence of human persons in general with the character and actions of God. Barth refers to these from time to time throughout the *Church Dogmatics*. We will list some here in an abbreviated form: be perfect as... (Mt. 5:48); Love one another as... (Jn. 13:34); as I am sent so I send you (Jn 17:18); are all one as... (Jn. 17:21, 22); are loved as... (Jn. 20:21) be imitators as beloved children (Eph. 5:1) imitators as I am of Christ (I Cor. 11:1); become imitators of us and of the Lord (I Thess. 1:6); as death and resurrection came so... (I Cor. 15:21f.); forgive as... (Eph. 4:32); love as Christ loved us (Eph. 5:2); head as Christ, love as Christ, nourish as Christ (Eph. 5:23, 25, 29); and the theme of copy or shadow and reality throughout the book of Hebrews.

[110] *CD*, II/1, p. 150.

[111] See *CD*, I/1, pp. 53–54, 273, 447; II/1, pp. 61, 75, 223, 229, 232, 235. "He is the One who will appropriate us, and in so doing permit and command and...adapt us to appropriate Him as well" (II/1, p. 188).

[112] *CD*, II/1, pp. 230–232. Barth's most in-depth discussion on analogy is in II/1, pp. 227–247.

[113] *CD*, II/1, pp. 231–232.

projection is to empty the Gospel of its reality. And following this, one could only substitute another mythology which would appear, for the moment, to be less mythological and possibly more real. But this will be at the expense of the reality of the biblical witness, not in correspondence with it.

3. The Analogia Relationis *is the* Imago Dei

What this indicates is that the biblical witness points to a correspondence of relationships grounded in Christ as the essential analogy, not a correspondence of being abstracted and somehow lived out apart from such relationships. Thus, Barth speaks of an *analogia relationis* and not of an *analogia entis*.[114] There is a similarity and dissimilarity between the relationship of God to man and the relationship of persons to persons. It is the analogy of the relationships Christologically determined that are of ultimate concern for Barth. The biblical witness does not attempt to address the issue of some kind of ontology apart from an an ontology of God and mankind in relationship.[115] There is a relationship of correspondence between the relationships.

> But for all the disparity—and this is the positive sense of the term "image"—there is a correspondence and similarity between the two relationships. This is not a correspondence and similarity of being, an *analogia entis*. The being of God cannot be compared with that of man. But it is not a question of this twofold being [Father and Son]. It is a question of the relationship within the being of God on the one side and between the being of God and that of man on the other. Between these two relationships as such—and it is in this sense that the second is the

---

[114] See just above and note 16 in Chapter Four for a discussion of Barth's usage of the terms *analogia entis* and *analogia relationis*.

[115] We will not attempt to resolve the debate as to whether, as several have suggested, the *analogia relationis* presupposes *analogia entis* and or necessarily excludes it if not presupposed. See Lee, "Barth's Use of Analogy" for a survey of the options and his evaluation. Our view is that Barth has not absolutely dismissed some kind of similarity of the being of humanity in general which might be spoken of *subsequent* to reconciliation, faith and redemption in Jesus Christ by the Holy Spirit. He has on the one hand, however, rendered any such comparison of being, outside of faith, as totally speculative and totally inadequate for grounding any knowledge of God. On the other hand, from within faith, he has radically relativised its significance theologically, since the ultimate and overriding concern of the biblical witness to the Word is the Word itself and the relationships actualized there. In Jesus Christ being can only be understood in terms of the God-man and man-man relationships, and not *vice versa*. So while it may be argued that, given Jesus Christ and our being in Him, there must be some analogy of being, Barth's point is that even within faith this is an unhelpful abstraction and detraction from the (relational) reality of our being in Jesus Christ. Outside of an ongoing living relationship with God by the Spirit of Jesus there can be no correspondence at all. Deism is ruled out all together. This is Barth's way of acknowledging the theological uselessness of pure metaphysical substantival speculation, while maintaining a concrete relational and dynamic ontology of humanity in Jesus Christ.

image of the first—there is a correspondence and similarity. There is an *analogia relationis*.[116]

As such there is an original relationship and its reflection or copy. This relational image corresponds in a such a way that it may lead one from the copy to the original relationship. It is similar in that one leads to the other. It is dissimilar such that there is no confusion of that which is the copy and that which is the original relationship. The image that bears this kind of witness is the kind of analogy or correspondence to which Barth refers.[117] This distinction and ordering of the *analogatum* by the *analogans* is the crucial distinction for Barth because it follows the pattern of our justification by God's grace.[118] Our relationship to God and so the obedience of our speaking about God is possible only because of the grace of God. There is an essential asymmetry within the analogy.[119]

4. John 17: The Central Christological Grounding

His whole exposition of *analogia relationis* is Christologically grounded in Jesus' own understanding of the relationship between his relationship with the Father, his relationship with the disciples and their relationship with him and the Father by the Spirit. Barth refers specifically to the Gospel of John, Chapter 17. Here he finds the revelation of an original relationship of the Son with the Father which exists before His presence in the creaturely sphere of the world in Jesus. In this sphere the relationship of glory is to be repeated in Jesus' relationship to his disciples[120] and through their relationships to the world. "There could be no plainer reference to the *analogia relationis* and therefore the *imago Dei* in the most central, i.e., the Christological sense of the term."[121]

Here we have a concise grounding for the *analogia* and see how it is an interpretation of the, strictly speaking, more theological term *imago Dei*. Having defined what Barth means by the term *analogia relationis* and those related to it we can consider how it is that humanity does correspond within the creaturely sphere to the relationship of God to man in Jesus and the intra-trinitarian relations revealed in Him. We will briefly consider three spheres of human interrelationship. In marriage, in persons generally, and in the Church.

---

[116] *CD*, III/2, p. 220.

[117] *Ibid.*, pp. 219–222.

[118] *CD*, II/1, pp. 238ff.

[119] As noted above and in Chapter Four, this essential asymmetry and unidirectionality of theological analogy was indicated by Aquinas in his concern that primary analogy is not proportional but *unius ad alterum, per prius et posterius*. See Alan Torrance, *Persons in Communion*, pp. 135–142 for his discussion of the recovery of Aquinas's true position.

[120] *CD*, III/2, p. 220.

[121] *Ibid.*, p. 221.

Human Relationships as Image and Witness

1. I and Thou, Imaging One Another

In human relationships which bear witness to God's own relationships there is an imaging of one by the other. The one comes to know the other and himself by mirroring the other and seeing him/herself in the mirror of the other. This turns out to be not only a matter of knowing, but also a matter of being and becoming. Who one becomes is necessarily conditioned by the nature of the imaging that does or does not take place. This is of course primarily true in our relationship with God in Jesus Christ but is essentially true, if secondarily so, in our person to person relationships as well.

The most succinct development of this theme, although it is implicit in many places, occurs in Barth's three part explication of I and Thou and the following discussion of the four essential characteristics of humanity as being-in-encounter: seeing, hearing and speaking, assisting, and relating with gladness. We will not go over this again but will only point out the reciprocal nature of these seven characteristics of humanity in relationship. This is most clearly seen in his discussion of seeing eye to eye when he says "We give each other something in our duality, and this is that I and Thou are men. We give each other an insight into our being...This moment, this mutual look, is in some sense the root-formation of all humanity without which the rest is impossible."[122] In terms of mutual expression and hearing and mutual address and hearing we come to recognize that "I am for him the sum of something objective which he needs as a subject but which is in the first instance unattainable, being concealed in me...I have something decisive for him to give him."[123] Furthermore, there is danger in refusing to be in encounter: "Do I see what is really at stake? It is really a matter of myself. I cannot be I without accepting this claim of the other, without letting him come to me, and therefore without hearing him...I am affected myself if I do not hear him, and do so in all seriousness."[124]

Thus, by being in encounter as I and Thou mutually seeing, speaking, assisting and rejoicing in the other, we thereby serve each other by reflecting one another and so assisting each other in knowing and being known in the process of becoming who we are determined to be in Jesus Christ. We are to be to each other images and witnesses. And this is a further witness to Jesus Christ who originally shows us the Father and ourselves that we might become, through our dynamic relationship with Him, all that we are given to be in Him.

2. Marriage as Image and Witness

For Barth, following the biblical witness, marriage is "a typical representation of fellow-humanity, and therefore of man's determination as the

---

[122] *CD*, III/2, pp. 251–252.
[123] *Ibid.*, pp. 256–257.
[124] *Ibid.*, pp. 258–259.

covenant partner of God."[125] In the covenant relationship of marriage a man and woman live out a mutual and ordered relationship in which each mirrors and gives of themselves to the other that which they don't have in themselves. They may discover the meaning of creaturely, life-long history of union and the meaning of the polarity of their being in relationship as man and woman. The marriage relationship is uniquely an image in that the otherness of the partners, and so the obviousness of one having and being what the other is not (male and female), and of one being able to reflect to the other that which the other cannot of itself know or see in its own self-reflection, is acknowledged and structurally represented in a unique way in a life-long relationship of faithfulness. The duality points out and holds promise of each becoming completed through, and only through, mutual self-giving.

In this way the marital relationship is a type or representation[126] of God's own covenant relation with humankind. It bears unique witness to the absolute otherness and faithfulness of God and our need for His self-giving and exchange required for our completion and which occurs within the history of His covenant relationship with us. We may see how this is so when we consider how Barth describes marriage.

MARRIAGE AS AN IMAGE AND WITNESS

1) It is a vocation taken on freely by man and woman taken up on the basis of a God-given permission and so an obligation. It is an elected and so covenanted life-partnership between a particular man and woman such that the pair becomes "We."[127]

2) The fulfillment of this life-partnership is a task to be accomplished, an end in itself, the perfecting of this fellowship.[128]

3) It is a total and all-embracing fellowship of life together, a complete togetherness, a unity of life, so that each discovers a freedom in this fellowship with and for the other. This is no fusion of persons, but a true becoming of one's self in total mutual relationship. It is an unity of distinct persons.[129]

4) It is an exclusive life-partnership at the center of its existence as it seeks its fulfillment in the freedom of fellowship in the conviction that they belong to each other and are so meant for each other.[130]

5) It is a lasting life-partnership for all their common future.[131]

6) Marriage has its roots, its genesis, in the freedom of God's own election of grace and so is grounded in the being and action of God Himself, in the self-

---

[125] *CD*, III/4, p. 143.
[126] *Ibid.*
[127] *Ibid.*, pp. 183–187.
[128] *Ibid.*, pp. 187–189.
[129] *Ibid.*, pp. 189–195.
[130] *Ibid.*, pp. 195–203.
[131] *Ibid.*, pp. 203–213.

giving of God. Thus, marriage is the reflection of the love of self-giving culminating in a creaturely union, it is an act of obedient faith in this Covenant God.[132]

7) It must also have the character of a responsible act outwards in relation to those around. It is not a purely private undertaking, an egoistic partnership, but is to be an outward witness and help moving out into wider circles including extended family, the greater society, and most significantly the life of the Church, the Christian community.[133]

In each dimension of the covenant-relation of marriage noted above Barth brings out the corresponding reality of the covenant-relation of God with man in Jesus Christ. It should be noted that in this definition of marriage we not only see that marriage is an image but that, as an image, it reflects all six of the determinations of humanity as we have outlined. We will not comment on this as it should now be obvious enough.

3. Imaging: The Universal and Unchanged Form of Humanity

But we should note that Barth does not indicate that it is exclusively within marriage that we have a type of God's own relationship with His people. Rather, it is "only one possibility which might be exploited" to explore how, on the creaturely plane, humanity in its relationships may witness to its divine source. Mankind is to bear witness to this original relationship in all human relationships, even if they may be limited in some ways compared to the marital relationship. What is required of faithful obedience is that it utilize the freedom which it is granted, not that it take on **every** vocation and so responsibility, e.g. marriage.

From this perspective perhaps we can see more clearly why Barth also said that the image of God in humanity was not lost.[134] First, it cannot be conceived of as a kind of possession. It is a relational reality. Thus, it is improper, from the start, to say that mankind had/possessed this image. The image is a relational reality which must be a continually renewed gift of being-in-relationship, first and primarily with God and then similarly with others. So the image cannot be a quality or attribute of man.[135] As such, the *imago* is God's intention and purpose for humankind.[136] This was never put into question or rendered void,

---

[132] *Ibid.*, pp. 213–224.

[133] *Ibid.*, pp. 224–229.

[134] *CD*, III/2, p. 324.

[135] *CD*, III/1, p. 184.

[136] See II/2, p. 566 where Barth indicates that the restoration of the likeness is the restoration of fellowship and that this is the *telos* of grace. Cf. III/1, p. 200. In I/1, p. 273, Barth says that the image of God was "annihilated." He is using the term in that context in a restricted sense, speaking from the point of view of man himself. It refers there to "man's capacity for God." In the same context he indicates that something is preserved of the man, his *recta natura*, which is his humanity and personality. In his *Table Talk*, p. 41, Barth clarifies that the *recta natura* is not the image of God. Rather he indicates that even here man retains his humanity and does not become inhuman

by the Fall. The sin of man cannot undo the gracious determination of God.[137]

This means that humankind was not created *as* the image itself, but "to be in correspondence with the image of God,"[138] that is, in correspondence with Jesus Christ, the Image itself. Jesus alone possesses the image because in this image the reality itself is present. He alone *is* the image.[139] We will be changed, "converted" to have a share in this image.[140] The upshot of this is that the question as to whether there *is* a point of contact or how does man as man image God are made relatively unimportant. The most important question is, how might mankind become the image of God in his relationships. God's intention is that humankind *become* analogous to the Image of His Son, Jesus Christ.[141]

---

although in sin. "Man remains man, even as a sinner." Later, in III/2, Barth seems to enlarge and somewhat adjust his usage of the term "image" viewed from the more comprehensive perspective of God. There he says, "God is in relationship, and so too is the man created by Him. This is his divine likeness....It is not lost" (p. 324). What is lost is not exactly the image, but his ongoing faithful relationship with God. In his *Table Talk*, he clarifies that "What man has lost in the Fall is his *faith*, not some ontological relation. He has lost his relation as an obedient child of God and has gone out of *analogia fidei*" (p. 39). The interaction is disrupted. This does not mean that man has no relationship with his Creator, but rather that it is radically disrupted from his side to his own eternal peril. However, the gracious purpose of God remains and thus man remains in the presence of his God and so is sustained even in his sin (III/2, pp. 27–28). It was never in man's capacity, however, either to maintain or renew this relationship. Thus the relationship is established, maintained, and so must be renewed by man's Creator, Reconciler and Redeemer.

[137] *CD*, III/1, p. 200.
[138] *Ibid.*, pp. 201–203.
[139] *Ibid.*, p. 197.
[140] *Ibid.*, p. 239.
[141] *CD*, III/2, p. 52; III/1, p. 202; IV/3, p. 770. This makes the quest for the image as some sort of given substantival aspect of an individual person a relatively misconstrued theological task. The being of humankind, much less its particular characteristics, is constituted by its relationships. The question of what humankind is and becomes in the action of its relationships is far more significant than describing some theoretically neutral capacity that individuals might or might not have. In this understanding of the *imago* Barth is of course departing from most of Roman Catholic and Protestant theological tradition which identifies the *imago* with the nature of an individual and various aspects of his given being, such as rationality.

We will not attempt to resolve the infamous debate between Barth and Emil Brunner. See their "dialogue" in *Natural Theology*, trans. P. Fraenkel, (London: Geoffrey Bles, 1949) and Brunner's "The New Barth. Observations on Karl Barth's *Doctrine of Man*," *SJT*, Vol. 2, No. 4 (1951), pp. 123–135. We can make some response to Brunner's article. 1) To his question as to how creation and redemption are related for Barth, it is clear that they are not 'identical' as Brunner fears. They are analogically related. The One God with one purpose, fellowship with humankind, creates and redeems and renews man with this in mind. They are two works united without confusion of the One God differentiated as Father and Son with the one purpose for creation and redemption. 2) As to Barth's indication that all are in Christ, Brunner fails to appreciate (and acknowledges his 'incapacity to understand,' p. 132) how and why

This is a matter of humankind's action (in response to God's gracious action) in relationship to Him and secondarily to others, rather than a losing or gaining some attribute, quality or possession.[142]

4. Humanity: Imaging the Trinitarian Communion

What is more generally seen in the creation of all humankind for being in relationship and is particularly poignant in the marital relationship is its being an image which has its final grounding in the trinitarian fellowship of Father, Son, and Spirit. Thus, Barth concludes his section on "Humanity as Likeness and Hope":

> As man generally is modelled on the man Jesus and His being for others, and as the man Jesus is modelled on God, it has to be said of man generally that he is created in the image of God. He is in his humanity, and therefore in his fellow-humanity. God created him in His own image in the fact that He did not create him alone but in this connexion and fellowship. For in God's action as the Lord of the

---

Barth speaks as he does. Barth will call 'real' our condition as it is to be understood in Christ. We *are* reconciled-sinners—both. Man as separate unreconciled sinner is not the final NT interpretation of humanity. For Barth, faith is man's participation in his determination. Faith does not change mankind's actual situation, but is his participation in that situation. God determines the actual. Brunner's insistence(?) on describing humanity's situation in terms of his own action (having or lacking faith) is an anthropological perspective which Barth believes is untrue to the situation. Barth allows that not all participate in their election and that all are not a part of the Church, not all are Christians. But he will not describe humankind's actual situation from this vantage point. Barth insists on a Christological exposition of the ontological situation of humankind in spite of their response which can only affirm or deny the truth, but not change the truth of God's grace. Barth believes this squares with the biblical witness. Thus there is a difference as to what is meant by their respective notions of a Christological point of departure. 3) As to Barth's question to Brunner about the separation of form and content things remain unclear. While Barth insists on the unity of form and content in most every case, so that there can be neither a formal aspect of the imago left after the Fall nor a content of righteousness and obedience. However, in "Christ and Adam" (1956) Barth considers man from the perspective of two different sets of form and content (Man in Adam: death, and man in Christ: life) on the basis of Romans 5:12–21. The difference comes in the "how much more." What Barth discerns in the end is that "it is obvious that sin is subordinate to grace, and that it is grace that has the last word about the true nature of man" (p. 15). So it is not so much the relation of form and content that is the deciding issue, but the ordering of one set to another. Brunner insists on emphasizing man in Adam, Barth on man in Christ. For Barth the relationship between them (and so creation and redemption) is analogical: related, differentiated *and ordered*. Here is the continuity yet discontinuity yet final truth of humankind. Barth's final response to Brunner may very well be that there is certainly a place for the description of humankind in Adam, but it cannot be given the final place.

[142] Already Barth anticipates the dynamic and eschatological dimensions of relationship in this actional and relational conception of the *imago*.

covenant, and even further back in His action as the Creator of a reality distinct from Himself, it is proved that God Himself is not solitary, that although He is one in essence He is not alone, but that primarily and properly He is in connexion and fellowship. It is inevitable that we should recall the triune being of God at this point. God exists in relationship and fellowship. As the Father of the Son and the Son of the Father He is Himself I and Thou, confronting Himself and yet always one and the same in the Holy Ghost. God created man in His own image, in correspondence with His own being and essence. He created him in the image which emerges even in His work as the Creator and Lord of the covenant. Because He is not solitary in Himself, and therefore does not will to be so *ad extra* it is not good for man to be alone, and God created him in His own image, as male and female. This is what is emphatically said by Gen. 1:27, and all other explanations of the *imago Dei* suffer from the fact that they do not do justice to this decisive statement. We need not waste words on the dissimilarity in the similarity of the similitude. Quite obviously we do not have here more than an analogy, i.e., similarity in dissimilarity. We merely repeat that there can be no question of an analogy of being, but of relationship. God is in relationship, and so too is the man created by Him. This is his divine likeness.[143]

Thus, in the fact that we exist in the nexus of inter-human relations, we may see humanity imaging God's relation with his people in Jesus Christ. Further, this is a reflection of the inner Triune life of Father, Son and Spirit as a history of interaction of covenant love in unity of essence and distinction of persons that immeasurably exceeds its creaturely representation, but which nevertheless bears witness to this Triune Covenantal God of Jesus Christ.[144]

5. Imaging: The Church as Representative and Witness

Although in this section (III/2) Barth does not develop the concept of Israel and the Church being the image of God, he does so in depth later (in Volume IV) and has anticipated it earlier. In *CD*, II/2 it is the one community of Jesus Christ, in two forms, which is essentially elect. Because the community is elect, individuals are therefore necessarily elect, but only as members of His community, and not otherwise. They are essentially called to be in relationship with God and fellow humans and are not called otherwise. Thus, the relational purpose and ontology of humanity was already anticipated in Barth's understanding of election. They both exist to the end of attesting to Jesus Christ and representing God's judgment and mercy and man's hearing and believing, a

---

[143] *CD*, III/2, p. 324.

[144] As Alan Torrance puts it, there is not a vestige of the Trinity in humanity, but rather, a *vestigia creaturae in Trinitatis*, a vestige of the creature in the Trinity! *Persons in Communion*, p. 209.

passing provisional form and an anticipatory waiting form.[145] As communities they represent or image the relational character of humanity to the whole world and so summon the whole world into that one community. This community "points beyond itself to the fellowship of all men." Verne Fletcher summarizes Barth's exposition in IV/3.2 and says that the Church "makes visible and fulfils in a normative manner the basic human form of co-humanity."[146] Jesus is "fitting [the Church] to give a provisional representation of the sanctification of all humanity...as it has taken place in Him."[147]

In this task we should note further that the Church's mission is to bear witness to the state and help it to realize its "analogical capacities."[148] The state is also called to correspond to the coming kingdom. This can be true because Jesus is "the eternal brother and arch-type of every man."[149]

Thus, we can see that Jesus is both the Image of God for us and also within the trinitarian life. For humanity to be also an image of this Image it must be a fellowship, that is, essentially be His community. The Church, as a corporate witness to the Triune God of Jesus Christ, represents this God and His calling for all humankind to participate in that fellowship created in Him. It may thereby become an image of that Image in every dimension of human existence, even in those societal relationships (such as the State) which do not participate in the life of the Church, *per se*.

Theological Ethics as Image and Witness

1. Humanity as the Priest of All Creation as It Bears Witness to God

Barth does not limit the correspondence of humanity to just the sphere of inter-gender interactions. What he notes is that all human activity is done by either a male or a female person and so to a certain degree as a male or female. Therefore, what is true for that which is indicated even in the marital relationship applies *mutatis mutandis* to all human interactions. In fact it applies to humankind's relationship to creation as a whole.

The fact that creation is a reality distinct from God yet upheld in its existence in absolute dependence upon Him is a sign of God's own true being.

---

[145] *CD*, II/2, pp. 195–205. See also II/2, pp. 309–316.

[146] See his "Barth's Concept of Co-Humanity and the Search for Human Community" *South East Asia Journal of Theology*, Vol. 9, No. 1 (July, 1967), p. 49. This is an excellent overview of the whole of the *Church Dogmatics* and some additional addresses which Barth gave, but especially Part IV. Here again we anticipate our discussion of the extension of relationship to the end of inclusion in the acknowledgement of the representative mission of the Church. See also *CD*, IV/1, p. 41; IV/2, pp. 31, 275, 661–666, 690–719.

[147] *CD*, IV/2, p. 614.

[148] *Ibid.*, p. 168. See also Barth's 1956 address "The Humanity of God" in *The Humanity of God* (Atlanta: John Knox Press, 1974), where he indicates the universal scope of the Church's witness is that "the Church is the place where man's co-humanity may become visible in Christocratic brotherhood" (p. 65).

[149] *CD*, IV/2, p. 269.

Although the revelation only indicates how it is that humankind is created in the image of God, and so specially created to recognize and participate in being and becoming this image, humankind is given in faith the capacity to recognize God, on behalf of all creation, in all His works. So Barth says,

> creation denotes the divine action which has a real analogy, a genuine point of comparison, only in the eternal begetting of the Son by the Father, and therefore only in the inner life of God Himself, and not at all in the life of the creature.[150]

God's act of Creation does indeed have an analogy. It bears witness to the begetting of the Son by the Father. Humankind is to be a kind of priest over all creation bearing further witness to all creation as to how all of creation, including human persons, do indeed reflect the Creator, Reconciler and Redeemer of all creation revealed in the only begotten Son of God.

2. Jesus Christ: the Correspondence of Loving God and Neighbor

Our concern here is to point out that for Barth all humanity's being and so behavior in relation to all persons and even the non-personal aspects of creation are to correspond to his relationship with God. This is the place where what is usually called theological ethics has its origin. Ethics, for Barth, is grounded ontologically in God, the God-man relation in Jesus, and so in our horizontal relationships with one another.

There is, of course, similarity, difference and an ordering of the human copy of good and loving action by the divine original in Jesus Christ. The two-fold command to love God and the second "like" (ὁμοία) the first, to love neighbor, brings this out (Mt. 22:39). And if we are to designate a *locus classicus* in Barth's work for the *analogia relationis* we could do no better than this discussion of the relationship of the love of God and love of neighbor in the *Church Dogmatics*.

> It is clear that Jesus did not regard love for God and love for the neighbour as separate but conjoined. Yet they are not identical...God is not the neighbour, nor the neighbour God...A true exposition can only speak of a genuinely twofold, i.e., a distinct but connected sphere and sense of the one love required of man. It has reference to God, but also the neighbour...It finds in the Creator the One who points it to its creature, fellow-man. And it finds in this creature, fellow-man, the one who points it to the Creator...Thus, the structure of the humanity of Jesus Himself is revealed in this two-fold command. It repeats the unity of His divinity and humanity as this is achieved without admixture or change, and yet also without separation or limitation.[151]

---

[150] *CD*, III/1, p. 14.
[151] *CD*, III/2, pp. 216–217.

We find here again the grammar of both the form and content of humanity's being-in-relationship in Jesus' fulfillment of the two-fold commandment which reflects and so bears witness to his very being. The commands of God are grounded in the personal being-in-relation of Jesus Christ, that is in the unity, differentiation and ordering of his love for humanity on the basis of his love for the Father. This is the basis of theological ethics. The being of man is created to become the image of God, and so must reflect love in all his actions towards God and his neighbor, the latter being analogous to and so ordered by it, so as to bear witness to the loving humanity and divinity of Jesus Christ.

> An active life lived in obedience must obviously consist in a correspondence to divine action. We are careful not to say in a continuation or development of divine action. All continuations and developments of divine action are still divine and not human actions. We are concerned with the sanctification of human life, not, like pagans and fanatics, with its deification. But in the sanctification of human life we are necessarily dealing with the restoration of a correspondence of human action to divine. God commands, and by His commanding He sanctifies human life.[152]

3. The Basis of Ethical Imperative: the Indicative of God's Gracious Self-Giving

Because humanity is determined by God in Jesus Christ, so is the good of human action. That Jesus Christ is for us, with us, from us and to us means that He is God's unreserved giving of Himself to us. This has irrevocably altered our situation. The consequence of this is that, "I am not my own but belong to my faithful Saviour, Jesus Christ."[153] Consequently, it is "the obligation which derives automatically from the gift that He has made us Himself....All this is actual in Jesus Christ."[154] "It is the fact that God is for him which binds and commits man himself, and that unconditionally."[155] Since God is for humankind, humanity is irrevocably determined to be for God.

4. Ethics: Becoming the Image that We Are in Jesus Christ

Another way Barth demonstrates the Christological/trinitarian grounding of ethics is in his speaking of the indicative of grace as being also an imperative for humanity. This is parallel to our previous discussion of the indicative of election having within it the call to responsive hearing, speaking and a history of covenant relationship.

> As the one Word of God which is the revelation and work of His grace reaches us, its aim is that our being and action should be conformed to His."Be ye (literally, ye shall be) therefore perfect (literally, directed to

---

[152] *CD*, III/4, p. 474.
[153] *CD*, II/2, p. 562.
[154] *Ibid.*, p. 557.
[155] *Ibid.*, p. 597.

your objective), even as (i.e., corresponding to it in creaturely-human fashion as) your Father which is in heaven is perfect (directed to His objective)" (Mt. 5:48). The truth of the evangelical indicative means that the full stop with which it concludes becomes an exclamation mark. It becomes itself an imperative.[156]

The fact of the grace of God calls forth, summons, man's conformity to this reality.[157] Thus, Barth will, upon many occasions, say that humanity is to become what it actually is in Jesus Christ. In the Old Testament "Everything Israel shall do is only an imperative transcription of what Israel is, repeating in some sense only what Israel has become by God."[158] In the New Testament, e.g. Titus 3:4–7, we hear of one and the same aim: "...that we should be what we may and therefore ought to be in its sphere and under its order and authority."[159]

5. Grace: No Ground for Ethical Inactivity or Disobedience

The fact of the determination of who we are is no ground for inaction, but rather is the only sufficient ground for our action. The fact that humankind is the covenant-partner of God means

> in concrete terms that He directs him to his fellow-man. He wills that man's being should fulfil itself in the encounter, the relationship, the togetherness of I and Thou. He commands him, invites him and challenges him not merely to allow his humanity as fellow-humanity to be his nature, but to affirm and exercise it in his own decision, in action and omission. He commands him to be what he is.[160]

The corresponding action or obedience of humankind in correspondence with who he is by the grace of God does not offer him an option for disobedience.[161]

---

[156] *CD*, II/2, p. 512.

[157] The 1935 paper "Gospel and Law" in *God, Grace and Gospel* (Edinburgh, London: Oliver and Boyd, 1959) Barth summarizes quite well his crucial understanding of Grace and Law as indicative and imperative, God's gracious action "aimed at *our* action, at getting our action into conformity with His." The command by grace becomes a promise: 'Thou shalt be!' (p. 9).

[158] *CD*, II/2, p. 572.

[159] *Ibid.*, p. 607.

[160] *CD*, III/4, p. 116.

[161] "We can only will to be what we are in Jesus Christ or we will not be. It does not therefore give me the choice between obedience and disobedience as if they were two possibilities. The disobedience open to me can only be utterly unnatural... impossible...excluded" (*CD*, II/2, p. 610).

6. The Freedom of Obedience, not a Choice Among Options

The freedom of obedience is the faith to obey. The command of God is uniquely a "permission—the granting of a very definite freedom."[162] Consequently, "When we obey we do the only thing we are freed to do; the thing that we can do only in real freedom. We can be disobedient only as we are not free. Disobedience is not a choice, but the incapacity of the man who is no longer or not yet able to choose in real freedom."[163]

Our obedience then does not fundamentally change our situation. It adds nothing to what we are determined to be in Jesus Christ. Our obedience is an "endorsement" by our action of the obedience of Jesus Christ for us.[164]

7. Bearing Witness, the Ethics of Being a Covenant-Partner with the Triune God and Humankind

In this way the obedience of humankind, corresponding to the obedience of Jesus which establishes the identity of humanity, has the character of being an image and witness, essentially bearing the witness that "we belong to God."[165] The grace of God constitutes His claim upon us. It creates a relationship of covenant between God and man and so determines man to exist in this covenant and so to be a partner with God.[166]

a. A Participation in God's Action, not a Repetition

To take responsibility is to respond to the grace of God. This does not mean that we continue or repeat God's action. There is a distinction to be made. God's action "demands only that he [man] should attest to it in definite deeds and attitudes which correspond to it."[167] To the extent that our actions do correspond, they are not identical with God's action but are a participation in God's action. In this movement there is involvement in a real relationship. "We are made covenant-partners for a share in His own work, so a witness to Jesus Christ, as a person, not a thing, a partner. The question arises as to the human self-determination which corresponds to [God's] determination of him. How is he going to exist under it?"[168]

b. Ethical Reflection: a Being-in-Fellowship of the Community of Faith

Consistent with this, Barth indicates that even the process of determining the command of God must correspond to his determination as co-humanity if it is to be free and faithful witness. This means that discernment is the task of the

---

[162] CD, II/2, p. 584–585.

[163] Ibid., p. 779.

[164] Ibid., p. 540. In his "The Gift of Freedom: Foundation of Evangelical Faith," *The Humanity of God* (Atlanta: John Knox Press, 1974), Barth reflects on God's gift of freedom to mankind which is "a divine calling to human action" as His creature and partner.

[165] Ibid., p. 632.

[166] Ibid., pp 575–576.

[167] Ibid., pp. 577–79.

[168] Ibid., pp. 509–510.

believing community, not the isolated individual with his conscience, even though in the end the individual must shoulder his own responsibility. He must be open to others for assistance, speaking and listening, and this gladly.[169]

Thus, it is as Barth considers humanity as a correspondence to the reality of his existence as a being-in-relationship (originally and primarily with his Creator, and so similarly with his fellow-humanity), that we have the most comprehensive description of the form of humanity. This constitutes a description of humankind as created in the image of the Image, Jesus Christ and so created to be a witness to the Creator in His being and action.

Summary: Theological and Anthropological Ethics

In this section we can see how Barth's ethics is not only a theological ethics, but is an anthropological ethics as well. The action of humankind is good and right as long as it is a conformity to **who** mankind is. Ethics is ontologically grounded. Since the ontology of humankind is relationally grounded in its relationship with its Creator, Reconciler and Redeemer, we can say that his ethics is theologically and relationally grounded. The correspondence called for by God is not then externally imposed, but is intrinsically given in and with the being of humankind.

The foundation for a theological ethics is our ontological union with Christ, whether it is acknowledged or not. This is the most basic stumbling block for interpreters of Barth's ethics. Those who cannot follow Barth's insistence that we order our analogies from the original to the copy so that we understand ourselves and our relationships in terms of God and His relationship with us in Jesus Christ cannot grasp, it seems, what he is saying.

We have already pointed out Robert Jenson's critique that, in relation to "what we know and experience of our lives," what Barth says of our lives "as they are in God" "shifts and shimmers" and "seems a dream having nothing to do with us." His perspective, of course, assumes that we know perfectly well the true nature of our life and experience. It is the nature of our relationship with God which must conform to this knowledge. For Barth the exact opposite is true. What we know of our relation to God is what is real, actual, transparent—not our own understanding of our lives grasped apart from that truth in Christ. While both would undoubtedly agree that coming to the knowledge of the truth about ourselves and God is a process, the direction and priority of which interprets which is the opposite.

Barth, and many of those who criticize his ethics, seem to be at an impasse. The basic conflict, however is not over the ethical conclusions themselves but rather over the acceptance or rejection of the given reality of our real union with Christ. For example, the interpreter of Barth's ethics, Robert Willis, regards such an ontological union as allowing for "an absorption" of humanity and suggests

---

[169] *Ibid.*, p. 611.

that man is only "deficiently person and agent."[170] This interpretation misses the crucial nature of our union with Christ, a personal and covenantal unity, distinction and correspondence. Without grasping the nature of this relationship, ethical behavior will tend to be understood, even within an otherwise Christian frame, as either heteronomy and absorption or autonomy, with Christ essentially serving as no more than an example.

A few have recognized the nature of the relation between the ontological union with Christ and ethics. Thomas Oden sees Christian ethics grounded in "the new man created by God's decision."[171] He sees that the obedience of Jesus Christ constitutes the divine predetermination [which raises] the question of human determination. The election of God calls for and enables a fitting response" and raises the question as to how he will exist under this determination. Thus, "man's obedience to God is always a total self-determination under the total determination of God's summons." Furthermore, there is "nothing logically inconsistent about deciding to will the decision of another." "One can choose to be the man God has chosen him to be." This need not involve, observes Oden, a loss of the human subject, substance, freedom or make him a mechanism.[172]

Paul Lehmann is another who has made his way clear through Barth. He sees that Christian ethics must be grounded in "what God is doing in the world to make and to keep human life human, in other words, to bring to pass a new humanity."[173] In view of the fact that the first Adam must be interpreted in terms of the Second Adam, Christ, Christology is the norm of anthropology.

> The doctrine of the Second Adam thus fortifies the christological focus and foundation of behaviour in a twofold way. In the first place, the doctrine of the Second Adam means that it is the new humanity which is at once the subject and the aim or goal of ethical action. This new humanity is a present, not a mere future, reality. It has already become a fact with the reality of the life, death, and resurrection of Jesus Christ. Christian behavior is behavior with a *forward* look, not a backward look. And the actions which make up this behavior are significant not in themselves but as pointers to or bearers of the new humanity which in Christ has become a fact in the world and in which, in consequence of what Christ is and is doing in the world, we participate.[174]

Our actual transformation through our renewed relationship with God through Jesus Christ, at an ontological level, comprises the ultimate theological

---

[170] Robert Willis, *The Ethics of Karl Barth* (Leiden: Brill, 1971), p. 433.

[171] Thomas Oden, *The Promise of Barth* (Philadelphia, New York: J. B. Lippincott Co., 1969) p. 73.

[172] *Ibid.*, pp. 47–48.

[173] *Ethics in a Christian Context*, p. 117.

[174] *Ibid.*, p. 119.

grounding for both his anthropology and his ethics. To grasp Barth's contribution and his explication requires the acknowledgement of this nexus of the theological, anthropological and ethical.

Those who have failed to take into account this entire framework, which itself is a critique of all other frameworks, cannot comprehend the truth and reality Barth is attempting to convey. The often repeated critiques of Barth are that his ethics make no sense, have no import, are unscientific or are unreliable. These critiques appear accurate to the extent that Barth's critics refuse to interpret his ethics in terms of his own theological anthropological framework and attempt to use their own alien framework to comprehend Barth's presentation. Barth's ethical reflections do then appear to some degree to be "senseless" and do not often serve the ends of alien frameworks. A refusal at the outset to allow one's own framework to be challenged and the insistence that Barth's ethical conclusions be evaluated within a framework alien to them leads to a hopeless situation. Barth's essential contribution *is* the new framework out of which he develops his ethical considerations.

Given this ontological and relational framework for doing any further ethical consideration, we will go on to interpret his section on "Parents and Children" within it. In this way we can come to fully appreciate and understand Barth's contribution. It is this theological anthropological framework which provides the basis out of which he develops his ethical considerations.

Before we move to that task we must finish our exposition of Barth's theological anthropology in terms of the actual *content* of the interrelations among humankind and so the content of imaging and so ethical relationships. In three final sections we will see how Barth fills out the form of relationship on the horizontal plane of creaturely existence in terms of the personal, the dynamic and eschatological, and the extensive and inclusive activity in covenantal relationship.

IV. Personal-Being-in-Covenant-Love

For Barth, the grace of God has given humanity its being and so is also given its confirming action. Humankind's action is to correspond to God's own action. This activity is the living out of life within relationships. These relationships are not just empty forms to be filled with unspecified content. God's own content, God's own activity within His relationship to humankind has already provided the ontological framework and pattern for the activity within relationships on the horizontal plane. They are to image Jesus Christ in both form and content. We may characterize this corresponding action within the given relationships as a personal being-in-covenant-love. We will use this concept as our most comprehensive term. It will include within it the following two categories of personal being as dynamic and eschatological becoming and as extension for the sake of inclusion. These latter two we will take up separately.

Covenant-Love: Reciprocal Life-Giving Exchange

God's love is the basis of the reality and of our knowledge of what covenant love is.[175] No pre-understandings must be allowed to stand in the way of reformulating our conceptions of love in accordance with what has been revealed to us in Jesus Christ. God's love not only determines the noetic content but also the ontological order. It is only as God does indeed love humankind that human persons can love.[176] Our love is a love ordered by God's own love. This is a theme now quite familiar to us.

What Barth means by covenant love has already been anticipated in our discussions in two previous sections: "God's Loving Freedom" and in "I and Thou: the Form of Humanity." We will recall this later section first to outline the covenantal content of human being-in- relation and then fill this out by referring to the earlier section on the covenantal character of God's loving.

1. "I and Thou" in the History of Encounter

First of all, we should recall that Barth described the form of humanity as a being with the other in a relationship of I and Thou. We may summarize and say that this being-in-relationship was further subdivided into three parts: "I am and Thou art"—in identification and yet differentiation; I and Thou as a "being-in-relation"—corresponding and imaging one another; and "I am as Thou art"—a being-in-encounter and a history of relationship of one over against another, differentiated but not separated.

We further noted how Barth's threefold description of humanity as I and Thou corresponded to the first three of the six characterizations of the God-man relationship of Jesus to the Father, from, to and with God. This in turn is parallel to the first three criteria of the relationship of all other human creatures to God of being from, to, and with God. These then correspond to our three determinations of humanity as being in communion yet with differentiation, being differentiated yet in a history of being in communion, and finally as being in corresponding or imaging relation. This is the form of relationship reflected in all relationships with all their similarities and differences: the form of *analogia relationis*. This is the form of our being in covenant love.

Following this, Barth discusses the corresponding content of the relationship as he gives it in his four "constant, decisive and necessary elements in this history of encounter."[177] They are seeing eye to eye, mutual hearing and speaking, mutual assistance and all this done with joy and in freedom. Putting all this in a diagram:

---

[175] *CD*, I/2, p. 374.
[176] *Ibid.*, pp. 372–373.
[177] *CD*, III/2, p. 249.

I AND THOU: BEING-IN-RELATIONSHIP (Form)

Persons exist:
1. in the identification yet differentiation of I and Thou,
2. in being-in-relation, acknowledging the differentiation but realizing the communion of being in relationship or fellowship,
3. in the fact of being in a history of encounter by virtue of our mutually affirming and corresponding or imaging one to the other.

THE FOUR ELEMENTS OF BEING-IN-ENCOUNTER (Content)

1. Seeing eye to eye,
2. Mutual speaking and hearing,
3. Giving mutual assistance,
4. Relating/serving gladly.

It is these last four categories that define most succinctly the content of mankind's humanity as a way of covenant response within the form of relationship given to him by the Election, Summons, and history of salvation in which humankind exists.

At this point we want to highlight three aspects of this covenant love not made explicit previously. Covenant love is a dynamic history of mutual affirmation and confirmation a) *in an exchange of self-giving,* b) *in responsibility and freedom* and c) *which promises joy.*

a. A Dynamic History of Mutual Affirmation and Confirmation in an Exchange of Self-Giving

Barth emphasizes the fact that covenant relationships are a history, whether between the persons of the Trinity or among human creatures. "Man's being is a history..." not a state.[178] This history of covenant relation takes place when one's existence is interrupted from without. It occurs when someone addresses another and speaks a word or acts towards the other and so impinges in a new life-giving way upon the existence of that other in a way it could not itself. Where this has occurred a covenant history has been initiated. A dialogue between two persons might be one sort of image of this. This type of interaction is what Barth means by encounter.[179] When there is an encounter, something other, from the outside, even transcending my own nature, has an effect upon me, initiates a new unforeseen situation which places me in a new situation. In this situation there is a certain contingency. The pattern of interaction is not predictable or prescribed. The dialogue has its own pattern as each contributes in response to the other's input not intrinsic to the other.[180] True human being-in-

---

[178] *Ibid.,* p. 157.

[179] *Ibid.,* p. 158.

[180] Stuart McLean in his *Humanity in the Thought of Karl Barth* has emphasized this aspect of human relationships by calling it a "dialogical-dialectical" relationship. The term "dialogical" emphasizes the importance of the aural nature of human interaction

fellowship has this character of dynamic encounter; the enactment of a genuine history between persons who acknowledge one another as persons.

In covenant relations there is an openness to the other as different and yet similar. There is a genuine listening to the unique gift of the other because one realizes that what is being offered one cannot give one's self. There is a genuine responding and speaking in order to clarify and receive exactly what it is the other is offering, and perhaps also to offer one's self as well, knowing that this is why one has what one has. It is for the other who is distinct and whose life may be enriched by one's self giving. Covenant relationship is a dynamic, reciprocal, history of interaction; a history of initiative and response to one another with a view to enriching and being enriched by the other.

b. In Responsibility and Freedom

Following Barth, we may see that this covenant-relation also includes both responsibility and freedom. Responsibility as a covenant-partner of God means being in covenant relationship with other persons. It signifies that I am given the ability actually to respond in a way that is appropriate, in a way that correlates to who that other person is. This kind of responsibility is ordered by the truth of the one to whom response is made. There is no laziness in discerning who this other is, there is no projection of myself or someone else upon this other person, there is no attempt to remake this other into something else alien to them. Coming to see the truth of the other occurs through the effort of the history of a dialogue of self-exchange. It occurs through the reciprocal interaction of successive approximations for the sake of one for the other. As this process of discernment continues, it does not lead to passivity or avoidance of the other, but to taking responsibility to discern and confirm the truth about the other as being one who is in covenant relation with God. This means that one is led to engage in a continual dialogue of successive phases of interaction.

Taking up this responsibility to others in covenant love constitutes freedom, the only freedom belonging to humankind. It is the only action that is congruent with the being of humankind as created in the image of Who God is. It is only as we know God for Who He is and know ourselves for who we are in relation to Him (namely, those created to image Who He is) that we may live and give life. There is no antithesis between responsibility and freedom. There is only a kind of polarity between one person and another and God and humanity. We are not extensions of each other but rather stand over and against each other. We are nevertheless not opposed to the other, but exist in covenant relationship for their benefit. Thus, this otherness of the other is not to be overcome or synthesized,

---

which in turn reflects the primacy of the Word of God for human life, and also the reciprocal and personal nature of human interaction: speaking and listening, listening and speaking. The term "dialectical" indicates the pattern of interaction of one person somewhat independent of the other, yet through the dialogue, aligning itself through successive approximations to the other so that there comes to be a mutual understanding and mutual action on the part of both persons in covenant relation.

but provides the basis for the dynamic of real relationship and so the external possibility of covenant relationship.[181]

c. Joyful and Glad

We may finally say, with Barth, that this covenant relationship, as a history of relationship with reciprocal and responsible dynamic interaction in freedom, is also to be characterized as joyful and glad. The freedom in fellowship with God and humanity produces an overflow of joy beyond the mere health of life. It is a joy which "intensifies," "deepens" and "elevates" the whole of life. This joy is not acquired "automatically" by living in covenant relationship. Such a living is a preparation for receiving such a gift of over-abundant joy. It cannot be predicted, it can take many forms, such as in a very difficult work of service or even in and through suffering for the sake of Jesus Christ. It cannot be possessed, and, in fact, we can only "have" it as it is given and spread to others. It is actually a participation in the rejoicing that is "first and last in God Himself."[182]

---

[181] There is often confusion at this point regarding what is meant by "otherness." This is due in part to how Barth began, in his *Römerbrief*, to use it in a way nearly making God and man mutually exclusive terms. However, as he comes to use it in *CD*, III, it does not essentially stand for some kind of moral/spiritual opposition. God is not the enemy of humankind. He is not against it in that He wills its evil and its destruction. God is not Wholly Other in this way for Barth. When Barth uses the terms Other, or over against, or even opposition, he is emphasizing that God is distinct, independent from the creature. The creature is not God nor an emanation of God. God and man do not share a common being or subject. They are therefore appropriately called objects one to the other. There is no identity of God and man and their respective wills. In this way God and man stand opposite one another. It is true that humankind finds itself turned morally/spiritually against God in its fallenness. Humankind is opposed, is against, is at enmity with God but in a way different from God's opposition. God is always for man, living for his benefit, for his living in fellowship with Himself. The sinful opposition of man against God is his denial of this truth. Mankind comes to distrust the difference between God and man claiming that it is a threat to him and his welfare. He misperceives that God's infinite difference is a "No" to man's life and humanity. Man denies that God has eternally and irrevocably said "Yes" to mankind in his humanity and creatureliness. Now in response to this "No," this denial of mankind, God must say an absolute "No." But this is not a change of mind. God's "No" to man's "No" is a confirmation of His original "Yes." If He were to renounce His "Yes" to the life of humanity, He would reply "Yes" to mankind's "No" to God. God is faithful to Himself and man as He places man with his "No" under His judging and consuming "No." God's "No" is for the sake of His "Yes" and so is and remains for, and not against, man. It is because God is autonomous from man and not under his control or conditioning and so stands over against man as his Other that God can contradict man's denial. It is because God is Other that He can eternally be "for" mankind. This is the freedom of God's love as he responds to mankind in the history of his covenantal relation to him in Jesus Christ. See *CD*, IV/1, pp. 211–283, "The Judge Judged in Our Place," and "The Judgement of God," pp. 528–608. In an analogous fashion humans also exist over against one another. The temptation is to view this duality as being detrimental to our existence instead of being essentially good.

[182] See the wonderful section in *CD*, III/4, pp. 374–385.

The encounter of self-giving in responsibility and freedom as a preparation for having God's own joy is a large part of what Barth means by the personal nature of humanity, by our being persons-in-covenant-relationship.

2. *God and Humankind in Covenant Reciprocity*

Of course, such a dynamic and history of covenant relationship is original only in our relation to Jesus Christ. Apart from relationship to God we have in ourselves no capacity for entering into such relationships. Our relationships can only be the gift of participation in His Covenant made for us in Christ. God creates creatures which are not Himself or mere extensions of Himself. Thus, God becomes an object to those He creates. The relationship between God and humanity then is not "built-in" or "automatic." The relationship is one personally sustained and renewed by God. Consequently, Barth says that "there is a reciprocity of relationship between Him and these objects."[183]

This does not mean that we have impersonal relations with God. We are "objects" to each other inasmuch as there is not a common subject, person, between the two. The two are distinct, really independent, although humankind is not autonomous. There is a genuine reciprocity by God's own gracious act of creation. This means that there is a real openness of God to humanity in such a way that God may be said to receive from man. There is no necessity here, but a graciousness on the part of God towards man. This covenant reciprocity is the privilege of humankind.[184]

God in Jesus Christ inaugurates our true history. It is in relationship to Him, who addresses us, represents us, and comes to be with us that we have a history and so a personal life. He comes to take our humanity and to give us Himself for our sakes that we might have His life and His relationship with the Father.[185] Here is the original encounter from beyond ourselves, the true interaction and real exchange of persons which is of original benefit.[186] This is the enactment of the original covenant relation which then grounds all our other covenant relations in such a way that they might be an actual participation and so be a true witness to God's own covenant relation to us in Jesus Christ.[187]

Our covenant relations may take this shape only because it is given to us in God's affirmation and confirmation of us in His self-giving in Jesus Christ. We must recognize, then, that while there is a correspondence of action and a unity of action, there is also a distinction. Human covenant-partnership may be, but may only be, a representation and participation in the original covenant-partnership of God with humanity in Jesus Christ. There is no repetition or identity.

---

[183] *CD*, II/1, p. 58.
[184] *CD*, III/2, p. 71.
[185] See various passages: *CD*, III/2, pp. 48, 50, 778–780.
[186] See for example: *CD*, II/2, pp. 606–607.
[187] *CD*, III/2, p. 161.

Personal and Personifying Covenant Love

Our discussion, so far, has covered most of Barth's anthropological description in *CD*, III/2 of humanity as being-in-covenant love. However, there are a number of elements missing from his description there which are implicit in his discussion of the Triune God which we discussed in our section "God's Loving Freedom" in Chapter Two. We will now bring in this discussion to build up a more comprehensive understanding of humanity as being-in-covenant love.

1. The Triune Personhood of God and His Human Creatures

In attempting to set out the character of the personal nature of humanity as a being-in-covenant-love we should review Barth's findings covered in our discussion of the trinitarian character of God as the ground for theological anthropology.

We will begin with what seems to be for Barth a very comprehensive category of human action and being. The activity of being human is a *personal* action, the acts of persons. While Barth has reservations about speaking of God as a "person," especially as the term takes on modern connotations of "personalism" or "personality" and so may connote a tritheism,[188] he nevertheless finds it helpful to adopt the more appropriate term "personal" to speak of God and so, in a secondary and derived way, to speak of humanity.[189]

Barth begins the discussion—which ends with the affirmation "let us say it then—the *personal* God."[190]—at the most general level of Christian confession: that God "is." From this point he works his way along towards ever more comprehensive descriptions of who this God is. He must first affirm that we may confess that "God is" only on the basis of His revelation in Jesus Christ. Thus, the way God is, is already revealed in the act of revelation. This God is one who

---

[188] *Ibid.* Alan Torrance (*Persons in Communion*) has criticized Barth for shrinking from identifying the hypostases of the Trinity as persons. He finds the notion of "modes of existence" entirely inadequate because so impersonal, incapable of even analogously pointing to personal union and communion, *koinonia*, in the triune Life. The effect is to convey a unitary God. We concur with Torrance that Barth did not need to throw out the term because of its misuse, but rather he should have persisted on the basis of his proper theological method and argue that others should do so as well and so avoid the danger of defining God's triune persons in terms of human persons. However, as we will go on to show, Barth's actual grasp of the trinitarian nature of God proved better than his choice of terminology or even the constraint of first speaking of God in terms of revelation. This is clear as early as in II/1 where Barth discusses the perfections of God in being and act in inter-personal and relational terms. There the internal *koinonia* of the Triune persons is assumed. See the following discussion.

[189] See also the compendium of interesting essays in Edward Schillebeeckx and Bas van Iersel, eds., *A Personal God* (New York: The Seabury Press, 1977) for a wide variety of approaches to the question of the personal or impersonal character of God in contemporary religious philosophy.

[190] *CD*, II/1, p. 297.

acts in His self-revelation. Furthermore, this act of revelation is a self-giving of God.[191]

In the Word of God we see the "personalness" of God displayed for us. He is to be distinguished from material and impersonal things. God personifies Himself to us in his Word as a morally free subject who acts, wills, decides and relates in a personal way (that is, as subjects who act, will, decide) with others.[192]

This, notes Barth, is not a case of anthropomorphizing, but just the opposite. "The problem is not whether God is a person, the problem is whether we are."[193] The theological task is to interpret our lives in terms of the revelation, not *vice versa*. While we inevitably begin with ourselves and our experience, the question, for the theological enterprise, is what will serve as the final criterion? Will humankind insist on making God and itself into its own images, undoubtedly protesting that this is all it can do, or will it allow God's own revelation to reform man's image of God and man?

If we are to speak theologically about the God who has revealed himself in Christ and ourselves only in terms of this, then we must conclude that if and how we are personal must be dependent upon God's being the source of all personhood. "We cannot speak of 'personalizing' in reference to God's being, but only in reference to ours. The real person is not man but God. It is not God who is a person by extension, but we."[194]

If we take this path which Barth marks out for us, then the true personhood of God and humanity may be revealed in Jesus Christ.

> The One person, whom we really know as a human person, is the person of Jesus Christ, and even this is in fact the person of God the

---

[191] "What or who 'is' God? If we want to answer this question legitimately and thoughtfully we cannot for a moment turn our thoughts anywhere else than to God's act in His revelation.... What God is as God, the divine individuality and characteristics, the *essentia* or "essence" of God, is something which we shall encounter either at the place where God deals with us as Lord and Saviour, or not at all. The act of revelation as such carries with it the fact that God has not withheld Himself from men as true being, but that He has given no less than Himself as the overcoming of their own need, and light in their darkness—Himself as the Father in His own Son by the Holy Spirit" (*CD*, II/1, pp. 261–262).

[192] "The personification of the concept of the Word of God which we cannot avoid when we remember that Jesus Christ is the Word of God, does not signify any lessening of its verbal character. But it signifies...the knowledge of His personalness as distinguished from all thingness or materiality....Personalness means being one subject not only in the logical sense, but also in the ethical sense, being a free subject....[we] recognize him as a Person precisely in His Word" (*CD*, I/1, p. 157).

[193] *CD*, I/1, p. 138.

[194] *CD*, II/1, p. 272.

Son, in which humanity, without being or having itself a person, is caught up into fellowship with the personality of God.[195]

Barth finds himself compelled to sum up the being of God, at this point of acknowledging His act of revealing Himself, as unique triune event, as *life*. "Only the Living is God."[196] "God is also the One who is event, act and life in His own way, as distinct from everything that He is not Himself, even though at the same time He is its source, reconciliation and goal."[197]

Thus, as we turn to the knowledge of God in the Word, Jesus Christ, we see God necessarily as Triune. In this revelation "we always understand God as event, as act and as life" in the unique way revealed in Jesus Christ. In Him we see that this is God "in Himself free event, free act and free life."[198] In Christ we see God in His sovereign unity, distinction and correspondence in His self-knowledge, His self-willing, and his self-accomplishing. That is to say, He reveals himself as Father and Son, in the Spirit.[199]

Thus, as Triune God, Father, Son, and Spirit we come to terms with the nature of God as a personal existence. In this, Barth rejects a pure spiritualism or absolute spirit as being true to the reality of God. "Acts happen only in the unity of spirit and nature."[200] If these are disjointed then all the acts of God, internal or external, are not actual or true, but are images, similes, and there is no real revelation, reconciliation or redemption of God. The Spirit of God has a personal nature. God's being is a "being in person." And this personal being of God is not an it or a he but an "I."[201]

Barth has so far filled out the personhood of God in the light of the Word of God which reveals the Triune God as being event, act and life which is distinct and so is free from but is the source of every other created thing and being. Thus, God is Spirit, but not Spirit without a nature. The Spirit has the nature of a

---

[195] *Ibid.*, p. 286.

[196] *Ibid.*, p. 263.

[197] *Ibid.*, p. 264.

[198] *Ibid.*

[199] "The I who knows about Himself, who Himself wills, Himself disposes and distinguishes, and in this very act of His omnipotence is wholly self-sufficient. In this formula we are simply interpreting the triune being of God as Father and Son in the unity of the Holy Spirit proceeding from both" (*CD*, II/1, p. 268).

[200] *CD*, II/1, p. 267.

[201] "In accordance with the happening of revelation we reject a false spiritualising on the one hand and a false realism on the other, and have to understand God's being as 'being in person.' What is meant is certainly not personified being, but the being that in the reality of its person realises and unites in itself the fullness of all being. In its person means in its unity of spirit and nature. For in the due superiority of its spirituality, in the due inferiority of its naturalness, it is not an 'It' nor is it a 'He' like a created person. It is genuinely (and therefore also for a genuine understanding) always an 'I.' It is the I who knows about Himself, who Himself wills, and disposes and distinguishes, and in this very act of His omnipotence is wholly self-sufficient" (*CD*, II/1, p. 268).

divine person,[202] not of some abstract, absolute, "supernatural and imperceptible spiritual reality."[203] We see the divine act, life and event most particularly as God speaks as an I who is heard by the Thou who is addressed in the Word of God become flesh which is also poured out subsequently on all human flesh, i.e. persons.[204]

Thus, Barth concludes that it is most appropriate to speak of the whole Triune God as personal. "What we can describe as personality is indeed the whole divine Trinity as such...not the individual aspects by themselves."[205] There are not three faces, wills, Words or works of God but only one.[206]

Barth cannot remain for long at this generalized description of God's being as His own knowing, willing, deciding and acting as Father, Son and Spirit, because this "act of His, which is His being, is not actuality in general and as such, but is, in His revelation and in eternity, a specific act with a definite content."[207]

> This God is one who does not will to be God for Himself nor as God to be alone with Himself. He wills as God to be for us and with us who are not God...He places Himself in this relation to us. He does not will to be Himself in any other way than He is in this relationship...But his attitude and action is always that he seeks and creates fellowship between himself and us...God wills and does nothing different, but only one thing—this one thing. And this one thing that He wills and does is the blessing of God, that which distinguishes His act as divine and therefore also His person as divine.[208]

The action of this God is a fellowship or communion-creating action. It demonstrates that God wills to be for and with us and not without us, and not alone. The ground for this action *ad extra* is that God in Himself is not alone. He loves in Himself. God exists in fellowship and communion. We receive the gift

---

[202] *CD*, II/1, p. 271.

[203] *Ibid.*, p. 266.

[204] "The particularity of the divine event, act and life is the particularity of the being of a person. We speak of an action, of a deed, when we speak of the being of God as a happening. Indeed the peak of all happening in revelation, according to Holy Scripture, consists in the fact that God speaks as an I, and is heard by the thou who is addressed. The whole content of the happening consists in the fact that the Word of God became flesh and that His Spirit is poured out upon all flesh" (*CD*, II/1, p. 267).

[205] *CD*, II/1, p. 297.

[206] Alan Torrance's critique is again important here. Are the three hypostases of the Trinity not each to be regarded as persons as well who have their personhood by being Triune? Does not Barth's way of putting it here tend towards making them impersonal thereby rendering the Triune relations impersonal? See, *Persons in Communion*, pp. 213ff. Our concern is not to take up this issue, but to grasp how Barth conceives of personhood. We concur, however, with Torrance's criticism.

[207] *CD*, II/1, p. 272.

[208] *CD*, II/1, pp. 274–275.

of God's overflow of Himself to us for inclusion in that Triune communion of love.[209]

Barth continues, filling out this love which God is, under four headings:

1) "God's loving is concerned with a seeking and creation of fellowship for its own sake." In loving us He gives us Himself, He gives us everything, every good, every blessing. Consequently, in His loving us...He takes us up into His fellowship, i.e., the fellowship which He has and is in Himself, and beyond which there is no greater blessing."[210] We thus have a share, participate, have a place in the very inner divine relations of love between Father, Son and Spirit.

2) "God's loving is concerned with a seeking and creation of fellowship without any reference to an existing aptitude or worthiness on the part of the loved."[211] This is not a blind love but God's love for that which is lost to itself, a sinful, alien, and hostile creature.

3) "God's loving is an end in itself. All the purposes that are willed and achieved in Him are contained and explained in this end, and therefore in this loving in itself and as such." Even God's will for his own glory is willed for the sake of His love. "God loves because He loves; because this act is His being, His essence and His nature."[212]

4) "God's loving is necessary, for it is the being, the essence and the nature of God. But for this very reason it is also free from every necessity in respect of its object." He is sufficiently and eternally and completely Love in Himself, yet "in the fact that He determines to love such another, His love overflows. But it is not exhausted in it nor confined or conditioned by it...While God is everything for Himself, he wills again not to be everything merely for Himself, but for this other."[213]

Thus, the personhood of God, which is the essence of God, is that God is, in His Triune Self, Love. We become fully personal as we recognize that God is *the* person because He acts as a person inasmuch as He is the One who has loved us and enables us to love yet others in a way that God loves.[214]

---

[209]"As and before God seeks and creates fellowship with us, He wills and completes this fellowship in Himself. In Himself He does not will to exist for Himself, to exist alone. On the contrary, He is Father, Son and Holy Spirit and therefore alive in His unique being with and for and in another. The unbroken unity of His being, knowledge and will is at the same time an act of deliberation, decision and intercourse. He does not exist in solitude but in fellowship. Therefore what He seeks and creates between Himself and us is in fact nothing else but what He wills and completes and therefore is in Himself....He is the One who loves. That He is God—the Godhead of God—consists in the fact that He loves, and it is the expression of His loving that He seeks and creates fellowship with us"(p. 275).

[210]*CD*, II/1, pp. 276–277.

[211]*Ibid.*, pp. 278–279.

[212]*Ibid.*, pp. 279–280.

[213]*Ibid.*, pp. 280–282.

[214]"In the light of the definition of His being as a being in act we described God as a person....The One who (in His own way) loves us, who (in His own way) seeks and

It is in this way that Barth asserts that it is proper to speak of the Triune God as personal and also to speak of humankind as also personal, without engaging in anthropomorphizing. We are persons because we belong to the personal Triune God by virtue of our being graciously united to him in Jesus Christ.[215]

2. The Personal Triune God: Six Characteristics

In the section above we have attempted to encapsulate Barth's exposition of the character of the Personal God in six points. The first three points emphasize God's being-in-action. The second three emphasize the content of the action of God as being life-giving. These two divisions are parallel to our two primary categories of the grammar of Barth's understanding of personal-being-in-relation.

THE PERSONAL GOD

A. A Being-in-Act

1) As Triune, God's Being is a Being-in-Act, which is to say that God is a Living God.

2) God's Being is a Being-in-Person. His character shows us what personhood is originally. God is a self-knowing, willing, deciding and acting being in communion among the 'persons' of the Trinity.

3) God is a Being-in-Becoming by creating and maintaining a loving fellowship which extends to others to include them in the divine life. And the establishing and maintaining of this loving communion is an end in itself because it is God's own giving of Himself to others.

---

creates fellowship between Himself and us, also informs us what a person is, in that (in his own way! not as if we knew of ourselves what it is, but in such a way that we now come to recognize it for the first time) He acts as a person. The definition of a person—that is, a knowing, willing, acting I—can have the meaning only of a confession of the person of God declared in His revelation, of the One who loves and who as such (loving in His own way) is *the* person. Man is not a person but he becomes one on the basis that he is loved by God and can love God in turn. Man finds what a person *is* when he finds it in the person of God and his own being as a person in the gift of fellowship afforded him by God in person. He is then (in his own way as a creature) a person wholly and exclusively in the fellowship of Him who (in His way as Creator) is it in Himself. Therefore to be a person means really and fundamentally to be what God is, to be, that is, the One who loves in God's way. Not we but God is I" (*CD*, II/1, p. 284).

[215]T. F. Torrance noted this connection between humanity and God: "The Triune God is not only a fullness of personal Being in himself, but is also person-constituting Being. It was from the theological understanding of God's personal and personalizing self-communication, creating personal reciprocity between us and himself, that the Christian concept of the person arose, which is applicable in a creaturely way to persons in relation to one another but which reflects the transcendent way in which the three divine Persons are inter-related in the Holy Trinity." See his *Reality and Evangelical Theology*, pp. 43–44.

B. A Being in Life-Giving

4) As such the Triune God is a personifying person, one who enables others to participate in His personhood and so become created persons in their own right by participating in His loving communion.

5) The communion-creating God is lovingly free in all this because this act is completely congruent with Who the Triune God is in Himself and so towards others. Who He is towards us is the overflow of His inner-Triune life towards us and nothing else.

6) Finally, all the actions of God *ad extra* are then to be characterized and interpreted in terms of his personal, living, loving, fellowship-creating, person-making, freedom for others. God's working *ad extra* must be understood as those of Fatherly Creator, Reconciling Son, and Redeeming Spirit. And all His attributes are expressions of his Triune Being-in-Loving.

Now, what we propose is that taking Barth's discussion as a whole we have warrant to extend our understanding of humanity as being in correspondence with the above six characterizations of the intra-trinitarian love of God. The result is that we should understand persons *mutatis mutandis* as being creaturely copies of the Image in these six ways:

3. Humanity as Personal Being: Six Criteria

1) Beings who exist in their action, who are living beings to be understood inseparably from their particular actions in their relationships with others, primarily with God and similarly with others.

2) Who then in their own creaturely way know themselves, will, decide, and so act, corresponding in obedience to God's own doing so.

3) The total purpose of whose life is to live in communion with God to the end that all others live and share in this same communion of love for God and similarly love for one another.

4) And that this living is a history of ongoing interaction in which we may participate in God's own creating and recreating his human creatures into persons who image his own original Person. Our living is to consist in a humanizing of persons in the image of God.

5) In this communion with God and with others each one will not be absorbed or be co-opted but come into his own as a being-in-communion by entering into the freedom of becoming who he was created to be and finding a perfect congruence between his being and his acting.

6) That all human activity of the whole person is to be conformed to this image of personal, free and loving being and becoming in participation in God's own inner-life of communion, whether this be personal or social, vocational or avocational, in relations within the Church or beyond it.

These six characterizations fill out the nature of our two primary categories of the personal relational grammar we have used throughout this chapter. However, within them there are several themes that do not explicitly come out in Barth's discussion of humanity as I and Thou. From these corresponding characterizations of the Triune God and humanity we want to highlight three additional aspects of being-in-covenant-love.

Personal Being as a Being-in-Loving

1. Personal Being

From the section on "God's Loving Freedom" we discussed Barth's most comprehensive understanding (encompassing all six characterizations listed above) of God as Personal Being. However, the personhood of God, which is the essence of God, is that God is, in His Triune Self, Loving. Consequently, in perhaps his most comprehensive expression of the personal being of God, Barth inextricably binds personal being with loving.

On this basis Barth proceeds to understand humanity also as personal in a secondary and derived way, yet nevertheless personal as God is personal. Humanity is personal being to the extent that all its true living and acting, all its deciding, willing and doing are loving in a way that corresponds to God's own loving.

2. Personalizing Love

This means that living as personal beings we must be oriented to the creation and maintenance of fellowship or a communion of persons. Without this, humankind's personal being is threatened. True personhood is not merely personal but personalizing. In the gracious act of creation God acts as the personal God that He is. This means that Creation involves a personification by God. God is "the personifying person." Furthermore, His actions of Reconciliation and Redemption are the renewal and completion of God's personifying of his human creatures. To live in communion with this God is to be involved in the process of sharing in God's own personalizing of persons.[216]

Thus, to be a person, after the image of God, is to love others in such a way that they become persons, or we should say, our love is to be a personalizing love. Of course, following what Barth has indicated, this can only mean that this personalizing love in the creaturely realm arises out of relationship of one with another, a relationship in which there is a unity and fellowship of persons yet an inviolable distinction between persons as I and Thou, where there is an ordering within the relationship of one to the other, although there may be an oscillation of giving and receiving, and where this personalizing bears witness to God's own personalizing love in Jesus Christ. Consequently, humankind does not create persons or grant personhood to others, but we may participate in God's

---

[216]"Thus to know, to will, to act like God as the One who loves in Himself and in His relationship to His creation means (in confirmation of His I-ness) to be a person. God is a person in this way, and He alone is person in this way. He is the real person and not merely the ideal. He is not the personified but the personifying person—the person on the basis of whose prior existence alone we can speak hypothetically of other persons different from Him" (*CD*, II/1, p. 285). C. S. Lewis has said this in an interesting way: "We are the anthropomorphisms of God."

own personalizing activity of others as our witness to His love. God is the creator of relationships as well as of persons.[217]

We have characterized the form and content of humankind's humanity as a participation in God's own covenant love as actualized in Jesus Christ. In anticipation of our chapter on "Parents and Children" there are two more issues, those of human power and authority, which are important for filling out Barth's theological anthropology. While Barth's perspective on authority and power has been implicit all along, a discussion of his explicit presentation of these concerns in his section on the perfections of God will be helpful for achieving a more comprehensive understanding of personal-being-in-covenant-love.

Covenant Love, Power and Authority

For Barth the biblical witness to Jesus Christ indicates that loving freedom is essential to God himself, being freely loving in and of himself overflowing to the creature.[218] This has great implications for understanding all the perfections and actions of God. These must all be interpreted in terms of the essential character of God revealed in Jesus Christ. All the other characteristics of God and actions of God are to be seen in the light of *Who* God is, the God who has His being in Love of Father, Son and Spirit.[219] Thus, Barth, only after he has expounded the essential personal nature of God as love in Himself, then goes on to discuss the Perfections of God, His Grace and Holiness, Mercy and Righteousness, Patience and Wisdom, Unity and Omnipresence, Constancy and Omnipotence, the Eternity and the Glory of God. Each of these designations is understood as the "Perfections of Divine Loving and Freedom." "God's being is His loving. He is all that He is as the One who loves. All His perfections are the perfections of His love."[220]

We cannot take up at this point a discussion of Barth's recasting of all these attributes of God in the light of Who He is. However, we should consider briefly the nature of God's omnipotence and sovereign freedom as understood in the light of God's being as Love. God's love is uniquely His alone. He is the original source of all persons and so all loving. In this God's love is free and sovereign. Note that it is God's person, God's being as Love that is sovereign.

---

[217] So, Barth says, "He creates not only the I and Thou, man and woman, but also their mutual relationship." (*CD*, III/1, p. 298).

[218] *CD*, III/3, p. 107

[219] *CD*, I/1, pp. 345–346. Here Barth's insistence on the priority of the Who? question for Christian dogmatics matches Bonhoeffer's call for the same in his *Christ the Center*. Moving from the question of Who God is to the questions of whether and what God is is a radical reversal of the Medieval order (*an sit, quid sit, qualis sit*). For Barth, what God is, His so-called attributes, can only be known from Who He is. Barth believes this follows the structure of the biblical witness which attempts to lead us to ask the question Who? before any others and which offers a response primarily in terms of Who God is. Compare Jesus' central question to his disciples: "Who do you say I am?" and Jesus' self-designations: "I am..." and his "Son of Man" sayings.

[220] *CD*, II/1, p. 351.

Barth rejects any naked consideration of an abstract sovereignty of God apart from His personhood, apart from His essential character. There can be no general consideration of God, but only of this God, the One who has revealed Himself as Being in Love. Consequently, God cannot be understood as abstract, absolute, unconditional, or irresistible power, or causation. "Irresistible omnipotence cannot be made the beginning and end of the being of God..."[221] "The true God is the One whose freedom and love have nothing to do with abstract absoluteness or naked sovereignty."[222] God is not a tyrant or despot. Absolute will and power are not, for God, ends in themselves.[223] To think of God in this way, says Barth, is to regard God as "a sovereign caprice" rendering any knowledge of God incomprehensible and any obedience or submission to God is rendered contentless and so reduced to mere passivity, resignation.[224]

Consequently, a mechanistic model of the action of God as causation is entirely inappropriate. God and man are not things or objects (*Ursache*).[225] Man's relationship to God is not like that of a clock or machine.[226] The relationship of God and creature "must be quite free from mechanistic influences."[227] The primary *causa* of God is His grace. This means that mankind's own willing, choosing and determining is given a place to correspond to God's own electing him for eternal fellowship of life with Him. Mankind has a *causa secunda* which is enclosed within and grounded upon God's own *causa prima*. There is here an analogy between the divine and the human, but no more. Mankind's will is to bear witness to the divine willing.[228]

Barth's re-framing of the omnipotence and sovereignty of God within His essential person of love is extraordinary. It cannot be overemphasized how significant this is for Reformed theology. It is perhaps Barth's second greatest achievement of the *Church Dogmatics*. It grows out of his greatest achievement—his Christological and so trinitarian point of departure for his whole subsequent theological enterprise. If God is to be understood in terms of His self-revelation in Jesus Christ, then all the attributes and works of God must also be interpreted in the light of Jesus Christ. Thus, "attributes" such as sovereignty and omnipotence, as well as all others, must be interpreted in terms of *Who* God is, the one who has His being as love in Jesus Christ. Jesus Christ

---

[221] *CD*, II/2, p. 45.
[222] *Ibid.*, p. 49.
[223] *CD*, III/3, pp. 92–93, 30–31.
[224] *Ibid.*, p. 113.
[225] *Ibid.*, p. 101.
[226] *Ibid.*, p. 12.
[227] *Ibid.*, p. 139.
[228] *Ibid.*, pp. 98–107.

shows us Who God is. All that He does and is must be interpreted in terms of Who He has revealed Himself to be.[229]

Consequently, as the Personhood of God is revealed as a trinitarian fellowship of love, the human creatures of God created to image His Image must be correspondingly understood. The nature of human personhood is transformed. It is to be similarly characterized by being in relationships of love as known in Jesus Christ and so in the inner trinitarian life. In fact, human personhood is constituted by its participation in God's own inner-trinitarian love in and through Jesus Christ Himself by the Holy Spirit.

Any consideration of human authority must have as its norm this true account of the nature of human personhood. Authority must be a form of love, and not be a mechanistic control over others nor a mere show of power over another. The human exercise of un-Christ-like authority has a dehumanizing effect on those who are the initiators as well as those who are the objects of such action. This results not in a personalizing of humans, but in a de-personalizing of humans. This is to bear false witness to the Image of God.

Finally, to complete our picture of human being-in-covenant-love it will be helpful to recall our discussion and bring to bear what Barth has said concerning God's love in his discussion on "The Being of God as the One who Loves."

Covenant Love: An Unconditional Communion

We want to recall two points here. God's love is one that seeks, creates and maintains fellowship. First, this fellowship is a communion of persons in a history of interaction of self-giving and receiving and so a reciprocal exchange of life to the benefit of the other. This is what God is in His Triune Self and so is towards us. Consequently, humanity also is so constituted. We are to seek, create and maintain a communion among persons by mutual self-giving and receiving, and an exchange of life. It is a communion of mutual seeing, hearing, helping, rejoicing. Of course it is in the Church where this communion is provisionally enacted, made provisionally manifest.

Secondly, this communion is unconditional. We recall Barth's discussion of the four characteristics of God's love: 1) The creation of this fellowship is for its own sake because it is the sole good. 2) The seeking and creation of this communion is done without reference to the worthiness or anticipated reciprocity of love. The reason for its being sought is in itself. God's covenant love is its own ground. 3) God's loving is an end in itself. The creation of the communion of love is not instrumental to some other end. It is its sole aim. 4) Finally, God's communion-seeking and creating love is free and unconstrained because it perfectly coheres in who God is in His own Triune life. His love towards us is the overflow of his own blessedness for our sakes, for the sake of our participation in it.

---

[229] This also has for Barth tremendous hermeneutical import. It means that ultimately the biblical witness is to be interpreted in the light of who God is as revealed in Jesus Christ.

Thus, in a corresponding way, human covenant love is the seeking and creation of a fellowship which is a participation in God's covenant love as our sole good, sole ground, sole aim, and only blessedness.[230] This means that covenant love is unconditional. It is not a contractual agreement between two parties on the basis of mutually agreed terms which if violated annuls the contract. It is a commitment to the benefit of the other by doing whatever is lovingly necessary to include them in the fellowship we have with God in Jesus Christ.

Summary

We may summarize and say that humanity is determined as a being-in-covenant-love which may be characterized as a personalizing relation between those who recognize and act towards others as persons, persons in a history of dynamic, reciprocal, responsible, free and joyful interaction for the sake of others in the light of and in correlation with the person Jesus Christ and the unconditional communion-seeking, creating, and maintaining love of the personal Triune life of God revealed in Him.

V. Being-in-Becoming

In the next to last section of this chapter we must consider the fifth designation of humanity, as a being-in-becoming. The sense of what Barth means by "becoming" is unique because it, too, is fashioned Christologically.

Creaturely Being-in-Becoming

As humanity exists in a covenant-relationship of love or fellowship, reflecting the covenant fellowship of and within God Himself, humanity becomes what it was determined to be in Jesus Christ. This does not mean that humanity becomes other than what it was. It means that what it is determined to be is a being-in-becoming in relationship to God through Jesus Christ. Human existence itself is not static. This, of course, is congruent with everything else that Barth has been saying regarding humanity. The nature of humanity's being-in-relationship, as a history of loving/covenantal dynamic, reciprocal, responsible, free and joyful interactions between persons constitutes his becoming. Ultimately this becoming is grounded in God's own being as becoming.[231]

---

[230]See J. B. Torrance, "Covenant or Contract?" *SJT*, Vol. 23 (Feb. 1970) for a crucial distinction between the biblical concept of covenant and the notion of a contract. The notion of a contract between two parties based on mutual fulfillment of conditions is a denial of all four of Barth's characterizations of the communion-creating covenant love of God.

[231]For a most helpful and extensive exploration of this dimension of Barth's theology see Eberhard Jüngel's *Trinity*. See pp. vii–viii, for his warning concerning the possibility of misinterpreting what Barth meant by "becoming." See also Colin Gunton's *Becoming*

We have already become familiar with a number of places where Barth has indicated that there is a becoming of humanity. The fact of humanity's having its being-in-action, existing in the history of God's salvation, leads up to this more comprehensive category. The understanding of humankind existing as it engages in an interaction with those, God and others, outside and beyond themselves (each in their own way) and in being and becoming a living analogy or image corresponding in their relationships to God's own determination for them also leads up to this designation of existing as a becoming. More comprehensively yet, the fact that persons are personalized in their relationships with God and with others so that their actions take on a covenantal quality (love in freedom) points up this becoming of humankind. This totality of being in the image of God in form and content is not a static substantival possession or a faculty of humanity. It is a purpose, God's intention, for humanity that it reflects the character of God. Thus, God's creatures are to "become mirrors" of Him.[232]

1. Becoming: A Process of Transformation towards its Telos

The character of humanity's being is open, not fixed. Mankind is engaged in a process:

> "Become what you are," means therefore: "Grow into your character, accept the outline of your particular form of life, the manner of existence in which your special struggle of the Spirit against the flesh will emerge more clearly as your own, as the one which is intended for you, as the form of the life allotted and lent to you by God." For it is in this form that already in the eyes of the eternal God and therefore in reality, you are what you are.[233]

Humanity's being is one of growing up into one's character. As such there is a continuing "transformation"[234] towards one's God-given *telos*.[235] The presence of purpose in the life of humanity is given and unavoidable because we belong to Jesus Christ. This makes one's life not a static gift but a gift of a certain task to be taken up.[236] Life is a calling and summoning to "what one is becoming."[237]

---

and Being for a comparison of Barth and Hartshorne's approach to the dynamics of being.

[232] *CD*, III/3, p. 52.
[233] *CD*, III/4, p. 388, cf. p. 387.
[234] *CD*, III/3, p. 6.
[235] *Ibid.*, III/4, p. 53.
[236] *Ibid.*, III/2, p. 180.
[237] *Ibid.*, III/4, p. 606.

This becoming occurs originally in one's relationship to God, and essentially in both the horizontal and vertical planes of one's existence. By being loved and loving God and neighbor, we become the persons we are to be.[238]

This becoming in relation to God then unfolds on the horizontal plane. In Christian love or *agape* we come to recognize others as brothers and sisters who also become whom God intends them to be by His grace.[239]

Thus, our being unfolds in its determination to become as it participates in covenant relationship with God and correspondingly with others. We should not say that we are already covenant partners and then become something over and above this. We are summoned to become, in our relationships, the covenant partners we are with God and with others. This is the *telos* of our human existence. We become in ourselves what we are in Christ. As such the only one who embodies completely what we are to become is Jesus Christ.[240]

2. The Telos: *Becoming, in Christ, the Children of God*

Again, the knowledge of the actual *telos* of human existence and the possibility of its realization for every person are both grounded in the actuality of its being realized in the humanity of Jesus Christ for us. Jesus is the covenant-partner of God existing in the form of our humanity with God in His inner Triune fellowship of love. Because Jesus, the Son of God, has become by the grace of God, our Brother, we are to become the children of God who call God our Father.[241]

This becoming of humanity, the becoming of the children of God, is our becoming by God's grace. Grace means becoming. Not abstractly, but concretely: becoming the children of God. This becoming the children of God is not an original creation with each individual. Our being and becoming the children of God are a participation in Jesus' own Sonship with the Father. "He [Jesus] gives us His Holy Spirit in order that his own relationship to His Father may be repeated in us."[242]

3. *Becoming Sanctified, Humanized*

As such, our becoming is the sanctification and so the fulfillment of our humanity. We do not become something other than human in the fulfillment of our covenant-relation with God. And we certainly do not become "religious" in some abstract way. As we are sanctified in our relationship with God through and in Jesus Christ, we are humanized, we are personalized, become fully human. We should understand "Christian love as the awakening and fulfillment

---

[238] "Man is not a person, but he becomes one on the basis that he is loved by God and can love God in return" (*CD*, II/1, p. 284).

[239] *CD*, III/2, p. 275.

[240] *Ibid.*, p. 225.

[241] *CD*, IV/4, p. 73.

[242] *CD*, II/2, p. 780.

of humanity, of the distorted and perverted but not forfeited manner of the natural man, i.e. of man as God created him."[243]

Who we are and are to become is indeed not apparent in ourselves. It is realized and apparent only in Jesus Christ. Yet in Him we may see our union with Him and so see our own fulfillment in Him, in that we see our humanity in His humanity and see Him in full personal communion with His divinity, i.e., His complete fellowship with the Father in the Spirit. So in Him we see the fulfillment of our own fellowship with the Father by the Spirit. He

> takes from us what is ours...giving us what belongs to God, all the wisdom and righteousness and holiness of the Son of God, everything, as He is for us and represents us, everything, as we belong to Him and He treats us as His own, His members.[244]

4. Becoming: an Eschatological Hope for Life in the Triune God

Consequently, this life of becoming is to be characterized as a life of hope. Who we ultimately are cannot be completely manifested. Our becoming involves a waiting for the completion of what was begun in us and is as yet only completed in Christ. This hope is essentially our union with him.[245]

It is with this final clarification that we must indicate that the 'becoming' must be understood eschatologically. It is not yet apparent, yet it is the future held out and made actual for us by the promise of God in Jesus Christ. This future is our eternal sharing in the triune life of God.[246]

The fact that the completion of our participation in the life of God is future does not mean that it is any less real or actual in the present. It is the truth about ourselves in which we live. We regard ourselves as the new creations we are, as the children of God united with Him. It is this realism or actualism of our

---

[243] *CD*, III/2, p. 284.

[244] *CD*, II/2, p. 607. We could recall the witness of the New Testament here: "Beloved we are God's children now; it does not yet appear what we shall be, but we know that when he appears we shall be like him, for we shall see him as he is. And everyone who thus hopes in him purifies himself as he is pure" (I Jn. 3: 2–4). "For the creation waits with eager longing for the revealing of the sons of God...For in this hope we were saved" (Rom. 8:19, 24). "For you have died, and your life is hid with Christ in God. When Christ who is our life appears, then you also will appear with him in glory" (Col. 3:3, 4).

[245] *CD*, II/2, p. 607.

[246] *CD*, IV/1, p. 8; cf. II/1, p. 181 concerning our participation. See also Jüngel's comment on this eschatological dimension, *Trinity*, p. 61ff. The editors of *CD*, IV/4, Lecture Fragments titled *The Christian Life* (Grand Rapids: Eerdmans, 1981), Hans-Anton Drewes and Eberhard Jüngel have noted that on the basis of these lectures "The commonly expressed view that there can be no eschatology proper in the course of *CD* is thus shown to be even more unfounded than it previously was. In fact, indications to the contrary are innumerable" (p. xii). We would say that the theme of becoming throughout the *Dogmatics* is one significant way Barth presents the eschatological truth of the Gospel.

ontological relationship with God in Christ by the Spirit that is a hallmark of Barth's theology. It is a key to his ethics. It is also the stumbling block of so many of his interpreters. It raises the question as to whether we regard our present experience and perception as "reality" with the future as potential reality or regard the truth concerning ourselves as revealed in Jesus Christ as the present reality and actuality for us with the future as the unfolding and manifestation of it.[247]

The Becoming of the Triune God

We can see how Barth Christologically sees humanity as a being which becomes what it is determined to be in the grace of God: the covenant partner of God exhibiting the very character of God in creaturely form, embodying the personal and personalizing love of God. And ultimately, for Barth, this means our participating in the inner life of the Triune God.

There is also a proper way to consider God's own being as a being of becoming. Our becoming is an image of God's own becoming. In this way our becoming is a witness to the grace and glory of God, in Himself, in His becoming, in trinity in unity. God's own becoming may be explicated in four ways.

1. Christologically Actualized and Revealed

First, God's becoming is revealed to us in the "real becoming of Jesus Christ."[248] Thus, Colin Gunton, following Barth, says that this knowledge of God's being is derived from what we know of his becoming in Jesus alone, not becoming or being in general.[249] Thus, this analogy of becoming for God is a unique one such that His becoming is neither a transcendent version of

---

[247]Ingolf Dalferth has brought this out more clearly than perhaps anyone. He argues that Barth is "an unashamed realist" (p. 14). He further clarifies this by saying it is an "eschatological realism" of the risen and present Christ and the new life into which we are drawn by the Spirit" (p. 21). This is the personal presence of the risen Christ. It is this "reality which determines what is to be counted as real and what isn't" (p. 22). Dalferth's analysis of Barth's contribution is that it "constitutes a massive and conscious contradiction to everything thought epistemologically acceptable in the light of post-Enlightenment restriction of meaningful truth claims to the formal truth of logic and mathematics and the empirical truths of science and history" (p. 22). He sums up Barth's position: "...our world is permanently in the process of becoming real (or unreal for that matter) by its eschatological *assumptio in Deum*. What we experience is a preliminary, penultimate, abstract reality which as such is in a permanent danger of relapsing into non-existence" (p. 29). This points up both the radical claim that Barth is making and the inimical context into which his teaching comes. See "Karl Barth's Eschatological Realism" in ed. S. W. Sykes, *Karl Barth: Centenary Essays* (Cambridge: Cambridge University Press, 1989).

[248]*CD*, I/1, p. 430.

[249]*Becoming and Being*, p. 156, cf. Jüngel, where he says that "the concept of being must be measured by the revelation of God" (*Trinity*, pp. 62–63) and that "becoming" is essentially "a trinitarian category" (p. viii).

creation's becoming nor its negation but "has its own distinctive becoming."[250] For Barth this means that God assumes, without ceasing to be anything other than he was, time and humanity in the Incarnation of the Son in Jesus Christ. God becomes the God of humankind in Jesus Christ.[251] God becomes the revelation of his Lordship for humankind.

2. The Triune Becoming the Revealer

Secondly, Barth indicates that grounded in the fact of the revelation is the fact that God has become the Revealer. God determines himself to be and so become the God of humankind.[252] This becoming of God occurs originally in the inner-trinitarian relation of Father and Son, it is the determination of Father and Son to be the God of humanity in Jesus Christ, i.e it is the determination of the election of humankind in Jesus Christ.

There is in God, a history of free and unconditioned interaction, of love in the intra-divine life. This God is "established and confirmed in its unity by its trinity, by the inner movement of the begetting of the Father, the being begotten of the Son and the procession of the Spirit from both."[253]

This interaction constitutes the election of the Son by the Father and the Son's affirmation of His election by the Father. In this "primal decision"[254] of Father and Son there is an inter-action, an event, a movement of becoming on behalf of humankind which affects God in Himself in a way which God Himself has determined.

3. The Triune Becoming Revealed in the Spirit

Thirdly, there is a becoming of God in that he "becomes manifest" to certain persons in a certain time and place. This is the working of God apportioned to the Holy Spirit.[255] In this, God becomes revealed to human creatures. In this the God who is hidden and not knowable to humankind does indeed manifest himself, even while remaining who he is, one not intrinsically knowable to humankind.

4. Triune Becoming in the Inner History of the Triune Relations

Fourthly, we may say that this is a "movement of intra-divine life" which Eberhard Jüngel paraphrases as Barth's indication that in the inner trinitarian dynamics "each mode of being *becomes* what it is together *with* the two other modes of being...a *being in becoming*."[256] The unity of the Trinity is a

---

[250] *Ibid.*, p. 162, cf. Jüngel (*Trinity* p. vii), it indicates "neither an increase nor a decrease of God's being."

[251] See also Barth's *Humanity of God*, "His deity *encloses humanity in itself*" (p. 50).

[252] See *CD*, II/1, pp. 16–24, for Barth's exposition on the primary and secondary objectivity of God, the hiddenness and the revealedness of God.

[253] See *CD*, II/1, p. 615, cf. II/2, pp. 2–14.

[254] *CD*, III/2, pp. 68–77. This is Barth's term in his discussion concerning election and the Father–Son relation in the *Church Dogmatics* centered in II/2, p. 105.

[255] See *CD*, I/1, p. 448–516. Cf. Gunton, 133–135.

[256] *Trinity*, p. 63. Cf. Gunton, *Becoming and Being*, p. 143.

becoming itself. God's being is a fellowship which is "becoming one."[257] The three modes become united and are always becoming one. The Triune fellowship is an activity. This is what the concept of *perichoresis* comes to represent, the "involution and convolution" of God in Himself and in His work, which is indeed His being as love.[258]

As such, there is a self-giving, an exchange, a flow of life from one to the other. The Father gives Himself and glorifies the Son and the Son glorifies and gives Himself to the Father all by the Spirit. In the eternal begetting of the Son, the Father is/becomes Father. In the eternal obedience of the Son, the Son is/becomes the Son. There is a dynamic becoming in the history of the intra-trinitarian relations. "He is God in their concrete relationships, the one to the other, in the history which takes place between them."[259]

The essential place where we see God's being and man's being as dynamic, and a becoming, is exactly where God has revealed Himself to man, Jesus Christ. In Jesus Christ, God became that which He was not previously. Without ceasing to be what God was, He determined Himself *to be*, in Himself, the God of the creature, for the creature, with the creature. This is God's own self-determination, and so a determination of His gracious love. But God, in exercising the freedom of His love, is free and loving to become the free and loving God of the creature, creating humankind to share in His own intra-trinitarian life.[260] God determined Himself to be God with humanity and humanity to be with its God, and to be God only in this way. For the purpose of eternal fellowship with the creature, He becomes the God of humanity by taking humanity into Himself in the Son. God is sovereignly free to allow his intra-trinitarian love to create that which is not or other than Himself, then overflow, go out and gather in His creatures to Himself, giving them a place of creaturely being-as-becoming in His own being-as-becoming, that is, within the Triune life of God.[261]

---

[257] CD, I/1, pp. 369–370. See Jüngel, p. 32.

[258] Ibid., pp. 370–374, II/1, p. 284, "the One who loves in himself."

[259] CD, IV/1, p. 203. Further insight on the triune becoming is found in T. F. Torrance, *The Trinitarian Faith* (Edinburgh: T&T Clark, 1988), Chapter 8. There Torrance argues that the unity of the Trinity should not be located in the person of the Father. The unity is strictly a triunity. Thus, the Father does not give rise to the being of the Son, but only of the personhood, the Sonship of the Son.

[260] CD, III/3, p. 109f.

[261] There are some similarities here with some forms of Process Theology (especially Christological and trinitarian forms, e.g. Lewis Ford, John Cobb, and Anthony J. Kelley) however there seem to be some decided differences. In both there is a dynamic conception of being and there is a becoming for both God and humanity in distinct ways. For Barth (and some Process thought) this is understood in terms of the trinitarian relations, and the Incarnation, Crucifixion, and Resurrection, i.e. Christologically. However, Barth's Christology exhibits a realism and also emphasizes the all inclusive humanity of Christ, so that what is actual for all humanity is what is true in Him. Jesus Christ does not serve as example or symbol for Barth, but the creator (or re-creator) of a

We may thus say that, as persons exist in relationship to God and other human creatures, they are becoming. Persons exist in hope of the realization of God's loving and free intentions for them as realized in Jesus Christ and so promised to them as the fulfillment of their own humanity. This hope is the realization of God's filial or familial purposes of our becoming the children of God by our sharing in the Son's own fellowship with the Father in the Spirit, indeed in the communion within the Triune life of God.

---

new reality in which all humanity presently exists. Certainly for Barth Jesus did not realize some ideal out of the infinite possibilities in the mind of God. He is the reality for all humanity in which they may now themselves participate. Thus what is actual for Barth is most often understood at most as an ideal or a future potential in most Process thought. What might be potential for Process thought is more similar, if Christologically defined, to what Barth indicates is actual. Distinct from most if not all Process thought is the way Barth takes the sense of contingency in the being of God and in the future of mankind. While there seems to be some debate and ambiguity even within Process discussion, for Barth the sovereign freedom, although defined as sovereign love, is clearly not at stake, nor is humanity's determination or the providential outcome of the history of the world's reconciliation or renewal.

Additionally, for Barth there is no neutral reality, force or principle that is somehow neutral, such as certain Process notions of creativity. The omnipotence of God is not diminished here. It is interpreted in terms of His loving character and purposes which has indeed a dynamic dimension for God Himself and for humanity as well. While the trinitarian forms of Process theology relate their conceptions to the persons of the Trinity these relations seem to be significantly more abstract and of a logical nature and less personal than for Barth. For both there is a sense of contingency giving human action a real significance and independence, but for Barth this occurs within God's gracious determination. Evil as well, for Barth, is a real threat but does not have the same ontological status as God's determination of humankind, whereas for Process thought evil seems to be on much more of a par with good human action and the good that is given by God is a potential, not an already realized reality involving all humankind in the present. Both want to emphasize hope for humankind and call for humankind's involvement. For Barth this is a participation in a given actuality, while for most Process theologies this is realization of a given potential for one individual at a time. While we cannot compare Barth's view with all of what might come under the heading of Process theology, this sketch highlights at least what differentiates Barth from Process thought. See for comparison Gunton, *Becoming and Being;* John B. Cobb, *A Christian Natural Theology* (London: 1966) and *The Structure of Christian Existence* (London, 1968); Charles Hartshorne, *The Divine Relativity: A Social Conception of God* (New Haven, 1972); Schubert Ogden, *The Reality of God and Other Essays* (London, 1967); Lewis Ford, "Process Trinitarianism," *Journal of the American Academy of Religion,* Vol. 43, (1975), pp. 199–213; Anthony J. Kelley, "Trinity and Process: Relevance of the Basic Christian Confession of God," *Theological Studies,* Vol. 31 (1970), pp. 393–414.

VI. Being-in-Extension-for-Inclusion of the Other

As we come to this final determination of the content of the existence of humanity we reach a crucial point in fully understanding and appreciating Barth's explication of humanity in fellowship as an image of God existing in its activity as God's covenant-partner and becoming what God intends for it to be. Humanity, as it correlates to its Creator, engages in relationships which call for persons to go out beyond themselves to that which is distinct, other, even alien and alienated, to bring the other into intimate fellowship with themselves and so into their fellowship with God as a fellow-covenant partner, enjoying the same life which God has given them.

In Barth's anthropological work this concern does not quite receive its own thematic presentation. Rather, it, like the fifth determination, is implicit in his discussion of nearly every other determination. The significance of this concept comes into view by its pervasive and accumulative effect rather than its presentation in one single concentration. Thus, we will have to cover again some ground already considered but from the angle of this determination as its own theme. We will begin, then, with man's being-in-extension-for-inclusion as found in the God-man relationship and then proceed to show how this comes to play, for Barth, a part in the determination of person to person relationships.[262]

A further word of introduction. There does not seem to be any particular terminology suited to this dimension. Ecstatic,[263] exo-centric,[264] self-transcending, other or otherness are some possible descriptions of this determination of humanity. The ecclesiological term "mission" is also related. However, these terms overlook the *telos* for this going out beyond one's self and the elliptical nature of this dynamic. It is for the purpose of making room for the other in one's own fellowship with God. Thus, we adopt the terminology of "extension-for-inclusion" to bring out this emphasis.

---

[262] While there does not seem to be a particular passage which Barth uses to emphasize this theme it can be seen in I John 1:2–4: "the life was made manifest, and we saw it and testify to it, and proclaim to you the eternal life which was with the Father and was made manifest to us—that which we have seen and heard we proclaim also to you, so that you may have fellowship with us; and our fellowship is with the Father and with His Son Jesus Christ. And we are writing this that our joy may be complete." We should also mention John 20:21 where Jesus says, "as the Father has sent me even so I send you" and the parallel saying in the prayer of Jesus in Jn. 17:18 in which Jesus continues to pray "that they may all be one even as thou, Father, art in me, and I in Thee, that they also may be in us..."

[263] The term *ekstasis* used by John Zizioulas in connection with *hypostasis* to characterize the central aspect of human existence, namely, that personhood is a movement of communion. This is an understanding much like Barth's. See his "Human Capacity and Incapacity," *SJT*, Vol. 28 (1975).

[264] This is the key term used by Wolfhart Pannenberg in his *Anthropology in Theological Perspective* (Philadelphia: Westminster Press, 1985).

The Extension-for-Inclusion of the Triune God

1. God's Election of Humankind: A Movement of Double Transcendence

Each created person is summoned and called by God to enter actively into the relationship with Him provided in Jesus Christ. Barth defines this calling. "To be summoned is to be called out of oneself and beyond oneself."[265] Mankind is necessarily called beyond himself because originally the One who calls him into relationship with Himself is beyond him, is other than he is. In this relationship of unity and communion God remains distinct, other. Yet God gives of Himself to humankind in His Word.[266]

In communion with humankind, God remains "not man," "not creature" even though God is with him and for him in his creatureliness. God remains distinct. Meeting God always requires going out of one's way.[267]

However, the "otherness" of God is not bound up with some supra-human or supra-cosmic dimension of being unrelated to humanity. The "otherness" of God is actual and real and made known in Jesus Christ. He alone is mankind's true Other, true Counter-part. In Jesus humanity encounters "the wholly and true Other as the genuine counter-part who satisfies and justifies him and in relation to whom he is called out of and beyond himself, and may thus discover and actualize his own freedom."[268] In Christ it becomes clear that there is now no divinity apart from humanity. Even though God is not a creature, God is not without the creature. He is with and for the creature as its Counter-part. Thus, the revelation in Jesus Christ is not the information about or an example of this, but it is the event in which God is with and for all creatures in actuality. We see, in Jesus, the Creator coming to be with the creature forever affecting the life of God. That which is truly divine is that God has gone out of Himself to be with and for the creature. God is love.

Given the otherness of God and man, the establishment of the relationship calls for a double movement of transcendence, both instigated by God. God transcends himself to give himself to be known and enables us, by His Spirit, to transcend ourselves and receive a knowledge of God.[269] So humanity

---

[265] *CD*, III/2, p. 166.

[266] "If God gives Himself to man to be known in the revelation of His Word through the Holy Spirit, it means that He enters into the relationship of object to man the subject....Man knows God in that he stands before God.. But this always means: in that God becomes, is and remains to him Another, One who is distinct from himself, One who meets him....Man cannot and must not know himself apart from God, but together with God as his 'opposite' " (*CD*, II/1, pp. 9–10).

[267] *CD*, II/1, p. 9 and p. 274: "There is no lack of contrariety in this conduct. It establishes and embraces the antithesis between the Creator and His creatures."

[268] *CD*, III/4, p. 480.

[269] *CD*, III/2, p. 166.

is not enclosed within the circle of its intrinsic possibilities, but opened towards that other and new reality of God its Creator which has broken through to it in His Word, and in that Word as His promise has come to dwell within it...He is, as, called by this Word, he is ready, and already in the act of transcending himself.[270]

God in Jesus Christ initiates and establishes a history of interaction which is a double movement which constitutes the being of humankind. Speaking of Jesus Christ:

> But the fact of this one man is prior to the existence of all other men. It is thus through their relationship to Him that they are what they are...The new and other which God is directly for the man Jesus, Jesus Himself is for all other men, and therefore He is the basis which makes their being history, a being which is transcended in his limitation from without and transcends its limitation outwards. Man is what he is as a creature, as the man Jesus, and in Him God Himself, moves towards him, and as he moves towards the man Jesus and therefore towards God. Man is as he is engaged in this movement in this "to him" from without and "from him" outwards...[271]

God has come to His creature in the event of the coming of Jesus Christ and the creature has responded also in Jesus Christ, reaching out beyond itself back to its Creator. There is a double movement of divine, and then, on that basis, a creaturely, self-transcendence in a correlating response.[272]

2. The All-Inclusive Humanity of Jesus Christ

God in Jesus Christ has established a unique history of relationship not only with some persons but with all humanity. Everyone has in Him "a human Neighbour, Companion, and Brother...He is definitively our Neighbour."[273] Jesus is from the very outset of Creation and originally the "Counter-part of every man."[274] This means that "every man as such is the fellow man of Jesus."[275]

---

[270]*Ibid.*, pp. 165–166.

[271]*CD*, III/2, pp. 161–162.

[272]"[In the history of Jesus Christ we have] both the transcendence and transcending of such a sphere—its transcendence by a new and different factor and its transcending in response and relation to this factor. It is the identity of the Creator and the creature. And the Creator is for the creature the utterly new and other....This creature is what it is as creature in a dynamic movement of the Creator to itself and itself to the Creator. It exists in this movement from another to itself and itself to this other—a movement which, since God the Creator is the Other, it is quite impossible to describe as a movement within itself" (*CD*, III/2, p. 159).

[273]*Ibid.*, p. 133.

[274]*Ibid.*, p. 134.

[275]*Ibid.*

This relationship of God through Jesus Christ is not a series of events with isolated individuals. It means the formation of a universal humanity in communion, represented by the Church and signifying the coming of the Kingdom of God. Jesus is the "quintessence of all possible relationship and fellowship."[276] Jesus includes within himself all others. "The love of God in Jesus Christ brings together Himself with all men and all men with Himself" and this means a bringing together of all humankind with one another.[277] His work of reconciliation is on behalf of all humanity.[278] Along with Christ's known people He has "a much larger unknown people which He is not ashamed to call His brethren."[279] This reconciliation has taken place *de jure*, although not yet *de facto*.[280] Because Jesus Christ and His community are so related, Barth will say that "the calling of sinful man to faith in Jesus Christ is identical with his calling to the community of Jesus Christ...his encounter with this object of his faith will therefore be in some form his encounter with the Christian community."[281]

Thus, the movement of God to man and man to God is one of extension out to the other for the sake of the inclusion of all humanity in the Son's communion with the Father by the Spirit. This mission comprehends the person and work of Jesus Christ. Humanity is given the privilege of participating in this mission.

3. The Intra-trinitarian Extension and Inclusion

However, the very being of God, by grace, contains within it the movement of going out to the other and including it. This movement is not alien or arbitrary, or extrinsic to God. What God does in Jesus Christ arises out of Who this God is. What He is towards the creature He is in Himself. This movement of mission *ad extra* is evident in the Father-Son relationship itself. The Father and Son are eternally other to each other. The otherness of the world and creatures is a "natural" overflow of this out of the life of God.[282]

Thus, we see again, this time in terms of an extension and inclusion, that the Father-Son relationship is the original relationship which is repeated *ad extra* in God's relationship to the world and its creatures.

Furthermore, this extra-divine movement has the character of a free covenantal relation as does its internal expression. The reason for this outgoing of God is not because of any necessity, but arises out of the very freedom of relationship between Father and Son in the Spirit. Barth describes creation as the overflow of God. "He has that which he seeks and creates between Himself and

---

[276] *CD*, II/1, p. 317.
[277] *CD*, IV/1, p. 105.
[278] *Ibid.*, p. 106.
[279] *CD*, IV/2, p. 511.
[280] *Ibid.*
[281] *CD*, IV/1, p. 759.
[282] *CD*, II/1, p. 317.

us. We must certainly regard this overflow as itself matching His essence, belonging to His essence."[283]

The fellowship within God of loving covenantal communion gives shape to the creation which is to correspond to, and so participate in, this divine intra-trinitarian fellowship between Father and Son in the Spirit. As the Father, in order to have fellowship, goes out to His other, to His counter-part, the Son, so Father and Son create creatures as a further counterpart to themselves with the intention to include them within their own fellowship.

Humanity: Extension and Inclusion of the Other in Fellowship

Within the human and divine relationship actualized in Jesus Christ we see the original and its own reflection and both of these in the creaturely sphere. However, there is also a horizontal reflection of this dynamic as well from the person of Jesus to other human creatures and in turn in His sending out his disciples to yet others.

1. Humanity: Directed to Other Persons

Thus, Barth directs us to John's Gospel. In the Father's sending of the Son into the world (Chapter 17) and the Son's sending of the disciples "we are obviously reminded even in this context of the bursting of the inner circle of the community outwards in favour of all men of the whole world."[284]

Jesus directs us in his own person to other persons. As Jesus exists by His extension for the sake of communion, so does all humanity. Humanity cannot realize its true form through isolated individuals.

Humankind's existence is created to be in relation with others who are not extensions of one's self, but distinct, other, who stand over against it. Consequently, there is to be no preoccupation with the self. Barth picks up on Luther's terminology and says that humanity is no *homo incurvatus in se*.[285] This self-concentration and self-centeredness represents the sinfulness and lostness of humanity. We become our true selves only in relation one to another.[286]

A refusal to extend one's self to others constitutes a sinful existence. This self-enslavement is itself a refusal to live by God's grace, a refusal to acknowledge that God is with us and for us so that we exist in a blessed

---

[283] *CD*, II/1, p. 273, *cf.* p. 274. "If God comes to man in His divine Word He does not do so because He needs man. God does not flee to man for refuge. He is not obligated to be the Creator, nor be gracious to man. He is glorious in Himself. He could be content with that inner glory. The fact that He is the Creator of man and is gracious to man is a free overflowing of His glory" (*CD*, III/2, p. 187).
[284] *CD*, III/2, p. 221.
[285] *CD*, III/4, p. 473.
[286] *Ibid.*, p. 478.

fellowship with Him. Since God is for us, being merely for ourselves is excluded. We are relieved of this burden.[287]

The relationship with God through Christ sets persons free and constitutes the reality of humanity existing in fellowship. Jesus alone is uniquely related to all human persons. We recall that "every man as such is the fellow-man of Jesus."[288] Consequently, this means that relationship with Jesus necessarily points us to relationship with others and relationship with others points us to relationship with Jesus. So, Barth says that the "neighbour's humanity reminds me of the humanity of the Son of God."[289] There is a unity of humanity in Jesus Christ so that He shows me my neighbor and my neighbor shows me Jesus. Consequently, Jesus directs and sends his disciples to their neighbors to represent Him and also indicates that their treatment of others and others' treatment of them are both related to humanity's treatment of Him.[290]

Since Jesus is a man for others, having His whole being directed for their benefit and on their behalf, he consequently directs his disciples to others with the twofold command which correlates his love for them and their love for others: "Love one another as I have loved you." The disciples are directed away from themselves out to others.[291]

This is the meaning and purpose of creation, to find its being in fellowship with another. Again we see the ontological basis for the good of human relations, for ethics. It begins with the Trinity, moves through the incarnation of Christ, and then makes itself manifest within creation itself in terms of right human action

2. Humanity: Directed Ultimately to Its True Other

However, Barth is compelled to indicate that the fulfillment of creation cannot be accomplished within itself, but must come from beyond itself, beyond human relationship. There is an ordering of the copy to the original even in this

---

[287] *CD*, II/2, p. 597)

[288] *Ibid.*, p. 134.

[289] *CD*, I/2, p. 425.

[290] See Mark 9:37–41; Matt. 25.

[291] In Barth's section on "The Active Life" he writes: "Human life participates in the freedom of all God's creatures to the extent that it does not have its aim in itself and cannot therefore be lived in self-concentration and self-centredness, but only in a relationship which moves outwards and upwards to another. All God's creatures exist in a relationship of this kind. None exists for itself. None is self-sufficient. None can justify itself. None possesses meaning or purpose in itself. Each stands in need of another. Each exists only as another stands in need of it. The command of God the Creator which summons man to the active life always includes the fact that it places him in his general order of the creature and thus calls him out of himself. And if he is obedient to it, if his action is service, it always includes the general fact that he looks and strives beyond himself, that he actualizes his existence in his relationship to another, that he is thus integrated into the order of all creatures, and that he therefore participates at his own place and in his own way in the freedom of every creature" (*CD*, III/4, pp. 477–478).

going out to include the other. The humanity of mankind will find its true being only in relationship with its one true Counter-part.[292]

Ultimate preoccupation with human relationship can never be an end in itself. This will result in a suffocating dependency and constitute a demand that the other be what only God in Christ can be. This is the evil of existing in slavery one to another.

Rather, the obligation created by God's entering into a gracious relationship with man is man's own freedom. As we have noted in a previous section in this chapter, as God goes out to man and man to God, so there is communion, fellowship, even union, but not fusion and confusion. So also, in a corresponding way there is no fusion or confusion in the right and good communion and fellowship of creature with creature.

Ultimately, then, the neighbor must lead me to Christ. The secondary counter-part leads to the original counter-part. The humanity of humankind is meant to go outside and even beyond itself for a fellowship with its true Counter-part. Its life is to be a participation of obedience and service to Jesus Christ worked out within the creaturely sphere. The action and service which is a participation in communion with his Creator, Reconciler and Redeemer reaches out to yet others that they may have, not merely fellowship on the horizontal plane, but have that human fellowship fulfilled by being caught up in fellowship with its Creator and so be a participation in the divine fellowship of Father and Son in the Spirit.

Thus, when Barth goes on to explicate the doctrines of the Church and marriage and the parent-child relationship or any dimension of the Christian life, he always says something related to this extension-for-inclusion theme. Human relationships have their meaning by being real living signs and genuine participations in God's own relationship extended to us in Jesus Christ. We can see Barth develop this specifically in four areas: The Church and its mission, the service of work, the ministry of marriage, the ministry of parenting and serving the neighbor.

3. The Church: a Being in Community for the Other

Thus, the Church of Jesus Christ is 1)a community or fellowship in which persons are to attach themselves, be included, and be added to.[293] 2)The Church exists as a history of being and exercising a ministry of witness in its inner life as it corresponds to the life of the Spirit as a unity, with its humanity, its message, and in its loving service of freeing others to serve yet others.[294] 3)As a community which is called to bear witness and serve in the world by a) an "attempted imitation and representation of the love with which God loved the

---

[292]The mystery of creaturely existence is revealed in man "in the fact that he is summoned by the command of God to the active life and therefore beyond himself" (*Ibid.*, p. 478).

[293]*CD*, III/4, pp. 490–493.

[294]*Ibid.*, pp. 493–502.

world," i.e., being for the world, and b) by "the winning of new human members from the world around, of summoning non-Christians to an understanding of their call and therefore to faith, to obedience and to co-operation in the service of the community."[295] The Church is a missionary community and every Christian is a missionary.[296]

4. Work: Being of Service for the Other

From this center arises a person's calling to his work. This work then must be understood as an extension of this mission, and so creating fellowship in the sphere of his work. It will be work done for the sake of the service of the Kingdom of God.[297] Indeed all of mankind's activities and relationships are to be lived from this center, for this purpose.

5. The Ministry to Others of Marriage

Consequently, when Barth speaks of marriage he cannot consider it as an end in itself. It too has a mission. It too is a fellowship which will discover its freedom only as it moves out of itself to include others. "Marriage is not permission to establish an egoistic partnership of two persons." It is not and cannot be undertaken as a "purely private undertaking." The command of God regarding marriage "implies that its eventuality must have the character of a responsible act outwards in relation to those around." The marriage partners must exhibit a "willingness and readiness to undertake such active participation in the nearer, the more distant and the most distant events of the surrounding contemporary world."[298]

6. Parenting the Child and Serving the Neighbor

Finally, we should point out that Barth's development of the section on "Freedom in Fellowship" is itself structured along the lines of concentric circles becoming ever more inclusive as the circles of relationship continually move out beyond themselves to include yet others.

Barth begins with his exploration of the most basic and paradigmatic form of human fellowship, the relationship of man and woman. However, he cannot stop there. This relationship must include others. So, he next considers the parent-child relationship, not because all parents have children, but because all persons are children of parents and so exist already in a wider context than a marital one. Were they absolutely excluded from this circle of relationship they would not exist at all, and to the extent that they are excluded (orphaned, abandoned, etc.) it would mean for them the temptation and overcoming of great obstacles to extend themselves to include others. It would, indeed, jeopardize even their own potential marriages.

---

[295] *Ibid.*, pp. 502–505.
[296] *Ibid.*, p. 505.
[297] *Ibid.*, p. 521.
[298] *CD*, III/4, p. 224.

Barth does not stop at this point, either, as if the family were an end in itself. It too, must include yet others if it is to participate in its fulfillment as given to it in Jesus Christ. Thus, Barth concludes his section on freedom for fellowship with the part on the "Near and Distant Neighbours." Here Barth reaches out to the full extent of relationship paradigmatically present from the very beginning in the relationship of man and woman. Mankind's fellowship must include all humanity, near and far. Perhaps in this connection the enemy, rather than the opposite sex, or the "other" generation, or culture is the most distant. Thus, what begins as seemingly narrow and exclusive, the marital relationship, opens out to affirm that relationship can be fulfilled only in an all-inclusive fellowship of all humanity, no matter how distinct, different, other, and even alien. All relationships are included and established in the command of God for humanity to exist in fellowship.

Indeed, Jesus Christ is the One true Neighbor and the original and truly Other, far more distinct and alien, than any other human creature, and yet nearer than any other human creature to each and every human creature. To be rightly related to Him is to be in fellowship with all humanity through Him. For He is their Creator, Lord, Representative, Substitute, Savior and Redeemer. All persons, then, are a reminder of His own all inclusive humanity. To be in fellowship with the Neighbor must include a covenantal fellowship open to all neighbors. As Jesus has gone out of Himself to include others in His own relationship with the Father, so too we, as we are called to participate in this same fellowship, must also actively go out so that any and every other creature may also participate with us in God's calling to be his children, enjoying the same sonship which he has with His Son, Jesus.

We have now completed our survey of the six dimensions of the determinations of our humanity. We have summarized these six under two headings: The Form of Humanity as Personal-Being-in Relationship and The Action of Humanity as Being-in-Covenant-Partnership. We have seen how each of these determinations find their ground and root in the internal trinitarian relations of the Father and Son in the Holy Spirit and in the revelation in Jesus Christ. This constitutes their ontological determination as Christological and trinitarian. We have also noted how it is this same ontological grounding that forms the foundation for Barth's ethics.

With this as a foundation, we will now turn to the section on Barth's special ethics of "Parents and Children" prepared to appreciate and comprehend the full significance and weight of the exposition we find there. The coordination and interdependence of Barth's trinitarian and Christological theology, his anthropology and his special ethics will be quite evident.

Selected Bibliography

Anderson, Herbert. *The Family and Pastoral Care*. Philadelphia: Fortress Press, 1984.

Anderson, Ray S. *Historical Transcendence and the Reality of God*. London: Geoffrey Chapman Publishers, 1975.

_____. *On Being Human*. Grand Rapids: Wm. B. Eerdmans Publishing Co., 1982.

Anderson, Ray S., Editor. *Theological Foundations for Ministry*. Edinburgh: T&T Clark and Grand Rapids: Wm. B. Eerdmans Publishing Co., 1979.

Anderson, Ray S. and Dennis Guernsey. *On Being Family*. Grand Rapids: Wm. B. Eerdmans Publishing Co., 1985.

Balswick, Jack O. and Judith K. Balswick. *The Family: A Christian Perspective on the Contemporary Home*. Grand Rapids: Baker Book House, 1989.

von Balthasar, Hans Urs. *The Theology of Karl Barth*. Translated by John Drury. New York, Chicago, San Francisco: Holt, Rinehart and Winston, 1971. German title: *Karl Barth. Darstellung und Deutung seiner Theologie*. Köln: Verlag Jacob Hegner, 1951.

Barth, Karl. *Christ and Adam: Man and Humanity in Romans 5*. Translated by T. A. Smail. Edinburgh & London: Oliver and Boyd, 1963, reprint. *Scottish Journal of Theology Occasional Papers,* No. 5, German title: *Christus und Adam nach Römer 5*. Züruch: Evangelischer Verlag A. G. Zollikon, 1952. *Theologische Studien,* No. 35.

_____. *The Christian Life Church Dogmatics, Volume IV/4, Lecture Fragments*. Translated by Geoffrey Bromiley. Edited by Hans-Anton Drewes and Eberhard Jüngel. Grand Rapids: Wm. B. Eerdmans Publishing Co., 1981.

_____. "The Christian as a Witness." *God in Action*. Translated by E. G. Homrighausen and Karl J. Ernst. New York: Round Table Press, 1963.

_____. *Church Dogmatics*. Volumes I/1–IV/4. Translated by various scholars. General Editors: Geoffrey Bromiley and Thomas F. Torrance. Edinburgh: T&T Clark, 1955–1961. German title: *Die Kirchliche Dogmatic*. Züruch: Evangelischer Verlag A. G. Zollikon, 1948–1959.

_____. *Ethics*. Edited by Dietrich Braun. Translated by Geoffrey Bromiley. New York: Seabury Press, 1981. German title (two volumes): *Ethik I 1928* and *Ethik II 1928/29*. Zürich: Theologischer Verlag, 1973 and 1978.

_____. "Evangelical Theology in the 19th Century." *The Humanity of God*. Translated by Thomas Weiser. Atlanta: John Knox Press, 1974, pp. 11–33.

_____. "The Gift of Freedom: Foundation of Evangelical Ethics." *The Humanity of God*. Atlanta: John Knox Press, 1974. Eleventh priniting of 1960 first edition. Translated by Thomas Weiser from *Die Geschenk der Freiheit* originally published as a monograph in the *Theologische*

Studien. Zürich: Evangelischer Verlag A. G. Zollikon, no date. First given as an address, Sept. 1953.

———. "Gospel and Law." *God, Grace and Gospel.* Translated by James S. McNab. *Scottish Journal of Theology Occasional Papers,* No. 8, 1966 reprint of first English edition, 1959. Edinburgh, London: Oliver and Boyd, 1959. From the second German edition of *Evangelium und Gesetz.* München: Christian Kaiser Verlag, 1956.

———. "The Humanity of God." *The Humanity of God.* Atlanta: John Knox Press, 1974. Translated by John Newton Thomas. An address given in 1956 and published as a monograph as *Die Menschlichkeit Gottes* in the *Theologische Studien* series. Zürich: Evangelischer Verlag A.G. Zollikon.

———. *Karl Barth's Table Talk.* Edited and recorded by John D. Godsey. *Scottish Journal of Theology Occasional Papers,* No. 10. London & Edinburgh: Oliver and Boyd, 1962.

———. "The New Humanism and the Humanism of God." *Theology Today,* Vol. 8 (May, 1951), pp. 157–166, translated by Freidrich L. Herzog from "Humanismus in Theologische Studien." Heft 28. Zürich: Evangelischer Verlag, Zollikon.

———. "On Systematic Theology." *Scottish Journal of Theology*, Vol. 12 (1961), pp. 225–228.

———. *Die Protestantische Theologie im 19 Jahrhundert.* Zurich: Evangelischer Verlag A. G. Zollikon, 1952. English title: *Protestant Theology in the Nineteenth Century.* Translated by Brian Cozens, John Bowden, et. al. London: SCM Press Ltd., 1972.

———. *The Word of God and the Word of Man.* Translated by Douglas Horton. London: Hodder and Stoughton, 1928. German title: *Das Wort Gottes und die Theologie*, 1924.

Barth, Karl with Emil Brunner. *Natural Theology.* Translated by P. Fraenkel. London: Geoffrey Bles, 1949.

Barton, Stephen C., ed. *The Family in Theological Perspective.* Edinburgh: T&T Clark, 1996.

Baxter, Christina Ann. *The Movement from Exegesis to Dogmatics in the Theology of Karl Barth with special reference to Romans, Philippians and the Church Dogmatics.* Ph.D. dissertation, Durham University, 1981.

Beatty, Melody. *Co-Dependent No More.* San Francisco: Harper Hazelden Books, 1987.

Bender, Ross T. *Christians in Families: Genesis and Exodus.* Scottsdale, Pennsylvania and Kitchener, Ontario: Herald Press, 1982.

Berkouwer, G. C. *Man: the Image of God.* Translated by Dirk W. Jellema. Grand Rapids: Wm. B. Eerdmans Publishing Co., 1972. Dutch title, *De Mens het Beeld Gods.*

_____, *The Triumph of Grace in the Theology of Karl Barth*. London: Paternoster Press, 1956.

von Bertanalanffy, L. *General Systems Theory*. New York: George Braziller, 1968.

Biggar, Nigel. "Hearing God's Command and Thinking about What's Right: With and Beyond Barth." Oxford Conference in Commemoration of the Centenary of the Birth of Karl Barth, 1986—Proceedings. *Reckoning with Barth: Essays in Commemoration of the Centenary of Karl Barth's Birth*. Editor: Nigel Biggar. London: Mowbray, 1988.

Bonhoeffer, Dietrich. *The Cost of Discipleship*. Translated by R. H. Fuller. London: SCM Press, 1973 reprint of the Second Edition, 1959. German title: *Nachfolge*. Munchen: Christian Kaiser Verlag, 1937.

_____, *Ethics*. Edited by Eberhard Bethge. Translated by Nelville Horton Smith. New York: Macmillan Publishing Co., 1978. German title: *Ethik*. Munchen: Christian Kaiser Verlag, 1949.

_____, *Christ the Center*. Translated by Edwin H. Robinson. New York, Hagerstown, San Francisco, London: Harper and Row Publishers, 1978. From Bonhoeffer's *Gesammelte Schriften*. Vol. 3. Christian Kaiser Verlag, 1960. Published in Britain as *Christology*.

_____, *Creation and Fall*. Translated by John C. Fletcher. New York: Macmillan Publishing Co., 1971 reprint. German title: *Schöpfung und Fall*. Münich: Christian Kaiser Verlag, 1937.

_____, *Sanctorum Communio*. Translated by R. Gregor Smith. London: William Collins Sons & Co., 1963.

Bouillard, Henri. *The Knowledge of God*. Translated by Samuel D. Femiano. London: Burns & Oates/Herder and Herder, 1969. French title: *Connaissance De Dieu*. Paris: Aubier, 1967.

_____, *Karl Barth. Parole de Dieu et Existence Humaine*. Vol. III. Paris: Aubier, 1957.

Bracken, Joseph, S.J. "The Holy Trinity as a Community of Divine Persons, I & II." *Heythrop Journal*, Vol. 15 (1974) pp. 166–82 and pp. 257–270.

Bradshaw, Timothy. *Trinity and Ontology. A Comparative Study of the Theologies of Karl Barth and Wolfhart Pannenberg*. Edinburgh: Rutherford House Books, 1988.

Bromiley, Geoffery, *Introduction to the Theology of Karl Barth*. Grand Rapids: Wm. B. Eerdmans Publishing Co., 1979.

Bronfenbrenner, Urie. *The Ecology of Human Development*. Cambridge: Harvard University Press, 1979.

Brunner, Emil. *The Divine Imperative*. London: Lutterworth Press, 1953. German title: *Das Gebot und die Ordnungen*, Second Edition, 1932.

_____. *Man in Revolt*. Translated by Olive Wyon. London: Lutterworth Press, 1942. German title: *Der Mensch in Widerspruch: Die christliche Lehre vom wahren und vom wirklichen Menschen*, 1937.

_____. "The New Barth: Observations on Karl Barth's *Doctrine of Man*." *Scottish Journal of Theology*, Vol. 2, No. 4 (1951), pp. 123–135.

_____. *The Christian Doctrine of God, Dogmatics I*. Translated by Olive Wyon. London: Lutterworth Press, 1949. German title: *Die christliche Lehre von Gott*.

Buber, Martin. *I and Thou*. Translated by Ronald Gregor Smith. Edinburgh: T&T Clark, 1942 reprint of the 1937 English Translation.

Busch, Eberhard. *Karl Barth: His Life from Letters and Autobiographical Texts*. Philadelphia: Fortress Press, 1976.

Cairns, David. *The Image of God in Man*. London: SCM Press, 1953.

Camfield, F. W. *Reformation Old and New: (A Tribute to Karl Barth)*. London and Redhill: Lutterworth Press, 1947.

Campbell, Cynthia McCall. "Imago Trinitatis: An Appraisal of Karl Barth's Doctrine of the *Imago Dei* in the Light of His Doctrine of the Trinity." Ph.D. Dissertation, Southern Methodist University, 1981.

Chartier, Jan and Myron. *Caring Together—Faith Hope and Love in Your Family*. Philadelphia: Westminster Press, 1986.

Chartier, Myron. "A Theology of Parenting: An Incarnational Model." *American Baptist Quarterly*, Vol. 3 (1984), pp. 73–84.

Christensen, Torben. *The Divine Order. A Study in F. D. Maurice's Theology*. Leiden: E.J. Brill, 1973.

Clapp, Rodney. *Families at the Crossroads. Beyond Traditional and Modern Options*. Downers Grove, Ill.: InterVarsity Press, 1993.

Come, Arnold. *An Introduction to Barth's "Dogmatics" for Preachers*. Philadelphia: Westminster Press, 1963.

_____. *Human Spirit and Holy Spirit*. Philadelphia: Westminster Press, 1959.

Cousins, Ewert. "The Theology of Interpersonal Relations." *Thought*, Vol. 45 (1970), pp. 56–82.

Curran, Charles. "Toward a Theology of Human Belonging." *Journal of Religion and Health*, Vol. 4 (1964–1965), pp. 227–241.

Dalferth, Ingolf. "Karl Barth's Eschatological Realism." *Karl Barth: Centenary Essays*. Editor, S. W. Sykes. Cambridge: Cambridge University Press, 1989.

Daly, Mary. *Pure Lust*. Boston: Beacon Press, 1984.

Deddo, Gary W. "Jesus' Paradigm for Relating our Experience to our Language About God." *The Evangelical Quarterly*, 68:1 (1996), pp. 15–33. I. H. Marshall, Editor.

Dobson, James. *Dare to Discipline*. Eastbourne: Kingsway Publications, 1980.

Dreikhurs, Rudolf with Vicki Soltz. *Children the Challenge*. New York: Duell, Sloan and Pearce, 1964.

Ellis, Ieuan. "Jesus and the Subversive Family." *Scottish Journal of Theology*, Vol. 38 (1985), pp. 173–188.

Ellul, Jacques. *Ethics of Freedom*. Translated by Geoffrey Bromiley. Grand Rapids: Wm. B. Eerdmans Publishing Co., 1976.

Evans, C. Steven. *Preserving the Person: A Look at the Human Sciences*. Downers Grove, Ill.: InterVarsity Press, 1979.

Fallot, Rodger D. "On Narcissism and Post Narcissism: Psychology and Theology in Context." *Pastoral Psychology*, Vol. 33 (Sum. 1985), pp. 255–266.

Firestone, Shulasmith. *The Dialectic of Sex*. New York: Bantam, 1971.

Fletcher, Verne H. "Karl Barth's Conception of Co-Humanity and the Search for Human Community." *South East Asia Journal of Theology*, Vol. 9, No. 1 (July 1967), pp. 41–53.

Gibbons, Cecil. W. "The Theological Significance of the Family." *The Modern Churchman*, Vol. VIII, No. 4, N.S. (July 1965).

_____. "A Secondary Point of Reference in Barth's Anthropology." *Scottish Journal of Theology*, Vol. 16 (January 1963), pp. 132–135.

Greer, Germaine. *Sex and Destiny: the Politics of Human Fertility*. New York: Harper and Row, 1984.

Griffen, Karn. "The Church as a Therapeutic Community." *Theological Foundations for Ministry*. Editor, Ray S. Anderson. Edinburgh: T&T Clark and Grand Rapids: Wm. B. Eerdmans Publishing Co., 1979, pp. 734–751.

Guernsey, Dennis. *Family Covenant: Love and Forgiveness in the Christian Home*. Elgin, Illinois, Weston, Ontario: David C. Cook Publishing Co., 1984.

Gunton, Colin. "The Triune God and the Freedom of the Creature." *Karl Barth: Centenary Essays*. Editor, S.W. Sykes. Cambridge: Cambridge University Press, 1989.

_____. *Becoming and Being: the Doctrine of God in Charles Hartshorne and Karl Barth*. Oxford: Oxford University Press, 1978.

_____. "Karl Barth and the Development of Christian Doctrine." *Scottish Journal of Theology*, Vol. 22 (1972), pp. 171–180.

_____, *The One, The Three, and the Many: God, Creation and the Culture of Modernity*. The 1992 Bampton Lectures. Cambridge: Cambridge University Press, 1993.

_____, *The Promise of Trinitarian Theology*. Edinburgh: T&T Clark, 1991.

Guthrie, Jr. Shirley C. "Pastoral Counseling, Trinitarian Theology, and Christian Anthropology." *Interpretation,* Vol. 33, No. 2 (April 1979), pp. 130–143.

Hammond, Guy B. "Christopher Lasch and a Renewed Theory of the Family." *Perspectives in Religious Studies,* Vol. 10 (Spring 1983), pp. 15–32.

Handy, Robert T. "The Individualistic Spirit and Concern for Community: A Critical Tension in American Protestant History." *The Modern Churchman,* Vol. 12 (Oct. 1971), pp. 32–41.

Harrisville, Roy A. "Jesus and the Family." *Interpretation,* Vol. 23 (1969).

Hartshorne, Charles. *The Divine Relativity: A Social Conception of God.* New Haven: 1972.

Hartwell, Herbert. *The Theology of Karl Barth: An Introduction.* London: Gerald Duckworth & Co. Ltd., 1964.

Hendry, George. *The Holy Spirit in Christian Theology.* London: SCM Press, 1965.

Hugen, Melvin D. "Idolatry." *Calvin Theological Journal,* Vol. 7, 8 (1972–3), p. 54.

Hughes, Philip. *The True Image.* Leicester: InterVarsity Press, Grand Rapids: Wm. B. Eerdmans Publishing Co., 1989.

Hulme, William. *The Pastoral Care of Families: Its Theology and Practice.* Nashville, New York: Abingdon Press, 1962.

Hunsinger, George. *Karl Barth and Radical Politics.* Philadelphia: Westminster Press, 1976.

Jenson, Robert. *God After God.* Indianapolis, New York: Bobbs-Merril Company, 1969.

_____, "Karl Barth." *The Modern Theologians: An Introduction to Christian Theology in the Twentieth Century,* Vol. 1. Editor: David F. Ford. London: Basil Blackwell, 1989.

Jewett, Paul K. *Man as Male and Female: A Study in Sexual Relationship from a Theological Point of View.* Grand Rapids: Wm. B. Eerdmans Publishing Co., 1975.

Jungmann, Joseph. *Handing on the Faith.* West Germany: Herder, 1964.

Jüngel, Eberhard. *The Doctrine of the Trinity. God's Being is in Becoming.* Translated by Horton Harris. Edinburgh & London: Scottish Academic Press, 1976. German title: *Gottes Sein ist im Werden.* Tübingen: J.C.B. Mohr (Paul Siebeck), 1966.

_____, *God as the Mystery of the World. On the Foundation of the Theology of the Crucified One in the Dispute between Theism and Atheism*. Translated by Darrell L. Guder. Grand Rapids: Wm. B. Eerdmans Publishing Co., 1983. German title: *Gott als Geheimnis der Welt*. Tübingen: J.C.B. Mohr (Paul Siebeck), 1977.

_____, *Karl Barth. A Theological Legacy*. Translated by Garret E. Paul. Philadelphia: The Westminster Press, 1982. Published in German: *Barth-Studien*. Zürich-Köln: Benziger Verlag, 1982.

_____, *Theological Essays*. Edinburgh: T&T Clark, 1989.

Kaufman, Gordon. *Systematic Theology: A Historicist Perspective*. New York: Chas. Scribner's Sons, 1968.

Kelley, Anthony J. "Trinity and Process: Relevance of the Basic Christian Confession of God." *Theological Studies*, Vol. 31 (1970), pp. 393–414.

Klausner, S. Z. *Two Centuries of Child Rrearing Manuals*. Philadelphia: University of Pennsylvania Press, 1968.

Kuhn, Thomas S. *The Structure of Scientific Revolutions*, Second Edition. Chicago: University of Chicago Press, 1970.

LaCugna. *God For Us: The Trinity & Christian Life*. San Francisco: Harper Collins, 1991.

Lapseley, James N. "Personhood in a Technological World." *Princeton Seminary Bulletin*, Vol. 61, No. 3 (Sum. 1968), pp. 36–41.

Lasch, Christopher. *The Culture of Narcissism*. New York: W. W. Norton, 1979.

_____, *Haven in a Heartless World: The Family Besieged*. New York: Basic Books, Inc., 1977.

_____, *The Minimal Self: Psychic Survival in Troubled Times*. New York, London: W. W. Norton, 1984.

Lee, Jung Young. "Karl Barth's Use of Analogy in His *Church Dogmatics*." *Scottish Journal of Theology*, Vol. 22 (1969), pp. 129–151.

Lehmann, Paul. *Ethics in a Christian Context*. New York and Evanston: Harper & Row Publishers, 1963.

Lewis, Clive Staples. *The Four Loves*. New York: Harcourt Brace Janovich, Inc., 1960.

Lyon, David. *Sociology and the Human Image*. Leicester, England and Downers Grove, Ill., InterVarsity Press, 1983.

Macmurray, John. *The Clue to History*. London: SCM Press, 1938.

_____, *Persons in Relation*. London: Faber & Faber Ltd., 1966.

_____, *Reason and Emotion*. London: Faber & Faber Ltd., 1962.

_____. *The Self as Agent*. London: Faber & Faber Ltd., 1953. The Gifford Lectures, Vol. 1, 1953–54.

Macquarrie, John. *Principles of Christian Theology*. New York: Chas. Scribner's Sons, 1977.

Mascall, Eric. L. *The Triune God*. West Sussex: Churchman Publishing Ltd., 1986.

Maurice, Frederick Dennison. *The Kingdom of Christ,* in Two Vols., 1838.

McConnachie, John. *The Significance of Karl Barth*. London: Hodder and Stoughton Limited, 1931.

McCulloch, Joseph. "Persons in Relation." *The Modern Churchman*, Vol. 12, No. 1 (Oct. 1968), pp. 32–41.

McIntyre, John. "Analogy." *Scottish Journal of Theology*, Vol. 12 (1959), pp. 1–20.

McKelway, Alexander J. "Perichoretic Possibilities in Barth's Doctrine of Male and Female." *The Princeton Seminary Bulletin,* Vol. 1 (1986), pp. 231–243.

_____. "The Concept of Subordination in Barth's Special Ethics." *Scottish Journal of Theology*, Vol. 32 (1979), pp. 345–357.

McLean, Stuart. *Humanity in the Thought of Karl Barth*. Edinburgh: T&T Clark, 1981.

McNeill, John T. "Natural Law in the Teaching of the Reformers." *Journal of Religion*, Vol. 26, No. 3, (July 1946), pp. 168–182.

Minuchin, Salvador. *Family & Family Therapy*. Cambridge: Harvard University Press, 1976.

Mollenkott, Virginia Ramsey. *The Divine Feminine: The Biblical Imagery of God as Female.* New York: Crossroad, 1987.

Moltmann, Jürgen. *Man: Christian Anthropology in the Conflicts of the Present*. Translated by John Sturdy. London: SPCK, 1974. German title: *Mensch*, 1971.

_____. *The Power of the Powerless*. San Francisco: Harper and Row Publishers, 1983, German title: *Ohne Macht mächtig*, 1981.

_____. *The Trinity and the Kingdom*. Translated by Margaret Kohl. San Francisco: Harper and Row Publishers, 1981. German title: *Trinität und Reich Gottes*. Munich: Christian Kaiser Verlag, 1980. Originally published in Britain under the title *The Trinity and the Kingdom of God*. London: SCM Press, 1981.

Mondin, Battista. *The Principle of Analogy in Protestant and Catholic Thought*. The Hague: Martinus Nijhoff, 1963.

Morse, Christopher. "Raising God's Eyebrows: Some Further Thoughts on the Concept of the *Analogia Fidei*." *Union Seminary Quarterly Review,* Vol. XXXVII, Nos. 1 & 2 (Fall/Winter, 1981–1982), pp. 39–49.

Mount, Ferdinand. *The Subversive Family.* London, 1982.

Mühlen, Heribert. *Der Heilige Geist als Person.* Munster: 1963.

Narramore, Bruce S. "Parent Leadership Styles and Biblical Anthropology." *Bibliotheca Sacra* (Oct.–Dec. 1978), pp. 345–357.

Newbigin, Lesslie. *Foolishness to the Greeks.* London: SPCK, 1988.

Niebuhr, Reinhold. "The Quality of our Lives." *The Christian Century,* Vol. LXXXVII, No. 19 (May 11, 1960), pp. 568–572.

Niebuhr, Reinhold. *The Nature and Destiny of Man,* Two Volumes. London: Nisbet & Co. Ltd., 1942, reprint.

O'Donnell, John, S.J. "The Trinity as Divine Community: A Critical Reflection Upon Recent Theological Developments." *Gregorianum,* Vol. 69, 1 (1988), pp. 5–34.

O'Donovan, Joan. "Man in the Image of God." *Scottish Journal of Theology,* Vol. 39 (1986), pp. 433–59.

O'Donovan, Oliver. *Resurrection and Moral Order. An Outline for Evangelical Ethics.* Grand Rapids: Wm. B. Eerdmans Publishing Co., 1994. Second Edition.

Oden, Thomas. *The Promise of Barth.* Philadelphia, New York: J. B. Lippincott Co., 1969.

Ogden, Schubert. *The Reality of God and Other Essays.* London: 1967.

Osborn, Robert T. "A 'Personalistic' Appraisal of Barth's Political Ethics." *Studies in Religion,* Vol. 12, No. 3 (June 1983), pp. 313–324.

Oshima, Sueo. "Barth's *Analogia Relationis* and Heidegger's Ontological Difference." *The Journal of Religion,* Vol. 53 (1973) pp. 176–194.

Pannenberg, Wolfhart. *Anthropology in Theological Perspective*, English Translation by Matthew J. O'Connell. Philadelphia: The Westminster Press, 1985. German title: *Anthropologie in theologischer Perspektive.*

_____. *Grundfragen Systematischer Theologie.* Gessamelt Aufsatze Band 2. Göttingen: Vandenhoeck und Ruprecht, 1980.

_____. *What is Man? Contemporary Anthropology in Theological Perspective.* Translated by Duane A. Priebe. Philadelphia: Fortress Press, 1970. German title: *Was ist der Mensch? Die Anthropologie der Gegenwart im Lichte der Theologie.* Götingen: Vandenhoeck and Ruprecht, 1962.

Parsons, Michael. "Being Precedes Act: Indicative and Imperative in Paul's Writing." *Evangelical Quarterly,* Vol. 88, No. 2 (1988), pp. 99–127.

Peck, William Jay. "A Proposal Concerning Bonhoeffer's Concept of the Person." *American Theological Review*, Vol. 50 (1968), pp. 311–329.

Pfuetze, Paul. "The Concept of the Self in Contemporary Psychotherapy." *Pastoral Psychology*, Vol. 9 (Feb. 1958), pp. 9–19.

Piper, Otto. "The Broken Family in the Bible." *Pastoral Psychology*, Dec. 1967, pp. 14–21.

_____. *The Christian Interpretation of Sex*. London: Nisbet & Co. Ltd., 1942.

Polanyi, Michael. *Personal Knowledge: Towards a Post-Critical Philosophy*. Chicago: University of Chicago Press, 1974.

Pöhlmann, Horst Georg. *Analogia entis oder Analogia fidei?: Die Frage der Analogie bei Karl Barth*. Göttingen: Vandenhoeck & Ruprecht, 1965.

Prenter, Regen. "*Die Einheit von Schöpfung und Erlösung*," *Theologische Zeitschrift* II (May, June 1946).

Prestige, G. L. *God in Patristic Thought*. London: SPCK, 1985.

Pride, Mary. *The Way Home. Beyond Feminism, Back to Reality*. Westchester, Illinois: Crossway Books, 1985.

Prins, Richard. "The Image of God in Adam and the Restoration of Man in Jesus Christ." *Scottish Journal of Theology*, Vol. 25 (1972), pp. 32–34.

Rahner, Karl. *Theological Investigations*, Vol. 8. Translated by David Bourke. London: Darton, Longman & Todd; New York: Herder and Herder, 1971.

Ramm, Bernard. *After Fundamentalism: The Future of Evangelical Theology*. San Francisco: Harper & Row Publishers, 1983.

Ranson, Guy H. "F. D. Maurice on the Social Nature of Man." *Canadian Journal of Theology*, Vol. XI, No. 4 (1965), pp. 265–276.

Richard of St. Victor. "Book Three of the Trinity." *Richard of St. Victor*. Translated by Grover A. Zinn. London: SPCK, 1979.

Roberts, Richard H. "The Reception of the Theology of Karl Barth in the Anglo-Saxon World: History, Typology and Prospect." *Karl Barth: Centenary Essays*. Editor, S. W. Sykes. Cambridge, New York, Melbourne: Cambridge University Press, 1989.

Robinson, H. Wheeler. *The Christian Doctrine of Man*. Edinburgh, T&T Clark, 1934.

Rodiger, Georgiana. *The Miracle of Therapy. A Layperson's Guide to the Mysteries of Christian Psychology*. Dallas, London: Word Publishing Co., 1989.

Ruether, Rosemary Radford. "An Unrealized Revolution." *Christianity and Crisis*, (Oct. 1983), pp. 399–404.

———. "The Left Hand of God in the Theology of Karl Barth: Karl Barth as a Mythopoeic Theologian." *Journal of Religious Thought*, Vol. 25, No.1 (1968–1969), pp. 3–26.

———. *Religion and Sexism.* New York: Simon & Schuster, 1974.

Russell, Letty. *Becoming Human.* Philadelphia: Westminster Press, 1982.

Sanger, Margaret. *The Feminist Papers.* Editor, A. S. Rossi. New York: Columbia University Press, 1973.

Schillebeeckx, Edward and Bas van Iersel, Editors. *A Personal God.* New York: The Seabury Press, 1977.

Schleiermacher, Friedrich. *Die christliche Sitte. Werke.* Erste Abteilung, Bd. XII. Edited by L. Jonas. Berlin: G. Reimer, 1843.

Schoeman, Pieter. "A Spirituality of Humanity: An Interpretation of Karl Barth's View on Romans 5." *Journal of Theology for South Africa,* Vol. 32 (Sept. 1980), pp. 23–27.

Schwöbel, Christoph and Colin E. Gunton. *Persons, Divine and Human.* Edinburgh: T&T Clark, 1991.

Sears, Robert S.J. "Trinitarian Love as Ground of the Church." *Theological Studies,* Vol. 37 (1967), pp. 652–679.

Seeberg, Reinhold. *Text Book of the The History of Doctrines.* Translated by Charles E. Hay. Grand Rapids: Baker Book House, 1983.

Smail, Thomas A. *The Forgotten Father.* London: Hodder and Stoughton, 1987 reprint.

———. *Reflected Glory.* London: Hodder and Stoughton, 1975.

———. *The Giving Gift: The Holy Spirit in Person.* London: Hodder and Stoughton, 1988.

Soucek, J. B. "Man in the Light of the Humanity of Jesus." *Scottish Journal of Theology,* Vol. 2 (1949), pp. 74–82.

Stackhouse, Max L. *Covenant & Commitments: Faith, Family, and Economic Life.* Louisville: Westminster John Knox, 1997.

Stockton, Ian. "Children, Church and Kingdom." *Scottish Journal of Theology,* Vol. 36 (1983), pp. 87–97.

Strauss, R. L. *Confident Children and How they Grow.* Wheaton: Tyndale House Publishers, 1975.

Strommen, Merton P. and A. Irene. *Five Cries of Parents.* San Francisco: Harper and Row Publishers, 1985.

Sykes, S. W., Editor. *Karl Barth: Centenary Essays.* Cambridge: Cambridge University Press, 1989.

Teilhard de Chardin, Pierre. *The Phenomenon of Man.* London: Collins, 1960.

Thielicke, Helmut. *Evangelical Theology,* Vol. 1. Grand Rapids: Wm. B. Eerdmans Publishing Co., 1974.

_____. *Being Human...Becoming Human.* Translated by Geoffrey W. Bromiley. New York: Doubleday and Co., Inc., 1984.

_____. *The Ethics of Sex.* Translated by John W. Doberstein. Grand Rapids: Baker Book House, 1964.

_____. *Theological Ethics.* Editor, William H. Lazareth. London: Adam & Charles Black, 1968. An abridgement and translation of *Theologische Ethik, 1. Prinzipienhehre* (2nd Edition, 1958) and *II. Entfaltun: Mensch und Welt* (Second Editon, 1959).

Thompson, John. "The Humanity of God in the Theology of Karl Barth." *Scottish Journal of Theology,* Vol. 29 (1976), pp. 249–269.

Tillich, Paul. *Systematic Theology,* Vol. 2. Digswell Place, Great Britain: James Nisbet & Co. Ltd., 1960.

_____. *The Courage To Be.* London: Nisbet & Co. Ltd., 1955.

Torrance, Alan. *Persons in Communion: Trinitarian Description and Human Participation.* Edinburgh: T&T Clark, 1996.

_____. "The Self-Relation, Narcissism and the Gospel of Grace." *Scottish Journal of Theology,* Vol. 40 (1987), pp. 481–510.

Torrance, David W. Torrance, Editor. *God, Family & Sexuality.* Carberry, Scotland: The Handsel Press, 1997.

Torrance, James B. "Covenant or Contract?" *Scottish Journal of Theology,* Vol. 23, No. 1 (February 1970), pp. 51–76.

_____. "The Place of Jesus Christ in Worship." *Church Service Society Annual,* No. 40 (May 1970), pp. 41–62.

_____. "The Vicarious Humanity of Christ." *The Incarnation: Ecumenical Studies in the Nicene-Constantinopolitan Creed, A.D. 381.* Edited by Thomas F. Torrance. Edinburgh: The Handsel Press, 1981.

Torrance, Thomas F. "Athanasius: A Study in the Foundations of Classical Theology." *Theology in Reconciliation.* New York: Geoffrey Chapman, 1975.

_____. *Calvin's Doctrine of Man.* Westport, Connecticut: Greenwood Press, Publishers, 1977 reprint.

_____. *The Ground and Grammar of Theology.* Belfast, Dublin, Ottowa: Christian Journals Limited, 1980.

_____. *Karl Barth: An Introduction to his Early Theology, 1910–1931.* London: SCM Press, 1962.

_____. "Karl Barth." *Scottish Journal of Theology,* Vol. 22 (1969), pp. 1–9.

_____. "The Problem of Natural Theology in the Thought of Karl Barth." *Religious Studies,* Vol. 6 (1970), pp. 121–135.

———, *Reality and Evangelical Theology*. Philadelphia: Westminster Press, 1982.

———, *The Soul and Person, in Theological Perspective*. Editor, Stewart R. Sutherland & T. A. Roberts. *Religion, Reason and the Self. Essays in Honour of Hywel D. Lewis*. Cardiff: University of Wales Press, 1989.

———, *Theological Science*. Oxford, London, New York: Oxford University Press, 1978.

———, *Transformation & Convergence in the Frame of Knowledge: Explorations in the Interrelations of Scientific and Theological Enterprise*. Grand Rapids: Wm. B. Eerdmans Publishing Co., 1984.

———, *The Trinitarian Faith*. Edinburgh: T&T Clark, 1988.

———, "The Word of God and the Nature of Man." *Theology in Reconstruction*. Grand Rapids: Wm. B. Eerdmans Publishing Co., 1975.

Vitz, Paul. *Psychology as Religion: The Cult of Self-Worship*. Bath: The Pitman Press, 1979.

Watson, Hood, Foster and Morris. "Sin, Depression and Narcissism." *Review of Religious Research*, Vol. 29 (1987–1988), pp. 295–303.

Webb, C. C. J. *God and Personality*. London: Library of Philosophy, 1918.

Weber, Otto. *Karl Barth's Church Dogmatics: An Introductory Report on Volumes I/1 to III/4*. Translated by Arthur C. Cochrane. London: Lutterworth Press, 1953.

Webster, John. *Barth's Ethics of Reconciliation*. Cambridge: Cambridge University Press, 1995.

Wells, Harold G. "Karl Barth's Doctrine of Analogy." *Canadian Journal of Theology*, Vol. XV, 3 & 4 (1969), pp. 203–213.

Whitehouse, W. A. "The Christian View of Man: An Examination of Karl Barth's Doctrine." *Scottish Journal of Theology*, Vol. 2 (1949), pp. 57–74.

———, "The Christian View of Man." *Creation, Science & Theology: Essays in Response to Karl Barth*. Grand Rapids: Wm. B. Eerdmans Publishing Co., 1981.

Willis, Robert, *The Ethics of Karl Barth*. Leiden: Brill, 1971.

Yu, Carver. *Being and Relation: A Theological Critique of Western Dualism and Individualism*. Edinburgh: Scottish Academic Press, 1987.

Zizioulas, John D. *Being as Communion*. New York: St. Vladamir's Seminary Press, 1985.

———, "Human Capacity and Incapacity: A Theological Exploration of Personhood." *Scottish Journal of Theology*, Vol. 28 (1975), pp. 401–448.

Indexes

Names

Anderson, Herbert, 306n., 335n., 341n., 342n., 346n., 369n., 395n.
Anderson, Ray S., xv n., 14n., 266, 281ff., 283n., 315f., 325n., 340n., 383n.
Anderson, Ray S. and Guernsey, Dennis, xv, 366n., 403n.
Aquinas, Thomas, 95n., 133n., 135n., 139n., 414n.
Aristotle, 367, 369n.
Athanasius, 413
Augustine, 369n.
Bailey, Sherwin, 375n.
Balswick, Jack and Judith, 270n., 285n., 299n., 343n.
Balthasar, Hans Urs von, xiv n., 135n., 225n., 379n., 394
Baxter, Christina Ann, 414n.
Beatty, Melody, 371n.
Bedouelle, Guy, 379n., 394, 400n.
Bender, Ross, 267, 325n., 331, 342, 370n., 383n., 403n., 404n.
Berkouwer, G.C., 386n.
Boggs, Carol, 373ff.
Bolich, Gregory, xiv n.
Bonhoeffer, Dietrich, 13n., 59n., 94n., 167n., 287n., 366n., 381n., 391
Bouillard, Henri, 132n., 135n.
Bracken, Joseph, 351n.
Bradshaw, Timothy, 14n.
Bromiley, Geoffrey, xvi, 12n.
Brunner, Emil, 143n., 221n., 229, 269, 320f., 343n., 345n., 346n., 383n.
Buber, Martin, 103n., 367n.
Bultmann, Rudolph, 208n.
Busch, Eberhard, xix n.
Camfield, F.W., 136n.
Campbell, Cynthia, 121n.
Chartier, Myron, 281n.
Clapp, Rodney, 267n. 270n., 333f., 338n., 403n., 404n.
Cobb, John B., 177n.
Cochrane, Arthur, xvi, xix n.
Come, Arnold, 208n.
Cousins, Ewert, 351n.
Culley, Iris, 400n.
Curran, Charles, 335n.
Daley, Mary, 120n., 213n.
Dalferth, Ingolf, 174n., 419
Davies, John, 343n.
Dickson, Graham and Alison, 347n., 355n.
Dobson, James, 288ff., 352
Dreikhurs, Rudolph and Soltz, Vicki, 307ff.
Dring, Tom, 281n.
Ellis, Ieuan, 332, 333n.
Ellul, Jacques, 330n., 391
Evans, C. Steven, 328n.
Fagley, Richard M., 346n.
Fallot, Roger D., 336n., 369n.
Fletcher, Verne, 130n., 146
Ford, Lewis, 177
Freud, 207n.
Freuerbach, 207n.
Galdston, Iago, 341n.
Getz, Gene, 376n.
Gibbons, Cecil W., 227n., 276ff.
Gibbs, J.G., 109n.
Godsey, John D., 96n.
Greer, Germaine, 325
Griffen, Karn, 403n.
Guernsey, Dennis, xiv n., 267, 281ff., 303ff.
Gunton, Colin, 58n., 64n., 170n., 174f.
Guthrie, Shirley, 391n.
Hammond, Guy, 332, 404n.
Hampson, Daphne, 266n.
Handy, Robert T., 366n.
Harnack, Adolph von, 200n.
Harrisville, Roy, 333
Hartshorne, Charles, 177
Hartwell, Herbert, xiii, xiv, xvii n.
Hugen, Melvin, 227n., 335n.
Hughes, Philip, 48n., 113n., 386n.
Hulme, William, 402n.
Jenson, Robert, 133n., 151
Jewett, Paul K., 121n.

Jungmann, Joseph, 378n.
Jüngel, Eberhard, xvi n., xviii n., 21n., 26n., 34n., 58n., 64n., 73n., 74n., 170n., 173n., 174n., 175
Kaiser, Christopher, 415
Kelley, Anthony J., 177n.
Klausner, S.Z., 373
Koller, Alice, 368n.
Kuhn, Thomas S., 34n.
Ladd, George E., 217n.
Lapseley, James N., 335n.
Lasch, Christopher, 320, 325n., 326f., 328n., 329n., 331, 346n., 352, 366, 369n., 371n., 383n., 404n.
Lee, Jung Young, 135n., 138n.
Lehmann, Paul, 152, 382n.
Lewis, C.S., 166n., 259n.
Loades, Ann, 327n., 334n.
Luther, Martin, 193, 378
Lyon, David, 328n., 366n.
Macmurray, John, 59n., 100n., 369n., 370n., 379n., 404n.
Maurice, F.D., 276ff.
McConnachie, John, xv, xvi
McCulloch, Joseph, 370n.
McIntyre, John, 132n., 134n., 135n.

McKelway, A.J., 121n., 122n.
McLean, Stuart, xiv, 18n., 53n., 63n., 70n., 155n.
Mehl, Roger, 368f., 404n.
Minuchin, Salvator, 302ff., 371f., 392n.
Mollenkott, Virginia R., 201n.
Moltmann, Jürgen, 26n., 216n., 399n.
Mondin, Battista, 135n.
Morse, Christopher, 135n.
Mount, Ferdinand, 333n.
Mühlen, Heribert, 351n.
Narramore, S. Bruce, 376n.
Newbigin, Lesslie, 34n.
Niebuhr, Reinhold, 216n.
Nietzsche, Friedrich, 108, 209n.
O'Donnell, John, 351n.
Oden, Thomas, xiv, 152
Ogden, Shubert, 177
Oshima, Sueo, 135n.
Palmer, Russell, 209n., 221n.
Pannenberg, Wolfhart, 178n., 369n.
Parsons, Michael, 70n.
Parsons, Susan, 334n.
Paul, Garret E., xvii
Peck, William J. 381n.
Pfuetze, Paul, 367n.
Piper, Otto, 344n., 345n., 346n., 383n., 392n., 397n.
Plato, 58n., 63n., 367f.
Polanyi, Michael, 13n., 34n., 59n.

Pöhlmann, Horst Georg, 135n.
Pride, Mary, 325n., 326
Pryzwara, Eric, 95n.
Rahner, Karl, 379n., 394
Ramm, Bernard, xiii
Ranson, Guy H., 277n.
Richard of St. Victor, 351n.
Roberts, Richard H., xiii
Robinson, H. Wheeler, 278
Rodiger, Georgiana, 403n.
Rogerson, John, 339n.
Romero, Jane A. 120n.
Rosato, Phillip, 216n., 392n.
Ruether, Rosemary, 120n., 332
Russell, Letty, 121n.
Sanger, Margaret, 326n.
Schillebeeckx, Edward, 159n.
Sears, Robert, 351n.
Smail, Thomas, 415
Smedes, Louis, 383n.
Snyder, Ross, 399n.
Söhngen, Gottlieb, 135n., 414n.
Stackhouse, Max, 283n.
Stibbs, A.M., 335n.
Stockton, Ian, 330n., 397n., 401n.
Strauss, R.L., 375n.
Strommen, Merton P., 301n.
Thatcher, Adrian, 266n.
Thielicke, Helmut, 59n., 345n., 346n., 383n.
Thompson, John, 73n.
Thurneysen, Eduard, xviii n.

Torrance, Alan, 24n., 44n., 94n., 132n., 133n., 136n., 139n., 145n., 159n., 162n., 367n., 414
Torrance, David W., 283n., 343n.
Torrance, James B., 33n., 71n., 170n.
Torrance, Thomas F., xvi, 13n., 59n., 60n., 176n., 413n.
Vitz, Paul, 366n.
Walrond-Skinner, Sue, 266n.
Weber, Otto, xv
Webster, John, 2n.
Wells, Harold G., 134n.
Whitehouse, W.A., 12, 57
Willis, Robert, 151f.
Wynn, John C., 391n.
Yarbrough, O. Larry, 347n.
Yu, Carver, 34n.
Zizioulas, John D., 34n., 59n., 178n.

Subjects

abortion, 344f., 358
adoption, 348n., 357-366, 388, 390
analogy, *analogia*, 131ff.
analogia entis, 94, 95n., 134n., 138, 414
analogia fidei, 95n., 131f., 136, 414
analogia gratiae, 131f., 136, 414.
analogia relationis, xx, 2, 3, 15f., 42ff., 85n., 94f., 131, 133, 134n., 135-139, 147, 154, 181, 190, 199, 200ff., 280, 397, 414
analogia unius ad alterum, 95n. 136n., 139n.
anthropology, Christological, 15, 27, 36-45, 73, 88ff.
non-Christological, 40, 57n.
theological, 10-13, 28, 32, 63
as theology, 207n.
trinitarian grounding, 39-43, 72, 81, 83, 91, 103
anthropomorphism, 137f., 160, 164
authority, parental, 193, 206ff., 246ff., 290f., 298ff., 310ff., 372-376, 397
autonomy, 108, 111, 152, 208n., 210, 309, 311, 315f., 367f., 380ff., 388.
becoming, 25, 28-34, 44, 55, 64f., 71-78, 80, 96, 98, 105f., 115, 117, 140f., 148f., 153, 163ff., 170-177, 203, 219f., 284, 324f., 350, 360, 370, 375, 378, 389f.
being and act, 4-8, 15f., 27-30, 33, 36, 43-49, 54, 66, 69, 78, 81, 374
being-in-encounter, 104f., 153-155, 195, 399
being-in-loving, 166f.
being-in-person, personal, 23, 27-31, 46, 50, 79, 81, 163f., 166
being-in-relation, 4-11, 15-17, 20, 22-27, 33, 43-66, 69, 72-85
belonging, 28, 48, 57, 118, 141, 148, 150, 171, 173, 238, 242, 248, 268, 286ff., 288, 292, 302, 309f., 315-318, 323, 340, 350, 356, 358-363, 371, 379, 396f., 401, 402-405
birth control, contraception, 229ff., 237, 345
character indelibilis, 241
childlessness, 221-228, 236ff., 343ff., 401
children, ministry to, 399
Christocentrism, 15
Christocratic brotherhood, 338
Church, the, 128, 145, 184, 269, 286ff., 337, 370, 390, 396ff., 402
civil authority, 193f.
co-dependency, 371
co-humanity, 99, 285, 303
command of God, 188f., 190f., 197, 209n., 222n.
covenant: internal meaning, external basis, 88, 114, 117, 205, 300, 325, 349n., 350, 359f., 384, 386, 388ff., 418
covenant love, 153f., 167-170, 340, 348, 384

Indexes

covenant partner,
humanity as God's,
36, 80f., 88, 91, 99,
107, 117f., 141, 150,
158, 286, 388
with children, 399
covenantal relations, 8,
17, 64, 67ff., 72, 74-
76, 141, 156, 195,
204, 234, 243, 268f.,
285, 296, 299, 306f.,
325, 349n., 350, 354,
360, 369f., 377, 386,
389
creatio ex nihilo, 73
dehumanization, 127,
169, 355
depersonalization, 124,
169f., 286, 354, 355.
*See personalization,
dehumanization*
discipline, of children,
249ff., 293ff., 376ff.
double transcendence,
179f.
ekstasis, 178
election, 63f., 66-69,
145, 175, 179f., 348,
351, 361f.
equality, 121, 126-129,
195, 287, 308ff., 311,
313, 315f.
eschatological hope, 44,
72, 78, 81, 83, 133,
153, 173, 216n.,
216ff., 220, 287
ethics, trinitarian
grounding, 148. *See
theological ethics*
evil, 177n. *See sin.*
exo-centric, 178, 227
extension and inclusion,
179, 181

faith, 10-12, 19f., 38f.,
81, 131, 136f., 142,
147, 150, 181, 185,
215, 233-237, 242-
246, 254-258, 265,
268-275, 277f., 288,
291, 321, 330f., 335,
353, 359, 370, 382,
391, 403, 405
seeking understanding,
20
family, 191f., 321ff.
and community, 342
as covenant com-
munity, 268ff.
child-rearing, 350
democratic, 308f.
extent of, 339
idolatry of, 335
nuclear, 341
six-fold grammar of,
405
fatherhood, *See
motherhood* and *God*
Fifth Commandment,
193, 203f.
feminist critique, 334,
378n.
forgiveness, 215, 251,
253f., 259, 268f.,
286, 307, 312, 364,
377, 391, 393f., 396
freedom, human, 79f.,
150, 380ff.
for God, 79f., 150,
156, 189, 209n., 226
God's, 27, 31, 79,
167
gladness, 65, 105f.,
123f., 127, 129, 140,
151, 155, 157, 237
God,
fatherhood, 74n.,
198ff., 204, 259, 395

fellowship creating
love, 26-33 162
freedom, 79, 167
life, 161
love, 27-29, 162f.
167f.
omnipotence, 167f.
personal, 32-28, 31,
159-167
personifying Person,
30f., 166
godlessness, 60f.
gender, 111-117, 123-
127, 146, 269, 340,
383-391
Godward aspect, of
parenting, 196ff.,
207n., 208 *See
parenting, spiritual
mission*
grace, 149, 198, 212,
258, 323, 276, 382,
391ff.
grammar of relations,
being-in-relation with
God, 82
of family, 405
human being-in-
relation, 44
human personal being,
165
human with God, 56
humanity of Jesus, 91
I-Thou, 102
intra-trinitarian, 33f.
intra-triune, 93
in marriage, 141
parent-child, 190
personal covenantal,
17
personal in God, 164
six characteristics, of
Jesus Christ, 51
six-fold, 43

trinitarian and Christological, 55
gratitude, 59, 63-67, 75f., 80f., 297f., 300, 323
Hegelianism, 14n., 110n.
heteronomy, 210f., 152, 380ff., *See autonomy.*
hierarchy, 123, 126, 244, 246
history, of covenant, encounter, relationship, 12, 43, 45-48, 52, 55-59, 62-72, 75-78, 80-84, 88, 90, 93, 100-103, 115, 130, 141, 145, 148, 154-158, 165, 169f., 175-177, 180, 184
Holy Spirit, 21, 110, 169, 172, 175, 189, 219, 222n., 228n., 257, 273, 392f.,
homosexual parenting, 387f.
honoring, parents, 195, 204ff., 209ff., 241f.
hope, 220, 392f. *See eschatological hope*
humanity,
  its determination, 37, 73
  as image of Image, i.e. Jesus Christ, 39f., 82, 85, 96ff., 99-137, 142f., 148, 151, 165f., 169, 198, 260, 298, 323
  six-fold determination, 59ff.
  trinitarian grounding, 72-75, 81, 144, 159

humanization, 104, 110, 120, 165, 172, 285, 297, 310, 353, 381. *See personalization, sanctification*
I and Thou, 100-103, 118, 140f., 154f., 166, 195, 382, 399
identification, 378
imago Dei, image of God, 10, 33, 37, 39, 43, 92, 96-99, 116, 118, 135-140, 142-147, 347ff., 376, 376n.
independence, 61, 82, 110, 117, 210f., 247f., 257f., 282, 285, 295, 302, 306, 309, 312, 314f., 323, 340f., 370f., 380, 382
indicative/imperative of covenant, 70, 75f., 66f., 78, 148f., 217n., 220, 240, 247, 274, 286
individualism, 108-111, 304n., 366ff., 370f.
idolatry, 245, 394f.
indwelling, 378f.
infertility, 226n.
invocation, 63, 75, 78-81, 83 *See prayer.*
Israel, 116, 120, 128, 145, 149, 192, 199, 200f., 206, 223, 225, 267ff., 272, 283, 339
Jesus Christ,
  the Child, 398, 399n., 403
  his humanity, 89ff., 91, 180f., 183
  all inclusive humanity, 180f.
  as Image of Father, Trinity, 39f., 55, 85, 96ff., 99, 103, 137, 137, 143, 146, 169, 198, 260, 280, 323
  Image of humanity, 37, 39f., 48, 85, 94, 96ff., 136f., 144
  Kinsman Redeemer, 339
  man for others, 183
  Mediator, 215
  the Neighbor, 182, 186
  as Person, 47
  Person and Work, 45ff., 54, 181
  Sonship, 398
joy *See gladness*
justice, social/personal, 400
Kingdom of God, 216ff., 219ff.
the "least," 400f.
logos asarkos, 74n.
love, 147, 183, 294f., 374ff., 330ff. *See God*
male and female, 111ff., 119ff.
marriage, 111ff., 117, 120, 140ff., 185, 230f., 270, 345, 348, 385ff.
maturity, 209
mission, 402
motherhood/fatherhood, 195f, 198f., 201n., 228, 240
mutuality, 122f., 124ff.
mythologizing, 136ff., 208n., 213n., 291, 395 *See anthropomorphism*
narcissism, 366ff., 371

nuclear family, 341
non-being, nothingness, 68, 78f.
obedience, 77f., 150, 207f., 236, 382f.
  Jesus', 128
  in Trinity, 129
ontology, substantival vs. personal/relational, 58n.
otherness, 157n., 178f.
orders of creation, 2, 273n., 287f., 292, 349, 391
parent-child relation, trinitarian grounding, 197-200, 263
parenting, 238, 241f., 258f., 378
  authority, *See authority, parental*
  covenant form, 355
  godward aspect, 196ff., 207n., 208
  mission of, 197, 215, 244, 279, 291, 301, 311f., 357, 360, 373, 380, 403
  negative attitudes, 351ff.
  spiritual *See spiritual parenting*
  spiritual mission of, 403
parity, 287, 315
patriarchalism, 123, 206, 213n., 251, 332n., 334n.
perichoresis (*circumincessio*), 25f., 27, 31, 33, 50n., 62, 74, 176, 378
personalism, 159

personalizing, 160, 166f., 169f., 171f., 174, 285, 297f., 348, 353, 388 *See humanization*
personhood, being persons/human, 30, 44, 46, 50, 52f., 72, 79ff., 82f., 99, 100, 103, 105, 111, 153, 158ff., 160, 165f., 285
personification, *See Personifying love*
Personifying love, 159
person-making, 160, 166, 169f., 352f., 376. *See personalization*
phenomena, of the human, 58
prayer, 211, 269, 365, 378 *See invocation*
process theology, 176n.
procreation, 221ff., 327n., 343, 347ff., 350f., 353-356, 386
punishment, corporal, 295, 300
reconciliation with God, *de jure*, 181
recta natura, 142n.
relations,
  Christological and trinitarian, 55
  covenantal, *See covenantal relations*
  I-Thou, 52n.
  seven spheres, 41
  trinitarian, *See trinitarian relations*
repentance, 317, 364, 391, 396 *See forgiveness*

representation, substitution, 128, 132, 140, 141, 146, 158, 184, 193, 195-199, 208, 210, 212, 217, 228, 241f., 285, 291, 361, 377, 378, 381, 385, 398, 403
responsibility, 59, 63-67, 75-81, 104, 106, 111, 123, 126, 128ff., 130, 142, 150f., 155-158, 194, 205, 207, 210f., 211, 228, 232-247, 254-259, 285-290, 296-316
revelation, 10-16, 21-25, 27f., 31, 33, 36, 39-42, 47-52, 58f., 62, 67, 69, 71, 73, 76, 81, 83, 89, 92, 94, 99, 104, 129, 137, 139, 147f., 154, 159-162, 168f., 174-176, 179, 186, 188, 199, 204, 206, 239, 251, 253f., 260, 265, 278, 280, 395
roles, 115, 119, 125-127, 240, 242, 281, 287, 324f., 327f., 331, 339, 371, 374, 389
sanctification, 45, 146, 172, 189, 242ff., 317, 327, 334, 378, 381, 390, 393f. *See humanization*
self-assertion, 111
self-giving, 33, 51, 56, 78-80, 83, 90, 94, 127, 141f., 148, 155-158, 160, 169, 176, 274, 275, 312, 317,

323, 350, 361 *See responsibility*
self-revelation, God's, 16, 18, 19-22, 24, 27f., 104, 106, 131, 160f., 168, 291, 335
sexual relations, 230ff., 339, 344, 346, 350, 354
sexuality, 389, 390f.
sin, 60f., 68, 79f., 89, 91, 142, 182, 197f., 215-217, 220, 259, 286, 273, 206f., 288, 341n., 370, 381, 385, 391ff., 396, 398 *See evil*
single parenting, 387, 390
single (unmarried) persons, 226ff., 288, 401-403
spiritual authority, 197, 246, 331, 397 *See parental authority*
spiritual formation, 286, 293, 397-401
spiritual mission of parents, *See parenting, mission of* and *Godward aspect of*
spiritual parenting, 195, 228f., 357, 397
subordination, 120ff., 123, 125-128, 194ff.
theological ethics, xiv, 6, 41, 146ff., 148, 151, 188, 334
theological anthropology, xiv
Trinity, the doctrine of, 5, 18, 20, 23, 26f., 31, 33-39, 43, 54-56, 162, 164, 168, 175f., 367, 391
trinitarian relations, 15f., 18ff., 22ff., 26, 33f., 43, 51, 56, 67, 81f., 85, 9-98, 103-106, 118, 129f., 139, 144f., 155, 165, 169, 175f., 181-183, 385, 391
triunity, 18, 21, 22, 25, 44, 92, 388 *See perichoresis*
unity, its relational nature, 17, 21, 22, 25-32, 73, 108, 167, 282, 284, 311, 316-318, 362, 369-371
unity-in-differentiation, 19-23, 26-28, 34, 44, 49f., 55, 62f., 78, 81, 84f., 89, 93, 95, 101, 103, 108-130, 132, 141, 145-148, 152, 158, 161, 179, 190f., 196, 207, 211, 257, 285, 300, 305, 367, 369-372, 385, 401
unity-in-Trinity, 25, 174, 175. *See triunity*
unmarried mothers/fathers, 238f.
vestigia creaturae, 145n.
vestigia trinitatis, 145n., 203n.
witness, as image, 130ff., 140, 146, 148, 150
Word of God, the, 10, 12n., 13f., 19, 59, 63
work, 185

About the Author

Rev. Dr. Gary Deddo received his Ph.D. in Systematic Theology from the University of Aberdeen, Scotland. He is ordained in the Presbyterian Church USA and has served as a university campus minister for twenty years. Rev. Dr. Deddo also has taught college and seminary courses in theology and has written articles for several academic journals. He resides with his wife and three children near Princeton, New Jersey.

www.ingramcontent.com/pod-product-compliance
Lightning Source LLC
Chambersburg PA
CBHW070252230426
43664CB00014B/2509